UNIVERSITY OF NORTH CAROLINA
STUDIES IN THE ROMANCE LANGUAGES AND LITERATURES
Number 114

STUDIES IN HONOR OF
MARIO A. PEI

RALPH NAZOR
Ironton, Ohio

STUDIES IN HONOR OF
MARIO A. PEI

EDITED BY
JOHN FISHER and PAUL A. GAENG

CHAPEL HILL
THE UNIVERSITY OF NORTH CAROLINA PRESS

DEPÓSITO LEGAL: V. 68 - 1972

ARTES GRÁFICAS SOLER, S. A. — JÁVEA, 28 — VALENCIA (8) — 1972

FOREWORD

On the occasion of his retirement from Columbia University, where he held the chair of Romance Philology until 1969, and his seventieth birthday, we felt that it would be most appropriate to honor Professor Emeritus Mario A. Pei with a testimonial volume made up of contributions by his former students on philological and linguistic topics pertinent to his vast interests.

Indeed, we can think of no better way to express the appreciation and gratitude of students, colleagues, and friends of Mario Pei for the untiring interest and untold kindnesses that this truly great humanist has unselfishly lavished upon them.

THE EDITORS

TABLE OF CONTENTS

	Pages
FOREWORD	7
MARIO A. PEI Theodore Huebener	11
MARIO PEI'S CONTRIBUTIONS (1941-1945) TO THE DISCUSSION OF PROBLEMS IN FOREIGN-LANGUAGE TEACHING DURING WORLD WAR II Paul F. Angiolillo	17
UNE FORMULE D'EXORCISME EN ANCIEN FRANÇAIS Menahem Banitt	37
LEARNED WORDS IN THE EARLIEST FRENCH DOCUMENTS Dorothy R. Brodin	49
THE ETYMOLOGY OF FRENCH *DA* Henri Diament	63
THE FLOWER IN THE BOWER: *GARRIS* IN *AUCASSIN ET NICOLETTE* Eugene Dorfman	77
THE EVOLUTION OF THE STRESSED VOWEL SYSTEM OF VEGLIOTE Thaddeus Ferguson	89
THE VEGLIOTE-SARDINIAN LEXICAL AFFILIATIONS John Fisher	101
THE PLURAL *I*-ENDING OF THIRD DECLENSION MASCULINE NOUNS IN ITALIAN Paul A. Gaeng	105
THE CONCEPTS "DIFFICULT" AND "EASY" IN MEDIEVAL FRENCH Ralph de Gorog	115

	Pages
THE CONCEPT OF EUPHONY IN TRADITIONAL FRENCH GRAMMAR: MYTH OR REALITY? Jesse Levitt	127
GADDA'S "PLURILINGUISMO" IN THE *PASTICCIACCIO* Joan McConnell-Mammarella	139
LINGUISTICS, LANGUAGE TEACHING, AND PEDAGOGY Robert L. Politzer	149
THE *CONFRÉRIE DES JONGLEURS ET DES BOURGEOIS* AND THE *PUY D'ARRAS* IN TWELFTH AND THIRTEENTH CENTURY LITERATURE Louise Barbara Richardson	161
VOCALIC ALTERNATION IN THE SURSILVAN ROMANSH VERB Kenneth H. Rogers	173
FRAY MARTIN SARMIENTO, *AMADÍS DE GAULA,* AND THE SPANISH CHIVALRIC "GENRE" Barton Sholod	183
DRAMATIC TEXTS AND *ARS DICTAMINIS* IN MEDIEVAL ITALY Sandro Sticca	201
TABULA GRATULATORIA	223
BIBLIOGRAPHY OF MARIO A. PEI	213

MARIO A. PEI

By Theodore Huebener
Farleigh Dickinson University

In summarizing the career of a distinguished professor one is tempted to quote the somewhat hackneyed phrase of "a scholar and a gentleman." Nothing, however, describes Mario A. Pei better, for he is both of these and in a very unusual way. Whereas most scholars devote a lifetime to intensive research and fill the storehouses of knowledge with their findings, Pei has generously shared the fruits of his labor not only with his students but also with the general public. More than any other outstanding American linguist he has popularized philology and made the study of words and of languages attractive and interesting.

He has accomplished this largely by his remarkable skill in assembling and presenting countless linguistic morsels in a fascinating manner. His bright, entertaining, journalistic style is far removed from the pedantic prose of many a philologist.

Pei's sense of humor and his innate modesty are refreshing. Never has he assumed an attitude of professorial inviolability or scholarly infallibility. He has always been ready to admit his failures as well as to announce his successes. Although he is the successful author of countless articles and some forty books, he is absolutely without conceit or vanity regarding his publishing ventures. There is a disarming candor about Mario Pei. An extremely frank and open confession of his own struggles in the learning of languages is given in his book, *How to Learn Languages and What Languages to Learn*.

Born in Rome of a cultured middle class family, Mario Pei was brought up in standard, literary Italian. After two years of schooling, at the age of seven, he came with his family to New York. There he quickly acquired English, on the street and in the parochial school of St. John the Evangelist. His Italian, however, did not lapse, for it remained the language of his home. His early reading material, too, was entirely in his native language. Not until after three years of school, quite by chance and through a classmate, did he discover the 58th Street branch of the Public Library. It was a veritable treasure trove for the voracious young reader, who now delved into books in English. There he also found some in Spanish, which, because of his knowledge of Italian, seemed easy to read.

In his home the bilingual youngster had contacts with a fourth language, namely, French, of which his cultured parents had some knowledge. At the age of thirteen his formal school education turned his attention to the ancient languages.

He had won a scholarship to St. Francis Xavier High School, where Latin and Greek were major subjects. There the classically trained Jesuit fathers gave him a firm foundation in the ancient tongues. For his modern language Pei took three years of French. This, as he points out, was taught exactly like Latin, with much grammar, two-way translation, composition, and analysis of structure. There was little or no conversation. The teachers were not natives. His first two instructors in French were Irishmen; then he had an Alsatian, whose English had a heavy accent.

Pei comments that although this methodology would horrify modern teachers, it had its merits. The grammatical structure of the language was assimilated with absolute thoroughness. The two-way translation exercises eventually led to semi-automatic responses. Reading proficiency was developed. The greatest weakness was the lack of any training in understanding a native speaking at normal speed.

Because of his mental alertness, which impressed his teachers, and because of his outstanding scholarship, Pei was recommended for a teaching position as soon as he had his diploma. He was given a sixth grade class to teach, in the elementary division of St. Francis Xavier.

Strangely enough, despite Pei's remarkable aptitude in acquiring languages, he was not at first attracted to the study of linguistics. In fact, he wanted to become a civil engineer. He was eager to follow in the footsteps of an uncle who had come to New York from Rome in 1904 and had helped to plan the first city subway.

During his four years in high school Pei had been given a firm foundation in Latin and Greek. He had won the French prize for three years and he had also received awards in mathematics and science. On the basis of the latter he took courses in engineering at the night session of the City College for a year. Since he taught by day and spent six nights at the college, he was more proficient in languages than in science. In view of this, he transferred to the A. B. course. This required continuing his Latin; he took four more semesters of it in the day session. In the evening he had a year of French (Racine and Corneille) and a course in Spanish (Cervantes and Lope de Vega).

His energy and ambition were amazing, for he continued teaching in the Xavier Grammar School for two years. Then an unusual opportunity presented itself: he was hired for a year as a private tutor of the nephews of President Menochal in Cuba. This was a valuable experience; through it he acquired a firm hold on Spanish.

His interest in languages grew continually. In his spare moments he studied German, Russian, Hebrew, and even ancient Egyptian. He delved into these languages primarily because he wanted to read the great classics in their original version. In fact, his interest was basically literary; only gradually did he become fascinated by the purely linguistic.

From a Russian political exile he learned Russian; with a former German U-boat captain he practised German. Since his informants were not pedagogically trained, Pei developed his own method. This consisted of memorizing grammar rules and vocabulary from a textbook, writing out exercises, and engaging in conversation with his speakers.

Curiously enough, he did not always follow the same method. In fact, he once commented that he had learned each of his major languages in a different manner. Italian, his mother-tongue, he of course learned at home. English he acquired on the street and in the classroom. It was only in French that he received formal instruction. German and Russian he acquired through exchange lessons as described above. He learned Japanese by listening to a friendly waiter in a sukiyaki restaurant. He got his Chinese by sitting in on classes in the Army Language School in Monterey, where he was serving as a linguistic consultant. Other languages, like Portuguese, he learned entirely from the book through self-study. It is evident that Pei possessed the autodidactic facility of Schliemann, who claimed he could learn a modern language in six weeks.

In 1921, together with thirty-two students of Italian background, Pei was given a three months' scholarship by the Italian government. On his return to New York he secured a part-time teaching position in French and Spanish at Fordham Preparatory School. This was followed by a full-time assignment at the Franklin School. Finally he was appointed to the Romance Language Department of Townsend Harris Hall, where he had obtained his A. B. magna cum laude, in the evening session. There he taught French, Spanish, and Italian. In addition, he gave courses in Latin in the City College three nights a week. He was instructor in Romance languages and Latin in the City College from 1923 to 1937.

Pei continued his graduate studies at Columbia University, doing work in an amazingly wide field of linguistics. His courses included Sanskrit, ancient Greek dialects, Oscan, Umbrian, Old High German, Gothic, Old Slavic, Vulgar Latin, Old French, Provençal, and medieval romance dialects. In 1932 he obtained his Ph. D. and in 1937 he was appointed to the Romance Language Department of Columbia. He served at that institution as Assistant Professor from 1937 to 1947, as Associate Professor from 1947 to 1952, and as Professor of Romance Philology from 1952 to his retirement.

With his extensive teaching schedules and his intensive learning of more and more languages, one would think that Pei had little time for other activities. Nevertheless, he has written a great deal, beginning early in his career.

Articles by Pei have appeared in *The New York Times Magazine, This Week, Good Housekeeping, Saturday Review, Think, Coronet, This Month, The New Leader, The Saturday Evening Post, Holiday, Readers Digest, Town and Country,* and *Tomorrow.* He has also had articles in most of the major professional language journals here and abroad.

Mario Pei is a prolific writer. The extent of scholarly research and information presented in his books and articles is astounding. In his *Languages for War and Peace* (1943), he gives a practical summary of over forty of the world's leading languages.

The Story of Language, published in 1949 and revised in 1965, was a Book of the Month Club choice. Bernard Shaw commented on it: "After a glance at it I found it was readable, and, though the writer is an Italian, so much more idiomatically English than most natives could achieve." He added that Pei's "prodigious memory and knowledge remind me of Isaac Newton."'

Other books by Pei include *The Families of Words, Voices of Man, All About Language, The Story of English, Invitation to Linguistics, Language for Everybody, One Language for the World,* and *The Italian Language.* As practical guide books for the traveler there is the fascinating "Getting Along" series, which appeared in French, Spanish, German, Italian, Portuguese, and Russian.

Pei has written two successful novels, *Swords of Anjou* and *The Sparrows.* He has also ventured into the realm of politics and economics in *Our National Heritage* and *The Consumer's Manifesto.*

Mario Pei has been decorated repeatedly and has been given many awards. Among them are: Cavaliere Officiale of the Order of Merit of the Italian Republic, George Washington Honor Medal from Freedom Foundation at Valley Forge, David McKay Humanities Award (Brigham Young University), Townsend Harris Medal, etc. Pei has also held many honorary positions. In 1968 he was made honorary president of the American Society of Geolinguistics, a professional organization he founded in 1964.

In view of his many outstanding contributions to the study of modern languages, his diligent research in English, and his many stimulating and valuable publications, Mario Pei can be acclaimed as one of the foremost linguists of the day. His broadcasts for OWI, the Voice of America, and Radio Free Europe have included lectures and discussions in a half dozen languages. It has been said that, with the possible exception of one member of the United Nations Secretariat, Mario Pei reads, speaks, and understands more languages than any living man.

His students, colleagues, and friends are happy to honor him on this occasion and extend to him their warmest wishes for many more years of health and happiness.

MARIO PEI'S CONTRIBUTIONS (1941-1945) TO THE DISCUSSION OF PROBLEMS IN FOREIGN-LANGUAGE TEACHING DURING WORLD WAR II

By Paul F. Angiolillo
Dickinson College

In the general mobilization of human and physical resources during the Second World War for the achievement of final victory, special educational programs were instituted by the U. S. Armed Forces as part of the total war effort. The most widely-known and most important of these was the ASTP (Army Specialized Training Program). And within the ASTP it was the intensive foreign-language training provided by colleges and universities for servicemen that became the most noteworthy. [1]

The sudden discovery of a shortage of well-qualified persons truly knowledgeable in either the "ordinary" or "exotic" foreign languages and the throughgoing, intensive way in which the ASTP sought to fill the demand provoked a great deal of discussion among professional language teachers on the needs, rôle and methodology of language teaching in American education. Critical evaluations and implications of the so-called "Army method" occupied not only numerous pages of the professional journals, but appeared as well in newspapers and popular magazines. Many speeches, also, were made on the relation of the renewed interest in foreign languages to post-war curricula.

Despite a full program of teaching, a number of graduate candidates and his preoccupying research and writing in philology

---

[1] See Paul F. Angiolillo, *Armed Forces' Foreign-Language Teaching* (New York: S. F. Vanni, 1947).

and linguistics, Professor Mario Pei, to his great credit, found time and energy (one wondered from where) to take an active part in these discussions. Between 1941 and 1945, of the numerous articles he published and addresses he made, more than 30 of the former and about 20 of the latter were directly and exclusively on the general topic of language teaching during wartime. Our purpose now is to review the principal ideas and concerns of those contributions and their relationship to dominant trends in foreign-language study during the last quarter century.

I

Dr. Pei's predictive powers and intuitive sense of national needs as regarded general preparedness manifested themselves even before the U. S. became involved in World War II. In a remarkable little article, published in December 1941, [2] he foresaw the rôle foreign languages were going to play in global war and, more significantly, made suggestions that were to materialize, a year or two later, in specific programs and projects. After reminding his readers that "victory goes to the side that is better prepared" and that "preparation is not necessarily altogether military or mechanical," he called attention to the use the Germans were then making of linguistic mastery of the tongue of victim nations as a tool of conquest. He then set forth a multitude of useful purposes (military and personal) to which the ordinary soldier could put a knowledge of the language of an ally or enemy. He called for "an extremely *intensive* course of *conversational* instruction in one or more languages for *selected men* and units. Members of a given unit might all be trained in the same language, in anticipation of the unit's future use in certain special countries..." (italics mine, to draw attention to features that were eventually to characterize the ASTP). He recommended that such instruction should be "discussed and planned by military and educational experts working in close collaboration" — which was indeed to become the procedure followed. He drew a distinction between the more

---

[2] Mario A. Pei, "Languages for Defense," *French Review*, 15, No. 2 (Dec. 1941), 108-110.

"familiar" languages ("French, Spanish, German, Italian, with the addition of Portuguese") for the majority of trainees, and the less familiar ones — Japanese, Russian, Arabic — "To be imparted to specially picked units or individuals." After envisaging the setting up of volunteer bureaus and governmental agencies to implement these general objectives, he concludes the article by a truly perceptive assessment of the broad, future benefits of such military instruction:

> Nor, in our military emergency, should we lose sight of the vaster, more permanent benefits that would accrue from such instruction. The learning of a foreign language, even though imperfectly achieved, will contribute immediately to the soldier's efficiency and supply him with a recreational activity; but it will also linger with him after he leaves the service and perhaps be of later vocational use. It will form permanent part and parcel of his intellectual and educational equipment, broaden his cultural interests, aid him in business, in traveling, in human relations, and tend ultimately to contribute to that spirit of international understanding and cooperation which, it is hoped, will arise from the ashes of destruction and make a recurrence of the present conflict impossible.

It may be noted, in passing, that this article was sent to and acknowledged by the President, Secretaries of War and Navy, and Mortimer Graves, Chairman of the Committee on the National School of Modern Oriental Languages and Civilizations, of the American Council of Learned Societies, and Secretary, Committee on Intensive Language Instruction, the groups largely responsible for instituting the ASTP.

II

In 1942, besides a booklet for learning simple Spanish [3] and an article on the use and extent of French as a chief tool of com-

---

[3] Pei, *Simplified Spanish for the Use of the Armed Forces* (New York: Carranza Press, 1942).

munication throughout the world, [4] Dr. Pei wrote a letter to the *New York Times* [5] in which he re-emphasized the need of a knowledge of French, German and Italian among our servicemen:

> Now that we have guns and planes and tanks, it is time that we give some attention to the secondary problem of languages in connection with our armed forces. Knowledge, even in the form of a smattering, of the tongue of an ally or enemy may easily spell the difference between life and death, between escape and capture, to the individual soldier. To a military unit it may signify survival or extinction. To an army as a whole it may conceivably mean victory or defeat. To put matters mildly, it certainly will make the difference between comfort and discomfort, between making and not making his wants know, to each and every soldier who lands on European or North African soil.

He goes on to point out the contradiction between the de-emphasis of foreign-language study in high schools at the time and the crash programs instituted by the military to meet a keenly felt need.

III

The year 1943 saw in the list of publications by Dr. Pei three important articles plus a major book that was to have several editions, all of which were based on the whole question of foreign languages during the war itself, as well as probable impacts upon post-war education. The first article [6] continued the campaign of reminding the country of the importance of some foreign-language ability on the part of Americans directly involved in some aspect of the war effort:

---

[4] Pei, "French as a War Language," *French Review*, 16, No. 1 (Oct. 1942), 52-58.

[5] Pei, "Language Courses for Army," Letter to the Editor, *New York Times*, 11 Nov., 1942.

[6] Pei, "The Function of Languages in Global War," *Hispania*, May, 1943, pp. 194-201. Also reprinted in *Education Digest*, March 1943, pp. 7-9, and in *School and Society*, Nov. 1943, pp. 401-03.

To say that languages are important in the present emergency is an understatement. In actual combat, they may not play so paramount a role as guns and planes and tanks. But almost every dispatch from our far-flung battlefronts informs us that their role is of significance — often of absolute significance — to the men who are doing the fighting.

There followed the descriptions of specific instances in which an understanding of a particular foreign language aided in the accomplishment of a special military or diplomatic mission. Among such cases mention is made of President Roosevelt, "who found it expedient to address the population of France and French North Africa personally and in French when the American occupation began."

It was in this same article that Pei tackled forthrightly the thorny problem of the Army's new type of teaching, with its different objectives and procedures as it related to the traditional academic goals and methods of language learning. Answering colleagues who saw the ASTP work as "not quite in accord with our own rather severe cultural standards and ideals," he argued persuasively that the immediate needs are practical, limited, and urgent. There should be broader understanding and cooperation on the part of language teachers: "Must we be totally uncompromising in our cultural ideals? Are we unable to make concessions to the exigencies of the moment in our teaching aims and methods...?" Revealing himself to be a scholar-specialist still in realistic touch with the general thought and desires of the country, he continues:

If there is one thing that stands out clearly from the wealth of material that comes to our notice in connection with the linguistic demands of the public and the Government and the armed forces, it is that languages are urgently wanted for practical rather than for cultural purposes, temporarily at least. What is wanted is languages, many languages, for purposes of communication, not a few selected languages for grammatical and stylistic correctness and literary values. The Government and the people of America want more French, more Spanish, more German, more Italian than they have ever wanted before. They also want Portuguese, Russian, Chinese,

> Japanese, Arabic, modern Greek, Hebrew, even Malay and Pidgin English. It is up to us, the people with the linguistic training and background, to give them what they want and need....
>
> There are two things that we must learn to do, and learn fast, if we are to take advantage of the golden opportunities for service that the present moment offers. One is to be elastic in the matter of objectives, to be ready to shift at a moment's notice from the leisurely, cultured, literary reading approach to the practical, conversational, utilitarian language angle. It goes without saying that this need not be permanent.

We should draw attention to the fact that Pei's acceptance of "many languages" as worthy of serious study instead of the traditionally "selected few" was quite novel, if not revolutionary, for the time, and, again, quite predicative of what was actually to become the case later on.

Also presaging the increased importance of foreign-language study in the post-war world, Professor Pei warned in another article that America, after the war, must avoid the extremes of both linguistic isolationism and linguistic imperialism, counterparts or reflections of equivalent political attitudes. Instead we should strive for "linguistic collaboration if we are to convince other nations of our desire for peace and equality among nations." [7] He reiterates the paradox between the proven usefulness of foreign-language knowledge, on the one hand, and the then decreasing official interest in foreign language curricula in the schools and universities. Finally, once again he seems to have recourse to some sort of very dependable crystal ball:

> The post-war world, we hope, will behold commercial, political, and economic relations among the nations on a scale far superior to anything yet known. The languages that are now badly needed for war will be far more imperatively needed for peace, if we are to take full advantage of the opportunities for economic betterment

---

[7] Pei, "Languages in the Post-War World," *International Quarterly*, 7, No. 3 (Summer 1943), 111-14. (Reprinted in *Modern Language Journal*, 27, No. 7 (Nov. 1943), 481-85). The article was originally given as an address on March 14, 1943 before the student body of International House in New York City.

that the peace will bring in its wake. From a narrowly selfish standpoint, for the sake of our future commercial, economic, and diplomatic relations, even for the sake of the enjoyment we shall derive from our trips as tourists to foreign lands that the airplane will make easily accessible, it behooves us to become linguistically minded.

The publication that made the name of Professor Mario A. Pei known more broadly and outside the realm of academe was his tremendous descriptive compilation of most of the languages of the world.[8] In a Foreword, Pei explained the contents and aims of the book:

> The world's main languages and their geographical distribution, the linguistic families and the elementary relationships among their members, the identification of the written and possibly the spoken form of several important tongues, and lastly the description of the sounds and grammatical structure, together with a limited vocabulary, of seven of the world's most widely-spoken languages — all this will serve the purpose of giving the reader the elementary linguistic consciousness that the soldier of today needs in his military activities on foreign soil and that the man and woman of tomorrow will need in a world destined, by reason of the constant advances in our mechanical civilization and spiritual point of view, to become more and more a single political, economic and cultural unit.

In the same Foreword he collected the arguments he had used in previous articles and addresses for more and better foreign-language study both during the war and for the peace that would follow. Here, too, he pleads for more flexibility and broad-mindedness in our attitudes toward foreign-language study:

> But let us also have, for the people who do not wish to become specialists and literary and cultural experts in any one language, and for those who do, but who also want to know something about other languages, a method that will enable the individual of average linguistic ability to acquire the basic facts about the world's

---

[8] Pei, *Languages for War and Peace* (New York: S. F. Vanni, 1943).

chief languages, where they are spoken and by whom, to identify them readily, and to handle more than just one of them in a comprehensible and acceptable fashion, even if without absolute grammatical correctness and literary style.

The last article published in 1943 was one of particular interest and importance to the controversy that was evolving out of the new methods employed in foreign-language teaching under the ASTP. [9] After describing in concise, comprehensive fashion exactly how language was being taught in the ASTP (characteristics, aims, methods, personnel), Pei takes up the arguments one by one of those who favor and those who oppose the new methodological emphases. The latter, for example, are critical of the utilitarian nature of the work, the costliness of the low teacher-student ratio, and the special circumstances of high student motivation and exclusive concentration available to the Program but which would be impractical (if not impossible) in the normal classroom situation. He concludes by making a general prediction that, once more, is substantiated by what has occurred in modern-language teaching in the last decades with A-LM (audio-lingual method) and the "new key" of language learning:

> The Federal Government's present highly enlightened linguistic policy will bear fruit, in the sense that it will be followed by State educational institutions, private colleges and even local school boards. The super-intensive features of the present programs may be somewhat whittled down, the excesses of the oral-aural approach may be eliminated, and time and money may not be poured forth quite as lavishly as at present on the language courses of post-war America. But these language courses will, and can, survive, because they have proved their worth and because they meet a genuine popular demand. Foreign languages will never again be the orphans of high school and college curricula, as they have so often been in the past. The precise form that such courses will take is largely a matter of conjecture. More language work-time, more languages (not merely

---

[9] Pei, "Can the Intensive Language Course Survive?", *Comparative Literature News-Letter*. National Council of Teachers of English, 2, No. 3 (Dec. 1943), 1-3.

the French, German, Spanish and occasional Italian of pre-war days), and more direct conversational methods are certain.

IV

The year 1944 was a particularly prolific one as far as publications by Pei on the subject of languages in the war and the implications for the future were concerned. Some dozen articles in both professional journals and popular magazines appeared that year, as well as an equal number of reviews, published letters and rejoinders — all of which had to do with some aspect of effective language teaching. In addition, he became director and compiler of the World Language Series, published by S. F. Vanni, under whose auspices appeared a series of basic language booklets in German, Russian, Spanish, Italian, French, Japanese, as well as others devoted to linguistic geography and English as a worldwide tongue.

Though started the preceding September, the War Linguistic Course at Columbia, formulated by Professor Pei, was described in an article published only in January, 1944.[10] The course was six months long and open to high school and college students with average language training. The course had a three-fold aim, according to him:

> ...firstly, to inform the students concerning the languages spoken all over the world, where they are spoken, by what peoples, and by how many speakers, secondly, to acquaint the students with the characteristic features of some thirty languages in their spoken and written form, so that the problem of language identification may cease to be a problem for the man who is called upon to distinguish between Russian and Polish, Swedish and Norwegian, Chinese and Malay; thirdly, to impart an elementary smattering of seven of the world's most important tongues, for purposes of everyday speech and comprehension.

---

[10] Pei, "War Linguistics," *French Review*, 17, No. 3 (Jan. 1944), 182-83.

Unique among the language-teaching innovations originated in the war, the Columbia University War Linguistics Course was another worthwhile solution of one aspect of the many-sided problem of language needs in wartime.

A most important article appeared in March 1944 [11] — actually the printed version of an address delivered at the Annual Meeting of the New England Modern Language Association at Boston University, on December 4, 1943. It is here that Pei takes up in detail the bitter controversy that raged in the profession at the time concerning the relative merits of the new "Army" or "intensive" method. He divides the language teachers into three groups:

> Which of our three groups of language teachers is more nearly right: the innovators who "crow" about a so-called discovery which was discovered and discussed long before their time, and which the war, the Government's need for trained linguists, both civil and military, and the lavishly spent millions of the Government and some great Foundations have finally made possible on a grand scale; the restrictive scholars who see little or no merit in the acquisition of living languages unless they are applied to problems of literary or philological criticism; or the vast mass of professional (not improvised) language teachers, who stand, somewhat befuddled and bewildered, between the two adverse currents, and for lack of better directives continue teaching in the old way, with the written as well as the oral approach, the practical as well as the literary slant?

He answers his own question by pointing out that there is some measure of right and wrong in each position, and then goes on to establish the clear need for more and better trained foreign-language people in the post-war world. There will be a place for persons with all types of linguistic, scholarly and cultural interests and abilities as far as languages are concerned. He predicts that "the Intensive Language, ASTP and Foreign Area and Language programs will survive, probably in something like their present form, which is highly effective for their avowed

---

[11] Pei, "The Function of Languages in the Post-War World," *Modern Language Journal*, 38, No. 3 (March 1944).

purpose...." He concludes the article by a supposition whose logic is unimpeachable but whose validity, unfortunately and ironically, is not corroborated by the present-day state of international relations:

> ... the function of languages in the post-war world will be that of unifying rather than dividing the world's peoples. There is nothing like the study of foreign languages to arouse intelligent and sympathetic interest in the habits, customs, way of life and mental processes of alien peoples. And once we become familiar with those phases of their lives, they cease to be alien. They become friends.

Answering a need for accurate information about the geography of language in the world, Professor Pei published two articles in 1944 relating to French and Italian.[12] What interests us at this moment in the articles is that in both he pleads for greater understanding of the linguistic emergencies, as it were, provoked by the war, as well as a more sensible attitude among language teachers toward language study, both as regards "culture" *vs.* "practical use," and "familiar" *vs.* "exotic" languages: Swahili and Siamese are not overnight going to be placed on a par with the French and Italian languages, nor will the focus of cultural or commercial importance suddenly shift from "Europe and Latin America to the steppes of Siberia and the wild gorges of the Yang-tze."

During the course of the preceding year two major controversial issues relating to the ASTP foreign-language teaching stirred the profession. Professor Pei was to take a very active part in the discussion surrounding both of them during 1944. The first concerned a sweeping reproof by certain writers of all civilian language teaching in comparison with the new Army method.

Charles R. Walker had published an article in *School and Society*,[13] in which he drew a critical picture of the inefficiencies

---

[12] a. Pei, "French as a World Language," *French Review*, 17, No. 5 (March 1944), 255-62.
  b. Pei "Italian as a War Language - and Beyond," *Italica*, 21, No. 2 (June 1944), 67-71.

[13] Charles R. Walker, "Language Teaching Goes to War," 57, No. 1475, April 3, 1943, 369-73.

and failures of foreign-language teaching in the schools, and contrasted this with the good sense and logic of the new intensive method. The fact that the *Reader's Digest*, with its large popular circulation, reprinted the article, [14] aggravated the offense felt by many regular language teachers in schools and colleges. There were many replies of a defensive nature. Professor Pei's took the form of an "open letter" [15] in which he called attention to the gratitude expressed by former students to their "old" teachers:

> ... language teachers would like to remind your readers (those of the *Reader's Digest*) of the thousands of letters that pour in to them from real G.I.'s — former students who voice their thanks for the languages they learned in high school and college by the "old-fashioned" way ...

Furthermore, he challenged the repeated assertion, namely, that the "informant — linguistic scientist" set-up that characterized the ASTP was valid and warranted even for the more familiar languages because, it was claimed, bilingual ability for teaching purposes is rare or non-existent, by writing another Letter, this time to *Fortune*. [16]

> The overwhelming majority of American language teachers will strongly disagree with [the] claim that there are few people trained in the world combining perfect bilingualism with pedagogic training.

The second issue, closely related to the first but of a more technical nature, concerned the methodological claims and counterclaims of the "new linguistic" approach of the Army method. The issue ultimately took the form of a spirited dialogue in the journals between Professor Pei and Professor Robert A. Hall Jr. of Cornell, accompanied by much stimulating thought (and entertainment) for many of the language teachers of the time.

---

[14] Walker, "Teaching Languages in a Hurry," 42, No. 253, 40-42.
[15] Pei, "Open Letter to the Reader's Digest," *French Review*, 17, No. 5 (March 1944), 300-01.
[16] Pei, "A Letter to Fortune," *Bulletin of New England Modern Language Association*, 6, No. 2 (Nov.-Dec. 1944), 26-27; Also, *French Review*, 18, No. 1 (Oct. 1944), 64-65; also, in briefer form, *Fortune Magazine*, 30, Dec. 1944, p. 278.

The dispute started with Professor Pei's review [17] of Denoeu and Hall's *Spoken French, Basic Course* in the January issue of the *French Review*, in which he criticized the over-simplification of French phonetics, the limitations of the grammatical explanations offered (both as concerned accuracy and completeness) and the failure to make adequate distinctions between the spoken and written languages or even between colloquial (or dialectical) and standard speech. In addition, Pei remonstrated against the underlying assumptions of the new book and its slavish adherence to the intensive language approach with its belief that a child and an adult learn a language in the same way:

> The fallacy of the Berlitz schools, from which our intensive programs ... have drawn their methodology, lies precisely in the fact that they ignore the mental gap between a child and an adult, their respective equipment of memory and coordination abilities, the different functions that the two have to play in their respective environments. The child is learning not merely words, but concepts; the adult already has his concepts formed.

In a rejoinder to the review, [18] Hall rebutted by calling attention to the intended purpose of the book: "to teach basic spoken French in a minimum of time...." He also defended the language used as being that used every day by almost all French persons, not speaking formally from a pulpit or stage. (In the same issue, incidentally, Hall had presented rather vehemently a series of strong arguments in favor of the theory and practice of the Army method, as opposed to the "superstitions" of the traditionally-minded. [19]) Pei was allowed, again in the same issue, to reply to Hall's rejoinder. [20] With considerable feeling and some sarcasm, Pei unequivocally denounced as absurd the various "errors" (as he saw them) of the "new menace" represented by

---

[17] Pei, "Review of *Spoken French*, by Denoeu and Hall," 17, No. 3 (Jan. 1944), 168-70.

[18] Robert A. Hall, Jr. "Letter to the Editor," *French Review*, 17, No. 6 (May 1944), 383-84.

[19] Hall, "Language and Superstition," *French Review*, 17, No. 6 (May 1944), 377-82.

[20] Pei, "Reply to Hall's Rejoinder," *French Review*, 17, No. 6 (May 1944), 382-83.

Hall's ideas that: 1) correct speech is a relative matter; 2) written language is unimportant; 3) new grammars for French and German should be constructed in the same way as those for "Bantu, Quechua and Chin."

In much the same vein, Pei replied a few months later to the exuberant faith and claims for the "new method" expressed in the *Fortune* article (August, 1944), "Science Comes to Languages." [21]

This ideological difference of opinion was to continue through the next several years, and, in a real sense, of course, though in a different form, down to our own day.

Returning to the subject of languages and their strategic importance in World War II, Pei published an article in the *Modern Language Journal* [22] to correct the oversights of an article published in the *National Geographic Magazine* ("The World's Words") the preceding December, in which were left out of consideration French, German, Italian and Japanese as dominant and critical tongues throughout the globe.

Lastly, in 1944, Pei recounted in an informal, entertaining fashion a personal experience in teaching. [23] The technique he tried out was the "impromptu realistic situation" (or what was called "comédie spontanée") as a means of stimulating conversational drill in the classroom. His success, he concluded, lay "... in the theory that languages are primarily for spoken use rather than for literary introspection, and that if we can break down the students' inhibitions, built up by marks, corrections and insistence upon absolute perfection, we shall have gone a long way toward making language study effective and popular." However, in the same article, he took part again in the continuing polemic on the new methodological orientation of the "intensive method":

---

[21] Pei, "A Letter to Fortune," *French Review*, 18, No. 1 (Oct. 1944), 64-5; also *Bulletin of the New England Modern Language Association*, 6, No. 2 (Nov.-Dec. 1944), 26-7; and also, in briefer form, *Fortune Magazine*, 30, Dec. 1944, p. 278.

[22] Pei, "What Languages are Our Soldiers Up Against?" 27, No. 6 (Oct. 1944), 463-71. This was also issued as a booklet in the World Language Series (S. F. Vanni: New York 1944).

[23] Pei "An Experiment in Conversation," *French Review*, 18, No. 2 (Dec. 1944), 96-99.

The new "talkie-talkie" school of linguistics assures us that "reading and writing come very easily, naturally, gracefully," etc. to those who have "learned to speak and understand." My own personal experience has shown me that the converse is true; that if there is a good grammatical background, a fair vocabulary range, and a good reading knowledge, conversational ability comes rather easily once we find ourselves in the environment where the foreign language *must* be used. The fact that the environment and the incentive were almost invariably lacking in pre-war days was probably largely responsible for the lack of conversational achievement on the part of American foreign language students.

V

Of some half dozen articles by Pei, written in 1945, on some aspect of war-time teaching of languages, four are of particular interest: they reveal continuing notice and study of the dominant ideas and proposals.

The first [24] takes up again the argument with Hall and the "linguistic scientists" concerning the new ways of presenting grammar. Pei takes issue with the "linguistic science" approach and demonstrates, using the adjective in French as an example, the unnecessary complexity and, to some extent, inaccuracy of the new approach as compared to the traditional one. He summarizes his dissatisfaction by a general observation:

> The rules of grammar of the civilized languages were not devised by fools. The function of formal grammar is to facilitate the learning of a language by using a process which the child's mind lacks, but the adult mind possesses: the ability to generalize. The child, of course, learns his mother-tongue by trial-and-error, by hit-or-miss, and, above all, by a process of infinite correction. The adult needs short-cuts to grasp in one year, at the rate of three to five hours a week, what the child has learned in ten years, at the rate of sixteen hours a day. The languages of civilization generally taught in American

---

[24] Pei, "French Grammar and the Linguistic Scientists," *Trait d'Union*, 3, No. 3 (April 1945), 3-4.

high schools and colleges (French, German, Spanish, Italian) have had their grammatical rules elaborated by scholars and teachers over many centuries. It is possible that better generalizations may be evolved than those we have now. But what the linguistic scientists have to offer seems more like a retrogression to the child method of trial-and-error than a scientific improvement of the generalization devices we now possess.

The second article [25] is an incisive analysis and, for its time, a bold prediction of the proper place of various foreign languages in the American high school. Pei foresees the need for the opportunity of high school students to study languages other than the familiar ones. A changing world compels us, he says, to recognize the importance, for instance, of the Slavic and Oriental languages in the developing domination of new political powers. (There is no need to point out the remarkable prophetic nature of his views.) In practical terms, he outlines the ways and means by which certain large, centrally-located high schools can accommodate such teaching. Nor does he in the article forgo the opportunity to emphasize his underlying belief in the value of such teaching. "In the dynamic global world of today, no subject has shown itself more vitally important, more directly and immediately useful, more satisfactory as a builder of character, principles of tolerance and world citizenship, than modern foreign languages." And, in addition, he clarifies his position in regard to teaching methods:

> The matter of approach is, of course, something that applies to all modern foreign language study, not merely to the proposed newcomers. There is no doubt that a more conversational approach is in order, since the primary function of any language is to be spoken and understood. At the same time, modern civilization is such that the written form of the language cannot be neglected. What ought to be thoroughly eschewed in the case of high school language study is the literary, so-called "cultural" approach for which high school students

---

[25] Pei, "A Rational Program for Teaching Languages in American High Schools," *American Slavic and East European Review*, 4, Nos. 8-9 (Aug. 1945), 138-41.

are unfitted, both by age and by disposition, and which is embodied in the present "reading ability" objective.

All in all, the article strikes one today as a kind of blueprint for the future.

The third article, having appeared a few months earlier, got a larger exposure in October of the year when it appeared in the *Modern Language Journal*.[26] Entitled "The French Adjective and the Linguistic Scientist," it returned to an attack upon the unfounded enthusiasm and confidence of the linquistic scientists, and more especially Robert Hall, in their belief that the grammars of the traditional languages should be rewritten. In simply greater detail, Pei reiterates his previous opposition to the new linguistic approach:

> Robert A. Hall, Jr. urges us to "turn the traditional approach around, and derive the masculine from the feminine," whereupon "everything becomes crystal clear," because "if we take the feminine as the basic form, the masculine of each adjective is derived from the feminine by dropping the final consonant, whatever that consonant may be."
>
> The following are a few of the hypothetical masculine forms we would obtain by applying this miraculous invention...:
>
> | Feminine | Masculine |
> |---|---|
> | BREV | BRE |
> | PROPR | PROP |
> | GOSH (gauche) | GO |
> | BEL | BE |
> | ... | ... etc. |
>
> This would be, according to Mr. Hall, "in correspondence with the facts of the language as spoken." It "reflects the true state of the language."

---

[26] "The French Adjective and the Linguistic Scientist," *Bulletin of New England Modern Language Association*, 7, No. 1 (May 1945), 31. Reprinted in *Modern Language Journal*, 29, No. 6 (Oct. 1945), 545-46.

Lastly, and from our point of view, most important of all, was the article by Pei in the *Bulletin* of the AAUP. [27] It is here that Professor Pei reproves with eloquence, humor, sarcasm and some bitterness all the reckless claims (as he analyzed them) of the linguistic scientists. In the first place, he defends language teaching in the schools and reminds us that if after a lapse of 20 years a person doesn't remember much of two years of language in school it is because "... proficiency in a spoken language, as in everything else, calls for constant practice." Secondly, to claim that no one ever really learned a language in an American school or college is nonsense: "... It was mainly American language teachers, products of American high school and college language courses, who staffed the ASTP courses in those four languages, working for the first time in their lives under ideal conditions of hours, student-to-teacher ratio, and student interest." Thirdly, after a technical examination of various grammatical theories, rules and teaching procedures evolved by the "linguistic scientists" in charge of the ASTP development, Pei demonstrates, point by point, that they are most often "not merely weird, but misleading and impractical." Fourthly, he fears that perhaps it is the case that "the linguistic scientists would like to set up their own little methods — and — textbook hierarchy, to which they would like to see the much more numerous language teachers pay tribute." In short, the article is a sharp denial of what Pei considered an exaggerated and dangerous undermining of what was sound and proven over the years. There was room for change and improvement, he admitted, but not along the lines then proposed by the new methodologists.

It would be well to point out here that what might seem a change of attitude from Pei's earlier staunch support of ASTP to the eventual criticism of some of its attributes is actually a differentiation between the general emphasis on foreign-language study for practical purposes, which he could support, and the

---

[27] Pei, "A Modern Language Teacher Replies," *Bulletin,* American Association of University Professors, 31, No. 3 (Autumn 1945), 409-17. This article is in reply to "Progress and Reaction in Modern Language Teaching," by Robert A. Hall, Jr. which was published in the Summer 1945 *Bulletin.*

extreme forms of implementation of technical theories, which he could not.

VI

The next several years witnessed a continuation of these controversies with restatements of the same opposing points of view; Professor Pei pursued as energetically as ever with the exposition of his own strong opinions.

Largely out of all this discussion and argument have come down to us today renewed interest in foreign-language study and a re-vitalized sense of new goals for a more relevant program of language teaching within the schools. Whereas the problem of a best method has not been solved (if it can ever be), it cannot be denied that textbooks, classroom activity, supplementary aids and general achievement have all been directly and very favorably influenced by the experiences of the "war years." Professor Mario Pei, because of the active rôle he played, must be specially commended not only for elucidating for the general public the important rôle of foreign language competence in a world at war or peace, but also for prodding the profession into examining its own conscience and experience as a kind of national self-study in preparation for a future he could perceive with uncanny accuracy.

UNE FORMULE D'EXORCISME EN ANCIEN FRANÇAIS

By Menahem Banitt
Tel Aviv University

Au milieu du XIIIe siècle, à Chinon en Touraine, le rabbin de la communauté juive, Isaac fils d'Isaac, enrichissait son rituel de nouvelles prières, d'oraisons et de poésies pieuses "au hasard des trouvailles et des besoins." De l'avis de Mme C. Sirat, qui a consacré à ce rituel, manuscrit hébreu 633 de la Bibliothèque Nationale à Paris, une étude aussi méticuleuse qu'approfondie,[1] ces ajouts dénotent une "inspiration mystique et ésotérique." Sous l'action des persécutions chrétiennes, qui devaient aboutir à l'expulsion des Juifs de France en 1306, la pensée rationaliste, voire ratiocinante, des rabbins français inclinaient de plus en plus vers l'occulte. Il est cependant étonnant de trouver dans un rituel, et écrite de la main même du rabbin, une longue adjuration contre l'anthrax. Elle est inscrite aux folios 149^v et 150^r du manuscrit et reproduite sur la planche II de l'étude de Mme Sirat.

Le fait que, sauf la formule initiale *rephua(h) šelèma(h)*, le texte entier de l'exorcisme, bien que transcrit en caractères hébreux, soit du français, n'est pas insolite en soi. Les Juifs du moyen âge en France priaient et étudiaient en français.[2] Ce qui est inattendu, c'est l'exorcisme. Les rabbins se sont toujours,

---

[1] Mme C. Sirat, "Le rituel juif de France: le manuscrit hébreu 633," *Revue des Etudes juives*, 3e série, 2 [119] (1961), 7-40.

[2] Hiram Pflaum, "Deux hymnes judéo-français du moyen âge," *Romania*, 59 (1933), 154-182; Hiram Peri-Pflaum, *Tarbiz*, 24 (1955-56), 426-440 (en hébreu); Menahem Banitt, "Une langue fantôme: le judéo-français," *Revue de Linguistique romane*, 27 (1963), 245-294.

formellement du moins, opposés à la magie. Toutefois, nous trouvons, dès les temps les plus reculés et jusque dans le Talmud des incantations juives. Les gens du peuple, dans tous les pays et à toutes les époques, s'adonnaient, comme leurs voisins non juifs, à la magie: ils se servaient d'amulettes, de formules incantatoires, de recettes cabalistiques et exerçaient des rites divinatoires et des sortilèges. Dans des cas extrêmes, certains rabbins allaient même jusqu'à permettre d'avoir recours à des thaumaturges chrétiens. L'emploi des noms sacrés du christianisme était subtilement rationalisé.[3] Or, ce ne sont pas quelques simples paroles magiques que le rabbin de Chinon transcrit; c'est une longue adjuration, exorcisant le mal dans une suite de formules construites selon les règles de la magie et où les éléments non juifs ne font pas défaut.

Le déchiffrement de la page était particulièrement ardu. On s'en convaincra rapidement en jetant un regard sur le facsimilé reproduit dans l'article de Mme Sirat. Ni la loupe au-dessus du parchemin, ni la photographie infra-rouge n'ont pu remédier aux imperfections de la copie. L'écriture est irrégulière; les lettres se suivent sans intervalles entre les mots ni même entre les phrases; l'orthographe n'est pas fixe; les voyelles ne sont pas marquées; certaines lettres ont des valeurs multiples; l'n de la voyelle nasale, à l'intérieur du mot, n'est pas marqué; les signes diacritiques font presque complètement défaut; les erreurs de copie sont nombreuses; les signes à la fin des lignes sont presque illisibles. Il a fallu d'interminables tâtonnements avant d'arriver à dégager l'intention de l'auteur.

La langue est correcte. Les rares traits dialectaux sont ceux de Touraine: vélarisation de [ã] en [õ] et simplification de [aj] en [ɛ]. De même, la présence d'un subjonctif en [ʒ], dans

---

[3] J. Wellesz, "Volksmedizinisches aus dem jüdischen Mittelalter," *Mitteilungen zur jüdischen Volkskunde*, 36 (1910), 117-118. L'ouvrage d'initiation sur la magie chez les Juifs, abondamment documenté et pourvu de copieuses notes et d'une bibliographie exhaustive est celui de Joshua Trachtenberg, *Jewish Magic and Superstition*, New York, Behrman's Jewish Book House, 1939.

Jacob Hazan, Rabbin de Londres et contemporain d'Isaac ben Isaac de Chinon, condamne cependant, en des termes violents et d'une façon inexorable, toute magie et pratique conjuratoire dans son *Etz Hayyim*, p. p. Israël Brodie, Jérusalem, Mosad Harav Kook, 1964, II, 338.

onsanje et *sanje* (§10) de *(en)saner* ou *(en)sanir*, n'est pas faite pour nous étonner dans un texte de l'Ouest. Cependant, *somoyle* (§1) ainsi que *fèce* (§5, = fasses) n'étaient connus que dans les régions de l'Est et du Midi du pays d'Oïl et n'avaient pas été attestés si loin à l'Ouest. La graphie *celiâ*, dans l'indication finale, où *-iâ* correspond au francien *-el*, pourrait n'être qu'une transcription phonétique du *a* vélaire résultant de la chute du *l*, équivalente à la graphie *au* en caractères latins. Il est possible, d'autre part, que ces trois derniers mots, *somoyle*, *fèce* et *celiâ*, soient dus au dialecte champenois de l'original. Une fois le dialecte tourangeau établi, les notations équivoques ont été résolues en graphie de l'Ouest. Ainsi *vav*, qui peut être lu *o*, *u*, *ou*, sera transcrit d'après ses normes.

La syntaxe est normale. Les grammairiens considèrent plutôt rare l'extension de l'infinitif comme impératif négatif à la conjonctive dépendant d'un verbe de volonté; notre texte en offre trois exemples contre trois verbes au subjonctif.

Quant au vocabulaire, il n'a de juif que la formule initiale *rephua(h) šelèma(h)* et le nom *peloni* (§5). Dans le premier cas, il s'agit d'un titre: les mots ne font pas partie de l'exorcisme propre. *Peloni*, bien que courant en hébreu, n'avait pas de contrepartie en ancien français. Il tient lieu du nom propre qui éventuellement prendra sa place dans des formulaires rituelles et juridiques; il correspond à notre 'un tel' ou 'X'.

Le mot *amen* de la fin n'est pas spécialement hébreu et les mots *a siègle* qui le suivent le francisent encore plus.

Le vocabulaire français comme tel nous livre quelques emplois peu communs:

BON MALON (§1), sous la forme *bon malant*, est employé au moins six fois par Raschi dans ses Commentaires talmudiques, pour rendre le mot araméen pour 'diphtérie' et une seule fois pour 'carboncle' ou 'anthrax'.[4] Le *bon malon*, comme l'euphémie nous l'assure, est un mal plus grave que le simple *malon* ou *malant*, maladie bénigne comme l'eczéma et la gale ou dénotant un ulcère, une plaie infectée. Le furoncle est nommé *clog* 'clou' par

---

[4] Arsène Darmesteter et David S. Blondheim, *Les Gloses françaises dans les Commentaires talmudiques de Raschi*, Paris, Champion, 1929, I, § 125, p. 15.

Raschi (Blondheim, §215). La gravité du *bon malant* est confirmée par une décision rabbinique rapportée par Eliézer berabi Joël Halévy (1160-1235), permettant de profaner le sabbat pour le soigner;[5] ceci ne se fait qu'en des cas extrêmes. Comme on conjure le *bon malon* de ne pas *son suc muèr ne sa chèr domajièr* (§5), il paraît plus judicieux de conclure que l'exorcisme s'applique à l'anthrax et de traduire *bon malan* par 'carboncle', le terme qui le désignait dans l'ancienne médecine.

BONS OMES (§10) a le même sens qu'il a dans les textes chrétiens: 'justes', 'saints hommes', bien que les bénéficiaires du titre soient distincts.

CELÈL (indication finale), ici sous sa forme dialectale *celiâ,* est un doublet non attesté du picard *celet* 'châsse' mentionné par Godefroy.

CLÈR (§6) signifiant 'eau' n'est mentionné nulle part.

GÈ (passim) pour 'Dieu' est plus fréquent dans les textes juifs que *dè.*

ISSIR (§6) transitif est rare, mais attesté.

LASCHIÈR ENMI ESTÈR (§5). Si ma lecture de ces lettres est correcte, *laschier* serait employé ici dans le sens de 'laisser,' ce qui est courant en français moderne, mais n'est pas mentionné pour l'ancien français.

MARTURIÈR (§10) en soi n'a rien d'incongru, sauf le fait de le retrouver dans un texte juif. Les dictionnaires n'ont pas relevé la construction *martirier a martire* à côté de *faire, livrer* et *metre a martire.*

SANISER (§10)? 'guérir'; voir plus loin.

SANONCE (§7), correspondant a *sanance* en francien, est un dérivé de *saner;* il ne se trouve pas dans les dictionnaires, mais est conforme au génie de la langue.

SUC (§5), au sens de 'sève' d'être vivant, n'a pas été relevé avant 1488 d'après Wartburg, *FEW,* XII, 391a.

Pour éditer le texte, il a évidemment fallu séparer les mots et pourvoir la ponctuation. Pour faciliter les références, les paragraphes ont été mis en évidence et numérotés. Les lettres sup-

---

[5] *Sefer Rabia(h),* p. p. A. Aptowitzer, 2e éd., Jérusalem, Harry Fischel Institute, I, 329 nn. 30, 31.

plées sont inscrites dans des crochets aigus < >; les crochets droits [ ] renferment les lettres difficilement déchiffrables et de lecture douteuse; les parenthèses ( ), celles que le copiste avait oubliées et suscrites.

Dans la transcription de l'écriture hébraïque en caractères latins, j'ai évité toute rigidité encombrante et me suis tenu autant que possible aux habitudes graphiques de l'ancien français, sans pour cela sacrifier les indices phonétiques particuliers que la notation en caractères hébreux pouvait fournir. Ainsi le *qoph* hébreu sera rendu soit par *c* soit par *q* selon le mode français; *yod* par *i* ou *è* quand il désigne une voyelle, par *y* dans le cas de la semi-voyelle et par *j* lorsqu'il transcrit la chuintante. Dans notre texte, [ɜ] est rendu par un *guimel* surmonté d'un signe diacritique, uniquement dans le mot *gè*. Cette graphie remplace le *yod* dans la plupart des textes juifs du XIIIe siècle. Une autre graphie archaïque de notre texte est l'emploi de deux *vav* pour *v*. Les copistes de l'époque préféraient *beth* surmonté d'un trait, le *raphè(h)*. En général, la distinction entre [a] et [ɑ] est maintenue: la voyelle vélaire est notée d'un *aleph*; elle est transcrite par *â*. L'autre n'est pas marquée du tout. La voyelle *e*, rendue en hébreu par un *yod*, sera notée *è*; par deux *yod*: *ê*. Un *e* muet a été ajouté dans l'édition là où les textes en caractères latins en ont.

Le texte de l'adjuration se lit donc comme suit:

fol. 149ᵛ   Rephua(h) šelèma(h):
§1 je te conjure bon malon de par sire gè, qi ne fot ne ne mo<n>t, ne ne dort ne ne somoyle;
§2 je te conjure de gè le roy pu(y)so<n>t, se tu ièç ci, qe non ne ayles avo<n>t;
§3 je te conjure de gè lou grant, se tu iès ci qe tu ne amandes;
§4 je te conjure de gè dou ciel, se tu iès ci qe ne proyèr;
§5 je te conjure de gè lou vif, se tu iès ci qe ne trère on cel ile de mèr lac<han>t o<n>-[mi] èstèr ta lâstè è ta chètivetè remanèr; q'à peloni ne fèces mês son suc muèr ne sa chèr domajièr;

§6 je te conjure de sire gè, issi tâ feltè; e de pèn e de sèl, e de vin e de clèr è de c(o)<n>c qe fit gè;

§7 je te conjure de gè lou vif e de verê sano<n>se qe èl m[èje] se mèt; è de pèn e de vin è de conc qe gè fit qe tu ne aretèr ci;

§8 je te conjure de toutes lès oroyzo[n]s qi furt e qi so<n>t;

§9 je te conjure de toutes lè prière<s> qi furt e qi ièrt;

§10 je te conjure de touç le bo<n>s omes qe furt onqe nes, è de Abraham lou sire qi so<n> fiç vôt ocire pour omour gè marturièr a martire; o<n>sa<n>jes vrêmo<n>t come gè fit Miriam la profète sène qe fut mèzèle, è sa<n>jes vrêmo<n>t; châce i esanise (ou: châce e sanise) ce mal è cête dolour de ci; amen a siègle (ou: sêgle).

*fol. 150*ᵛ

Cette adjuration sera dite trois fois de suite et trois fois par jour et qu'on tienne lou celiâ o safir *au-dessus des jointures ou [qu'on le mette] dans sa main et l'effet se fera sentir, avec l'aide de Dieu.* [6]

Il y aurait quelques remarques à faire au sujet de l'édition du texte:

Au début du premier paragraphe, la base du *beth* de *bon* semble avoir été grattée pour faire lire *don* (=donc), en accord avec les formules chrétiennes *conjuro ergo*, ou *igitur*.

Au lieu de *trère* (§5), on pourrait lire *traïèr;* le copiste avait d'abord écrit *tahèr* (?), puis a maladroitement surchargé le mot. Quelques mots plus loin, là où nous lisons *lachant onmi*, seules les lettres לקט sont certaines.

Au §7, *de verê sanonse* n'est pas très sûr. Ce que nous lisons *-no-* est représenté par *nun vav*, qui ne sont peut-être qu'un *teth* mal formé. Notre lecture est d'autant plus contestable que la phrase obtenue n'est pas très claire.

---

[6] Les mots en italiques sont en hébreu dans le texte.

Au lieu de *qe furt onqe nes* (§10), le manuscrit porte
אוקמואונש . Il fallait considérer les lettres superflues comme une
dittographie.

D'après l'état actuel du texte, il faut lire, à la dernière ligne
de ce paragraphe et écrit en un mot: *è sanise;* mais il est précédé
d'un אי exponctué, ce qui permet de supposer qu'à l'origine il
y avait *i esanise,* correspondant à un francien *et essanice;* car
essanicier est attesté (*FEW*, XI, 189a) et *saniser* serait un hapax.
Quant à *i* pour la conjonction *et,* ce devait être la prononciation
normale devant *e* et *a* initiaux du mot suivant immédiatement,
d'après les manuscrits juifs ponctués.

Au milieu de la rubrique finale, écrite en hébreu, nous trouvons les lettres לוצליאהאוספיר que je décide de lire *lou celiâ o
safir* plutôt que *l'oncelée o safir*. Il est préférable de supposer une
formation en *-el* non attestée que d'attribuer à *encelée*, attesté
dans l'Ouest (*FEW*, II, 573a s.v. *celare*), un sens concret 'châsse'.

Avant de procéder à la traduction, notons encore quelques
graphies phonétiques: *ièç ci* (§1) pour *iès ci; issi* (§6) avec deux
sin; lès oroyzons (§8), *mais lè prières* (§9) et *le bons* (§10); *i* pour
et devant voyelle a déjà été vu plus haut; par contre, devant
consonne la conjonction *et* est souvent réduite à un chva.

Voici la traduction de l'exorcisme:

Guérison entière:
§1 je te conjure, carboncle, par le Seigneur Dieu, qui ne faut ni ne déçoit, qui ne dort ni ne sommeille;
§2 je te conjure par Dieu, le Roi puissant, puisque tu es ici, (au moins) ne progresse plus;
§3 je te conjure par Dieu, le Grand, puisque tu es ici, de ne plus profiter;
§4 je te conjure par Dieu qui est au Ciel, puisque tu es ici, de ne plus accaparer;
§5 je te conjure par le Dieu Vivant, puisque tu es ici, de ne pas te retirer dans cette fameuse île de la mer, abandonnant derrière toi ta misère et laissant demeurer ton mal; de ne plus faire tourner sa sève à un tel ni d'infecter sa chair;
§6 je te conjure par le Seigneur Dieu: emporte ta cruauté; et par le pain et le sel, par le vin et l'eau, et par tout ce que Dieu a créé;

§7 je te conjure par le Dieu Vivant et par la vraie guérison qui inspire le médecin; et par le pain et le vin et par tout ce que Dieu créa, de ne pas rester ici;

§8 je te conjure par toutes les oraisons qui ont existé et qui existent;

§9 je te conjure par toutes les prières qui ont été et toutes celles qui verront le jour;

§10 je te conjure par tous les saints hommes qui sont jamais venus au monde et par Abraham, le grand homme, qui était prêt à sacrifier son fils pour l'amour de Dieu [et à lui] faire souffrir le martyre; et guéris réellement, de la même façon que Dieu rendit la santé à la prophétesse Miryam après qu'elle avait eu la lèpre; et guéris réellement; chasse ce mal d'ici et soulage cette douleur;

ainsi soit-il de toute éternité.

Ajoutons que les mots français *lou celiâ o safir* au milieu de la rublique hébraïque signifient 'la châsse au saphir'.

La traduction de l'adjuration exige quelques éclaircissements:

CELE (§5), pronom démonstratif, a nettement cette connotation dénigrante que notre langue rend par 'fameux'.

ESANISER (§10) signifie 'soulager' et non pas 'guérir': il doit y avoir une différence entre ce verbe et *saner* employé deux fois dans le même paragraphe.

MUER (§5) ne signifie pas simplement 'changer' comme les lexiques se contentent de le traduire, mais bien 's'altérer'. C'est le sens qu'il a dès la *Vie de saint Alexis* (v. 116). 'Tourner' garde l'image; il se dit pour des liquides et pour le sang.

ORAISONS (§8) n'est attesté qu'une seule fois dans un texte juif, notamment dans la traduction, très libre, d'un hymne de Rosch Haschana, où il ne correspond pas à un mot bien défini de l'original. [7] Aucun des glossaires bibliques, publiés ou en manuscrit, ne le porte. En modernisant la forme, nous n'avons donc rien fait pour préciser la teneur du mot. Il est probable que le terme a été repris tel quel de la source chrétienne.

SE (§§ 3, 4 et 5) a été traduit par 'puisque' dans un sens de causalité atténuée: 'puisque nous devons accepter le fait que tu

---

[7] Hiram Peri-Pflaum, *Tarbiz*, 25 (1956-57), p. 191 (en hébreu).

te trouves ici'. Il ne peut en aucun cas être considéré comme conditionnel pur.

Bien que nous ayons tendance à nier toute logique dans des textes de ce genre, nous devons admettre que, dans le cadre de la croyance qui sous-tend cet exorcisme, nous sommes en présence d'une organisation rationnelle très nette et d'une composition réfléchie. Il est vrai que les paragraphes 5, 6, 7 et 10 manquent d'unité et semblent n'être que des amalgames, alors que, d'autre part, les paragraphes 8 et 9 ont l'air d'être tronqués; on serait tenté de supposer une disposition originale différente. Mais le nombre 10 est bien un nombre magique ayant trait à l'action en question. Nous le trouvons présidant à la Création du monde, déterminant le choix de l'homme élu, Noé, et du peuple élu issu d'Abraham (*Mischna Abot*, IV, 1-4). Nous le retrouvons dans la création du macrocosme et du microcosme (*Séfer Yecira*). Il se divise en deux, 5 pour le macromosme et 5 pour le microcosme, quand ils s'affrontent: division observée dans notre adjuration. Dans chacun des cinq premiers paragraphes, Dieu (*gè*) apparaît attitré d'un attribut différent: *sire, roy puissant, grant, du ciel, vif*; au sixième paragraphe la série recommence. A la division de la formulation correspond une division interne, qui est celle de l'action qu'on attend des formules. Les cinq premières formules ne doivent servir qu'à arrêter le mal; à partir de la sixième commence la marche vers la guérison: *issi, mèje, sanje, chace, esenise*. De passif qu'il était dans les cinq premières conjurations, grâce à l'invocation des puissances du macrocosme, le démon est obligé de passer à l'action et aider à la guérison dans le cadre du microcosme: le pain, le vin, le sel, l'eau, le médecin, les prières, les saints, etc. A l'intérieur des deux groupes aussi, la progression se fait logiquement. D'abord *aler avant, amander, proïer* et finalement l'adjuration de ne pas partir en laissant le mal agir; dans le deuxième groupe, enchaînant sur la fin du premier: emporter le mal, faire agir le *mèje*, guérir et, enfin, adoucir la douleur.

Dans leurs efforts de s'assurer l'aide des puissances occultes, les exorcistes ne s'arrêtent pas aux limites de leur religion individuelle. Au contraire, regardant l'existence des autres religions comme des manifestations du Mal, ils s'empressent de se servir des noms des divinités étrangères afin de s'emparer du pouvoir sur lui.

C'est ainsi que les adjurations chrétiennes interpellent Adonaï, Elohim, Schaddaï, Sabaoth, Ehyeh. [8] Elles parlent de *deus vivus* et de *deus verus* qui sont des formules spécifiquement juives; du Dieu Créateur de toutes choses, du Dieu d'Abraham, Isaac et Jacob; elles conjurent au nom des *orationes Patriarchorum*, mais n'invoquent jamais les miracles de Jésus. Ce sont plutôt les Actes de Josué, de David, de Daniël et surtout de Moïse qu'on invoque. Par contre, notre texte fait mention du pain et du vin (transsubstantiation), du sel et de l'eau (baptême). [9] A côté d'expressions fondamentalement juives comme *ne ne dort ne ne somoyle* (Psaumes cxxi: 4) et *amen a siègle* (Rituel juif), nous trouvons des mots comme *oroyzons*, qui peut être soupçonné d'origine chrétienne et *marturier a martire* qui ne laisse aucun doute quant à l'origine, surtout dans ce contexte où le terme consacré est un mot courant, *akèda(h)*. La réunion d'Abraham, son fils qu'il voulait *ocire* et Miryam, rappelle de trop près, malgré les résonances juives, les trois personnages principaux du christianisme: Dieu le Père, son Fils et la Vierge. Si Miryam, la sœur de Moïse, a de sérieux titres à l'inclusion dans une prière pour la guérison d'un malade, c'est tout de même Moïse, celui qui a obtenu la guérison, qu'il faudrait invoquer. C'est ce que font, en effet, les conjurations chrétiennes. Répétons, c'est la juxtaposition, auprès du mot chrétien *martire*, du fils sacrifié et de la prophétesse Miryam, qui, en premier lieu, fait penser à une origine chrétienne. La prière

---

[8] Cf. Adolf Franz, *Die Kirchlichen Benediktionen im Mittelalter*, Freiburg i. B., 1909, 2 vol; plus spécialement p. 425. En général, les manuels d'exorcismes sont des ouvrages rédigés sous les directives de l'Eglise. Ils ont tendance à substituer des prières et des oraisons aux adjurations magiques. Le *Thesaurus exorcismorum atque conjurationum*, Cologne, 1608, bien que composé en latin et portant la marque de l'Institution, m'a semblé, entre tous, le plus proche des coutumes populaires et probablement françaises (nous y trouvons, par exemple, très souvent le verbe *baiulare* dans le sens de 'donner'). La formule la plus fréquente pour le début d'une adjuration est: *conjuro te ergo per nomen Dei Adonay*...
Cf. aussi Henri Leclerq, in *Dictionnaire d'Archéologie chrétienne et de Liturgie*, Paris, 1907-, I, col. 527, s. v. *adjuration* et V, coll. 964-978, s. v. *exorcisme*.

[9] Un recueil de pratiques magiques, du nom de *Clavicula Salomonis*, circulait en de nombreux manuscrits au moyen âge. Dans l'édition qu'en publia Hermann Gollancz (Franckfort et Londres, 1903), nous retrouvons, en hébreu cette fois, une adjuration "au nom de pain, d'eau et de vin" (App. 6b).

synagogale officielle en faveur d'un malade invoque le Dieu d'Abraham, Isaac, Jacob, Moïse, Aaron, David et Salomon.

La greffe a laissé une cicatrice: l'exorcisme oublie qu'il s'adresse au Mal et lui demande, comme s'il était Dieu, de guérir le malade comme Il avait guéri Miryam de la lèpre. La fin: "chasse le mal d'ici et soulage la douleur" est clairement l'écho d'une prière à Dieu.

L'adaptation du texte magique chrétien au goût rabbinique perce, d'ailleurs, dès les premiers mots. Au lieu d'invoquer Satan, le *malin*, le rabbin s'adresse à la maladie, le *malon*. On pourrait, à la rigueur, croire à une personnification de la maladie, mais on ne peut aller jusqu'à lui demander d'agir en *mèje*. L'accoutrement du *malin* en *malon* expliquerait l'erreur de *bon* pour *don*.

Allusion est faite, au paragraphe 5, à l'île de la mer, où le *malon* pourrait se rendre. Les exorcistes avaient coutume d'envoyer les démons au fond des mers, *ad profundum abyssi* (*Thesaurus*, pp. 339, 376, 440 et passim). Mais une île? Nous savons que les ermites se retiraient sur des îles désertes et nous connaissons des îles magiques dans les légendes arthuriennes. Tout cela est un peu loin.

Un mot encore sur la rubrique finale. Il est de règle de répéter une formule trois fois de suite, et de le faire trois par jour est un procédé élémentaire en magie. Répéter n'importe quel mot magique trois fois a en soi déjà une force curative (Trachtenberg, p. 201).

Le saphir, d'après Marbode et les lapidaires qui s'inspirent de lui,[10] a, parmi ses vertus, celle d'être *bon a malanz saner*. Un lapidaire hébreu assez étriqué (Trachtenberg, p. 226) attribue au saphir la seule vertu de guérison, mais recommande spécialement l'imposition sur les yeux. Le glossaire biblique hébreu français, qui forme le ms. 1099 (catalogue Vollers) de la Bibliothèque Universitaire de Leipzig, contient un lapidaire plus étendu (fols. 23^r-24^r) très proche des français: la guérison est une des vertus du saphir.

La châsse *(celiâ)* semble, elle aussi, naturalisée. Il ne s'agit, bien entendu, dans la pensée de l'exorciste juif, que d'un saphir

---

[10] Paul Studer and Joan Evans, *Anglo-Norman Lapidaries*, Paris, Champion, 1924.

encastré. Mais en gardant la formulation originale, l'accent dévie sur la chaton, comme si la vertu curative avait passé du saphir à l'encastrement; ce qui est absurde. D'ailleurs le terme employé n'est pas 'chaton', mais un mot pour 'châsse', objet spécifique du culte chrétien. C'est une châsse qu'on met dans les mains du malade; une amulette est tenue au-dessus de la plaie.

En concluant l'exorcisme par l'expression pieuse 'avec l'aide de Dieu', Isaac ben Isaac revêt sa dignité de rabbin.

LEARNED WORDS IN THE EARLIEST FRENCH DOCUMENTS

By Dorothy R. Brodin
Herbert H. Lehman College of the City University of New York

It has long been established that from the moment of its first appearance in the *Serments de Strasbourg*, the French language contained, side by side with the vocabulary regularly derived from Latin, an impressive number of so-called "learned" words, words borrowed directly from Latin and little changed by the forces of philological development. On the subject of this relatively large number of learned words found in early French documents, Ferdinand Brunot [1] emphasized the role of the "Renaissance" of Charlemagne's time and then called attention to the fact that the 12th and 13th century manuscripts contain learned forms to which Littré has ascribed a much later date of entry into the language. Brunot saw the Church as responsible not only for most of the terms used to describe religious ideas and practices, but also for those which composed the technical vocabulary of the "scientific" writings of the Middle Ages.

Eduard Schwan in his *Grammatik des Altfranzösischen* [2] also stressed the influence of religion on these early borrowings, but attributed them to the Church on the one hand and to the scholars (clerici) on the other. Such a division seems a bit arbitrary, since

---

[1] Brunot, Ferdinand, *Histoire de la langue française des origines à 1900* (Paris, 1905), I, p. 292.

[2] Schwan, Eduard, *Grammatik des Altfranzösischen*, dritte Auflage neu bearbeitet von Dr. Dietrich Behrens (Leipzig, 1898), pp. 15-16.

it is difficult to see, for instance, why a word like *epistre* should figure in the second category rather than in the first.

That there was a tendency to sweeping generalizations about the nature and origin of learned words is perhaps best seen in the work of Nyrop who had first stated categorically that there were no verbs or adjectives but only substantives among the learned words,[3] but who later revised his statement to read: "parmi ces mots d'emprunt on trouve surtout des substantifs, très peu d'adjectifs et de verbes..."[4]

The aim of this paper is not to lead to such conclusions as those made by Nyrop, who suggested that a study of early learned forms would shed light on the origins of the French epic, but merely to make an actual count and tabulation of the learned words in six early French documents, ranging from the 9th to the 12th centuries. Of these documents, the first is a political one, the *Serments de Strasbourg;* three, the *Cantilène de Sainte Eulalie,* the *Vie de Saint Léger,* and the *Vie de Saint Alexis,* are religious poems; one, the *Passion du Christ,* is merely a paraphrase of the Gospels, and finally one, the *Chanson de Roland,* is an epic poem.[5]

In counting the words of these documents, to determine what percentage of their vocabularies are actually learned, I have not taken into account frequency of occurrence, but have counted a word only once, whether it occurred one or many times, whether it appeared in one or several forms. A certain standardization had, of course, to be decided upon. This standardization, although

---

[3] Nyrop, Kristoffer, *Grammaire historique de la langue française,* I: *Phonétique* (Copenhaguen, 1899), pp. 25-26. "Il faut remarquer que parmi ces mots d'emprunt, qui appartiennent presque tous à la langue religieuse, on ne trouve ni verbes ni adjectifs, mais seulement des substantifs; il est aussi curieux de constater que les poèmes guerriers, tels que la Chanson de Roland, contiennent, moins de mots savants et plus de mots d'origine germanique que l'Alexis et les autres poèmes dévots. Ce fait suffit à montrer combien l'épopée française était populaire et quels rapports intimes elle avait avec la race germanique."

[4] Nyrop, *Grammaire historique,* 3rd edition (Copenhagen, 1914), I, p. 27.

[5] The editions used were the following: Koschwitz, Eduard, *Les plus anciens monuments de la langue française* (Leipzig, 1913) for the *Serments de Strasbourg,* the *Eulalie,* the *Saint Léger,* the *Passion,* and the *Alexis;* Dedeck-Héry, V. L., *The Life of Saint Alexis* (New York, 1931); Jenkins, T. Atkinson, *La Chanson de Roland,* Oxford Version (Boston, 1924).

highly arbitrary, makes little difference in the final results arrived at because of the large number of words dealt with. Moreover, the same rules were followed in studying all the documents so that comparisons between documents are perfectly possible.

1. All forms of a verb have been considered as a single word, whether they are derived from one Latin verb or from several. Thus, *sarai, sui,* and *etais* were all considered as one word.

2. Verbal nouns have been considered as words separate from the verbs from which they are derived. Thus, *departide* (separation) and *departir* (to separate) are counted as two words.

Likewise verbs have been considered as separate from the nouns from which they are derived. Thus, *herberge* and *herbergier* have been counted as two words.

3. All forms of a noun have been counted as one word, whether singular, plural, subject, or object case. Thus *ber, baron, barons* have been counted as one word.

4. All forms of an adjective have been counted as one word, whether masculine, feminine, singular, plural, subject or object. Thus, *bon, bonne, bons, bonnes* have been counted as one word.

5. Adjectives or adverbs have been counted only once, even if occasionally used as substantives. Thus, *bien* and *le bien* have been counted as one word.

6. Adverbs and adjectives have been counted separately, but an adverb has been counted only once, even if sometimes used as a preposition. Thus, *bel* and *belement* have been counted as two words, but *avant* has been counted only once although it is used both as an adverb and as a preposition.

7. In the case of possessive adjectives each person has been counted as a separate word, but all forms of the same person have been counted as one word. Thus, *mon, ma, mes* have been counted as one word, *ton, ta, tes* as another, *son, sa, ses* as a third, etc.

8. In the case of personal pronouns, each person has been counted as a separate word, but all forms of the same person have been counted as one word. Thus, *je, me, moi* have been counted as one word, *tu, te, toi,* as another, *il elle, le, la, lui* as a third, etc.

9. All forms of the definite article have been counted as one word. Thus *le, la, les* have been counted as one word.

10. Reflexive pronouns have been counted separately from personal pronouns. Thus *se, soi* have been counted as a separate word.

11. All forms of the relative pronoun have been counted as one word. Thus, *qui, que, dont* have been counted as one word.

12. All forms of the interrogative pronoun have been counted as one word. Thus *qui?, que?*, have been counted as one word.

13. The various forms of the demonstratives have been counted as separate words, but the various cases, numbers and genders of the same form have been counted as one word. Thus, *cil, cele, celui*, etc., have been counted as one word, *icil, icele, icelui*, etc., as another, *cist, ceste*, etc. as a third, *icist, iceste*, etc. as a fourth, etc.

14 Proper nouns have been omitted except *Dieu, domnedeu*, and *diable*.

15. Proper adjectives have been omitted except for *français, chrestien*, etc. which are so often used that they lose their proper character.

16. Lastly, it will be seen that the lists of learned words contain some purely Latin forms, while others are learned Romance forms, and still others show only the barest trace of a learned influence. No distinction as to "learned" or "semi-learned" has been made. A word has been called learned as soon as it showed any deviation from popular development. There are cases where words termed learned by Koschwitz and Dedeck-Héry seem to have had little chance of developing otherwise than they did. These have been included but will be noted in the body of this paper.

SERMENTS DE STRASBOURG (842 A.D.)

Total number of words	65
Total number of learned words	6
Percentage of learned words	9.23

Learned words:

chrestien	Deo	pro
conservat	nunquam	salvament

The word *Deo*, although learned in form, is not learned in the same way as the other words in the list. It was not so much borrowed from the Latin as always used, and it remained conservative in form for that very reason. (The same can be said for a word like *diable* which appears in later documents.)⁶ I have counted words like *Deo* and *diable* because their form is not popular, but with the realization that they are not true borrowings. It is often difficult to say whether a word is learned or not. There has been a tendency to call a word learned as soon as it fails in the slightest way to behave according to the strict rules of development. The lists given here contain such words, but for each document a second percentage is established to provide for their elimination.

If *Deo* is eliminated from the above list, the percentage of learned words in the Serments de Strasbourg is 7.67.

CANTILENE DE SAINTE EULALIE (early 10th century)

Total number of words	108
Total number of learned words	18
Percentage of learned words	16.67

Learned words:

anima	empedementz	paramenz
chrestiien	figure	post
clementia	honestet	preiement
Deo	inimi	presentede
diaule	menester	rex
element	ment	virginitet

---

[6] Cf. Brunot, p. 292.

The words *ment, preiement* and *presentede* are listed as learned by Koschwitz. It is difficult to see, however, what other development they could have had.

Leaving out *ment, preiement, presentede, Deo* and *diaule* reduces the percentage of learned words in the *Cantilène de Sainte Eulalie* to 12.03.

VIE DE SAINT LEGER (late 10th century)

Total number of words	319
Total number of learned words	53
Percentage of learned words	16.61

Learned words:

abbas	dominat	lauder	quandius
anatemaz	dominedeus	lingua	regne
anima	exaltat	litteras	regnet
caritet	exaudis	luerat	restaurat
carnels	exercite	magistre	rex
causa	fincta	mistier	semper
claritet	furor	observer	sermons
communiet	gladies	occidere	signes
conlauder	gratia	pasions	spiritiel
consolament	honorez	percutan	super
Deus	humilitet	perfectus	tiranz
devastar	inimix	perfides	veritiet
diable	labia	prediat	visitet
			vituperat

While it may be claimed that the words *exercite* and *gladies* appear in the Bible, they are military rather than religious in nature and cannot be considered as belonging to the same category as *anatemaz* or *lauder*. It is interesting to see how many different types of words this list contains. They cannot be dismissed by a wholesale ascription to religious influence. *Anima, caritat, communiet,* etc. were part of the cult; but what of *labia, lingua, tiranz* and others? There are also adverbs and prepositions which subsist in their Latin form.

Eliminating *Deus, diable* and *sermons*, which is called learned by Koschwitz but could not have developed otherwise than it did and is therefore only "functionally" learned, brings the percentage of learned words in the *Vie de Saint Léger* to 15.67.

PASSION DU CHRIST (late 10th century)

Total number of words	592
Total number of learned words	86
Percentage of learned words	14.53

Learned words:

adducere	esvegurad	passiuns	sanctificat
aloen	extendent	passus	sanitad
alta	fili	pax	secula
angeles	finimunz	pensar	semper
anma	flagellar	pietad	sepulcra
aromatizen	gloriae	pimenc	sermon
babzizar	gratiae	pius	signa
benedis	humilitad	podestad	sit
caritad	inimic	pontifex	spiritus
carnals	ipsum	postque	suscitet
cena	judicar	prophete	suspensus
confession	lagrimez	pugnar	templum
confirmet	lapider	pugnes	tradetur
conjuret	lauder	purpura	unguement
cortine	lingues	quasi	usque
crucifige	magnes	redemptionis	veritad
custodes	nona	redemptor	verus
deitat	nunc	regnaz	vestimenz
Deus	nuncer	regnum	vobis
diable	osanna	rex	voluntaz
emperador	palmes	sacrament	
errors	paradis	sanctus	

In the *Passion* it is not always clear whether a word is learned or popular, since a Provençal linguistic influx often obscures the issue. The word *anma*, for instance, might be a natural development. On the other hand, however, the actual use of the word is a learned one, and it is probably reasonable to classify it as learned.

Here again, side by side with words which have been taken bodily from the Gospels, there are others, like *pugnar* which seem military rather than religious in origin.

Eliminating *Deus, diable,* and *sermon* brings the percentage of learned words in the *Passion du Christ* to 14.02.

VIE DE SAINT ALEXIS (early 11th century)

Total number of words	767
Total number of learned words	63
Percentage of learned words	8.21

Learned words:

adjutorie	dignes	justisie	pueple
afflictions	emperedre	leticie	regenerer
alienes	emperie	memorie	regne
angele	enemis	miracles	regner
apertes	enfermetet	nobilitet	sacrarie
apostolie	enque	noble	saintismes
astenir	ereditez	noster	servisie
avoglet	escole	onorer	servitour
avuegles	feconditet	ories	siecles
batisiez	felix	palie	terrestre
celeste	fraieles	paradis	trinitet
crestiiens	glorie	pater	umilitet
cretiantet	grabatum	penitencie	usque
Damnedeu	gracie	pietet	veritet
declinant	imagene	porpenset	virgene
Deus	ipse	precious	

Dr. Dedeck-Héry calls *astenir* learned. The prefix, however, seems isufficient reason for such a classification. *Palie*, which he also lists, seems to be a case of learned spelling.

Damnedeu appears in a more popular form than the *dominedeus* of the *Vie de Saint Léger*.

Leaving out *Deus, astenir* and *palie* brings the percentage of learned words in the *Vie de Saint Alexis* to 7.82.

CHANSON DE ROLAND (late 11th or early 12th century)

Total number of words 1738
Total number of learned words 114
Percentage of learned words 6.56

Learned words:

acomingier	defension	martir	regne
adorer	Deu	martirie	regnet
affliction	diable	matice	relique
agut	discipline	miracle	resurrexis
altisme	domnedeu	mirre	saintisme
angele	dragon	monie	salvement
antiquitet	drodmond	navilie	salvetet
apostele	dux	nobilie	savie
arcevesque	emperedor	noble	sceptre
astenir	empirie	oblider	science
baptestirie	encenser	ocision	sermon
baptizier	enemi	offrende	siecle
benediçon	enluminer	olifant	signacle
benedir	escarboncle	olive	sinagoge
carboncle	essample	omnipotente	tables
celeste	evesque	ordre	tenebres
chameil	galee	oriente	tenebros
chanonie	geste	palie	terremoete
chrestiien	glorios	paterne	timome
chrestientet	herite	patriarche	topaze
confes	humele	pelerin	tradison
confusion	humilitet	penitence	traditor
contrarie	judisie	perdition	victorie
coronet	jugedor	piment	vigor
criminel	justisie	pitiet	violer
cristal	leon	pedestedif	ydele
croce	leupart	podestet	ymagene
declin	livre	principal	
decliner	magne	prophete	

Geste has been listed as learned because it has remained in the language as a learned word, and may have been a learned word at the time of the *Chanson de Roland*.

Astenir, sermon and *palie* have already been discussed (supra p. 55, p. 56).

There are in the *Chanson de Roland* many words like *hui, henir, herbe*, etc. in which an initial *h* has been either preserved or added. Where this *h* appears before a *u*, it was probably kept so that the *u* might be distinguished from a *v*. Although this process could be considered learned, these words are learned in spelling only and obviously depend for their form on the scribe who wrote the manuscript.

As regards the intervocalic dental found in the *Chanson de Roland*, Jenkins says:

> For the present edition, the intervocalic dental has been restored: the last copyist leaves it untouched in a large number of cases *(fedeilz, lodet, vode, aiude, poedent, odum, sedeir, ad une ewe, cruisiedes, edet)*, while in *tuele* 200 (for OF *Tudele*) he dropped it wrongly. In *ve. eir* 2853, the *-d-* was expunctuated and then erased; so also *pre.* (for *pret* PRATUM) 2871. As the space of three generations may separate the language of the copyist from that of the poet, it is a safe conclusion that the intervocalic dental should be regularly restored. [7]

In counting the words of the *Chanson de Roland*, I have omitted those which Jenkins brackets. Of those Jenkins says:

> Words in brackets... mean that the word or form given is not precisely the reading of the Oxford MS, but has been placed in the text of this edition because required by the assonance, by the meter, or by some other imperative consideration. [8]

The learned words in the *Chanson de Roland* have already been counted by Paul Blunk. [9] Although I have consulted his list

---

[7] Jenkins, p. cvi.
[8] *Ibid.*, p. 282.
[9] Blunk, Paul, *Studien zum Wortschatz des altfranzösischen Rolandsliedes*, Diss. (Kiel, 1905).

as a possible check on mine, I have not followed it, since many of the words which be calls learned, such as *clerc, conseil, anme,* etc. seem to be popular, whereas he leaves out such words as *terremoete,* which seem definitely learned.

If we were to omit *Deu, diable, astenir, sermon* and *palie,* the percentage of learned words in the *Chanson de Roland* would be 6.27%.

In looking over the percentages obtained, we find the following results:

Serments de Strasbourg	9.23%
Cantilène de Sainte Eulalie	16.67%
Vie de Saint Léger	16.61%
Passion du Christ	14.53%
Vie de Saint Alexis	8.21%
Chanson de Roland	6.56%

In view of the arbitrary rules that had to be established (cf. *supra* pp. 51-52, in order to obtain the count, it is better to quote these percentages as whole numbers since percentages taken to the hundredth place would indicate a degree of accuracy impossible to obtain in a work of this nature. The corrected percentages therefore read:

Serments de Strasbourg	9%
Cantilène de Sainte Eulalie	17%
Vie de Saint Leger	17%
Passion du Christ	15%
Vie de Saint Alexis	8%
Chanson de Roland	7% *

---

* If we were to leave out the words *Deu, diable, sermon, ment, preiement, presented, astenir,* and *palie,* the percentages would be:

Serments de Strasbourg	8%
Cantilène de Sainte Eulalie	12%
Vie de Saint Léger	16%
Passion	14%
Vie de Saint Alexis	8%
Chanson de Roland	6%

The influence of ecclesiastical language is, of course, very great, and the greater number of learned words are religious in origin. Yet, as one looks at the percentages obtained, the most striking feature is that, although the *Eulalie, the Léger* and the *Passion* all have a high percentage of learned words, the *Passion* which, by its very nature, must stay close to the language of the Vulgate, nevertheless has slightly less learned words, proportionately speaking, than the preceding religious poems.

On the other hand, the *Alexis*, which is also a religious poem, falls far below the two other lives of saints, and has scarcely more learned words than the epic *Chanson de Roland*. By its vocabulary, then, the *Alexis* seems to be closer to the *Roland* than to the religious poems of the 10th century. This might very well be true, since, where the *Eulalie* and the *Léger* are more or less the vernacular equivalent of Latin lives of saints, the *Alexis* is a true literary document; its subject may be similar to that of the earlier poems, but its treatment is much more self-conscious. From the point of view of literary style, the *Alexis* is definitely closer to the *Roland* than to the *Eulalie* or the *Léger*. The language of the *Alexis*, moreover, is a more general one than that of the other two poems. It is therefore not surprising that the vocabulary of the *Alexis* should show the percentage of learned words that it does.

The results obtained by calculating the percentage of learned words in the six early French documents studied may possibly indicate that while, at first, literary documents were still leaning heavily on their Vulgar Latin precursors, the number of learned borrowings gradually lessened as the language became better established, reaching a low just before the first period of wholesale borrowing.

Most of the learned words in the documents studied are religious in nature. Some of these are so much a part of the religious life of the Middle Ages that they can scarcely be called learned; others are part of a specifically religious vocabulary. Amongst the latter we can include such words as *anima, abbas, caritet, gracie,* etc... There are many other words which, at first glance, do not betray their religious origin so clearly, but which nevertheless stem from the same source. *Rex* and *regne*, for instance, in themselves have no religious connotations; yet they are constantly used in prayers and litanies. The adverbs *nunc* and *semper* which, in the *Passion*, appear in their Latin form are words used at the end of almost all liturgical prayers.

Along with the words which have a religious character, there are a few military words, *gladies, exercite, pugnes,* etc. Several other words seem to belong to the language of scholars, *livre, enque, escole,* etc. Still others do not seems to belong to any particular class or group, *fraieles, oblider,* etc.

Thus the learned words found in the earliest French documents are quite varied. They are derived from several different sources, and represent many different parts of speech. Verbs, prepositions, adverbs, adjectives and interjections are found together with substantives. Although most of them show the influence of the liturgy and of ecclesiastical writings, many have entered the language through other channels. Their number and kind seems to be little influenced by the document's origin, since the *Vie de Saint Alexis,* a religious poem, contains a percentage of learned words only slightly higher than the epic *Chanson de Roland* and lower than the political *Serments de Strasbourg.* It would seem that as Old French matured and developed to the point where it gave its masterpiece, the *Chanson de Roland,* it became increasingly self-sufficient, and the proportion of learned borrowings decreased markedly.

THE ETYMOLOGY OF FRENCH *DA*

By Henri Diament
University of California, Irvine

Contemporary popular French — especially as spoken in rural districts and by older speakers — still occasionally affords the linguist an opportunity to hear a most venerable word: *da*. Though it falls within the lexicographical definition of the *word*, since it is listed in all French dictionaries, it enjoys no separate existence in the modern language, though it did at one point in the history of the French tongue. It is always connected in speech to either *oui* or, rarely, to an archaic negative expression *nenni* < Latin NON ILLUD [1] (or < Old French *nen il* traceable to NON ILLUD [2]), sometimes used in place of *non*. The total dependence of *da* on these two words is further illustrated graphemically by the use of a hyphen: *oui-da, nenni-da,* plus the fact that one can never find it capitalized. This utter dependence gives *da* the status of a "bound morpheme" in French. Semantically, it acts as a reinforcing marker: "da (peut-être contract. de *dis, va*). Particule qui, jointe à un trait d'union au mot *oui,* ou, quelquefois, à *nenni,* donne plus de force à l'affirmation ou à la négation... (Fam.)" [3] This reinforcement may, in turn, have been at the origin of further semantic overtones: "*Oui-da,* volontiers, de bon cœur, vraiment! (marque souvent l'ironie ou l'étonnement)." [4]

---

[1] *Larousse Universel* (Paris, 1949), 1965 reprint, under "nenni".
[2] A. Dauzat, J. Dubois et H. Mitterand, *Nouveau Dictionnaire étymologique* (Paris, 1964), under "ne".
[3] *Larousse Universel,* under "da".
[4] *Larousse Universel,* under "oui-da".

The etymology suggested above by Larousse, i.e. < *dis, va* (preceded, significantly enough, by "peut-être") is the one most commonly proposed, and meets with varying degrees of acceptance by scholars. But an aura of doubt seems to permeate this explanation. While Littré, for instance, finds it to be an "explication... satisfaisante,"[5] Clédat declares flatly: "Origine incertaine."[6] Without necessarily rejecting the traditional etymology *dis, va*, the wide disagreement registered among scholars would seem to warrant a fresh approach and new hypotheses: that is the aim of this article.

A brief review of the attitudes of various authorities on the subject is now in order, before we undertake to advance a new hypothesis. What is most noteworthy at the outset is that recent work generally seems to merely repeat previous explanations. Thus Dauzat, Dubois and Mitterand give us the following: "*da* 1160, *Charroi de Nîmes (diva)*; XVe s. *(dea)*; XVIe s. *(da)*, dans *oui-da*; du double impératif *dis va*; nenni-da (XVIIe s., Molière)."[7] The etymology *dis, va*, suggested a long time ago by Diez, thus still seems acceptable to the three French authorities. Admittedly their entry is a rather brief one, with no elaboration, but then so was that of Larousse, which still added a precautionary "peut-être." Moreover, it could be pointed out that the *Nouveau Dictionnaire* entry is misleading on two counts. It states that the association of *da* to *oui* is first found in the fifteenth century as *oui-da*, whereas it is attested a bit earlier as *oïl dea* in Coyfurelly's *La manière de language*, first published in 1396.[8] The *Nouveau Dictionnaire* further contradicts itself on the chronology of first attestations in a separate entry, under *oui*, in which a sub-entry *oui-da* is now supposed to have first appeared as *oui-dea* in the sixteenth century. This could be construed as correct only if we deliberately ignored the previous form *oïl-dea*. Cf. Bloch & Wartburg, who state: "oui-da, XVIIe, d'abord oui-dea, XVIe..."[9] And

---

[5] E. Littré, *Dictionnaire de la langue française* (Paris, 1961), under "da".

[6] Léon Clédat, *Dictionnaire étymologique de la langue française* (Paris, 1930), under "da".

[7] *Nouveau Dictionnaire étymologique*, under "da".

[8] *La manière de language*, Gessler edition (Brussels & Paris, 1934). Authorship attributed to Coyfurelly.

[9] Oscar Bloch and Walter von Wartburg, *Dictionnaire étymologique de la langue française* (Paris, 1932), 1964 reprint, under "il".

yet Tobler and Lommatzsch, as long ago as 1936, gave two examples of *oïl dea,* both taken from *La manière de language:* "Voullez vous rien que je puisse faire? — Oïl dea." (383) "Janyn, estes vous la? — Oïl dea, ne me peux tu vëoir?" (388). [10] It seems a bit odd that two dictionaries, both published in the mid-sixties with a combined authorship of three living scholars (out of the original five) should both ignore a form which their predecessor of the thirties had already listed.

Bloch and Wartburg go on with what has become the classical explanation of *oui-da*: "...formé avec la particule *da,* qui se combinait aussi avec *non, nenni,* et, en outre, était employée isolément; *da,* qui a succédé à *dea* (parfois *dia*), usuel au XVe et au XVIe s. (et encore signalé fin XVIIe) est une altération, due à son emploi interjectif, de *diva,* XIIe, formé des deux impér. *di* et *va.*" [11]

Hatzfeld and Darmesteter agree with Clédat in being less peremptory than the Dauzat team or Bloch and Wartburg, and in suggesting caution about the *diva* etymology: "DA... ETYM. Origine incertaine. Au XVe et au XVIe s. *dea* (orth. qui se maintient jusqu'à la fin du XVIIème s.), très rarement *dia;* plus ancienne. *diva,* où qqns voient un composé de di (anc. forme de dis) et de va, imp. des verbes dire et aller." [12] The two scholars then quote the passage alluded to in the *Nouveau Dictionnaire,* from the *Charoi de Nîmes,* and this is apparently the earliest literary monument of the form, *if* one accepts *diva* as the *exclusive* etymology of *da*: "XIIe s. Diva, vilain... Fus-tu a Nîmes?" (904). Their explanation of the usage of *da* is "Particule qui, dans le lang. rustiq. ou famil., s'ajoute à oui, non, nenni, ou termine une phrase, avec un sens analog. à celui de 'vraiment'." [13]

Robert seems to share this skepticism: "DA... contract. de *dea...* qui paraît être une altér. de *diva...*" [14]

---

[10] Tobler-Lommatzsch, *Altfranzösisches Wörterbuch* (Berlin, 1936), under "da".

[11] Bloch and Wartburg, under "il".

[12] A. Hatzfeld and A. Darmesteter, *Dictionnaire général de la langue française* (Paris, 1888), 1954 reprint, under "da".

[13] Hatzfeld and Darmesteter, *loc. cit.*

[14] P. Robert, *Dictionnaire alphabétique et analogique de la langue française* (Paris, 1954), under "da".

Godefroy gives us the various spellings of the form: *Dea, dia, dya,* and *da.* He defines it as "sorte d'excl. d'éton. Quelquefois il n'est pas une excl. mais une affirm., et il équivaut à peu près à certes. Nicot donne *dea* comme une interj. qui sert à 'enforcer la diction'." [15] We find this observation to be of significance, in that it might pave the way towards consideration of *two* etymologies, corresponding to two different meanings and uses. The *exclamation* might indeed be < *diva*. The *reinforcement* might have an altogether different origin, and we suggest that it does.

That *diva, as an exclamation,* came about as a result of the coalescence of *dis* and *va* can hardly be doubted, if for no other reason than that there are instances of its being spelled as two separate words in medieval documents. That *diva* should then have simplified to *dea* (or *dia*) and *da* is also not surprising, phonologically speaking. Incidentally, both imperatives been — and still are — used separately as exclamations or interjections, e.g. *dis donc!, dis, eh!* or *va donc, eh!,* or simply *va* from which the actual idea of "going" is absent (e.g. the well-known "Va, je ne te hais point!" in *Le Cid*) as well as the very common "polite" form "allez!", the abuse of which as an exclamation or interjection has excited the raillery of Pierre Daninos. [16]

It is, however, interesting to note that inspection of available instances of literary occurrence of the forms, and statistical analysis of same, seem to show that *diva* is seldom, if ever, associated with any expression of negation or affirmation such as *oïl, non, nennil* etc., whereas most instances of *dea* or *da* are so associated. *Some* forms in *dea, da* are used in isolation and seem to convey exclamatory or interjectory meaning, *not* reinforcement. But the vast majority are used as reinforcements to words of affirmation or negation: *non-da, enda* (probably a misprint for *nen-da*), *non-dea, oïl dea, oui-dea, nanil-dea, voire dea, ouy dea,* and finally the modern versions *oui-da* and *nenni-da*. (See Littré, *op. cit.*) It is our first hypothesis that, on semantic grounds at least, *da* might reflect something different from an exclamation

---

[15] F. Godefroy, *Dictionnaire de l'ancien français* (Paris, 1881-1902), under "dea".

[16] P. Daninos, *Le Jacassin* (Paris, 1962), p. 114.

based on imperatives and designed to call attention. We therefore suggest that the origin of this *da,* associated with expressions of deictic origin, should be sought in connection with deicticity and allied concepts.

Oui < *oïl* < HOC ILLE and *nenni* < *nen il* < NON ILLUD show exuberant and redundant deicticity, which is in line with Vulgar Latin practices, especially in Gaul. But even such exuberance had its limits and usually consisted of the fusion of two elements, rarely more, though examples such as *aujourd'hui* < AD ILLUM DIURNUM HODIE, or *même* < METIPSIMUM, show this to have been possible. Semantically, it is not inconceivable that reinforcement should have been desired in the case of HOC ILLE, since this "primary deicticity" alone might not have given the listener the whole picture in some situations. And this is where a complementary expression of the totality of objects (or persons) *out of which* selection was made by deictic HOC ILLE or NON ILLUD could well have been added at one point in the evolution of synthetic forms of affirmation or negation. We would call such an additional expression one of "secondary deicticity." Some scholars suggest, for instance, that HOC ILLE was originally accompanied by the verb FECIT: "...probabl. condensation de *hoc ille fecit,* phrase de réponse, "il a fait cela," où *fecit* remplaçait le verbe de la question et pouvait être supprimé; *o il* l'a emporté sur *o je, o tu* et s'est cristallisé en *oui.*" [17] The same theory is applied by this author to *nenni* < *nen il,* the implication being that *il* in this case also represents the Latin *ille* (which would have acted as subject for the verb *fecit*).[18] Other scholars, however, consider *nenni* as < NON ILLUD, the latter neuter demonstrative being much less likely, in our opinion, to have served as subject of a hypothetical FECIT. Besides, if ILLUD is adduced for *nenni,* why not also HOC ILLUD for *oui?* The presence or absence of the verb in the immediate context, however, would still not preclude additional expressions of presumed "wide choice out of which a selection was made by reinforced deicticity through supplementary

---

[17] *Nouveau Dictionnaire étymologique,* under "oui".
[18] *Ibid.,* under "nenni".

demonstratives," i.e. expressions of secondary deicticity. There is no pleonasm in our sentence, as we wish to emphasize deicticity rather than the budding Vulgar Latin articular use of demonstratives. In our hypothesis, Latin demonstratives retain their basic classical meaning.

Our task is then to suggest an etymology for *da* in line with the above semantic theory, whereby *oui-da* might be considered as an originally reinforced expression of which later *oïl* > *oui* would be the elliptic outcome.

Setting aside, for the sake of argument, the etymology *diva* (which may still be recognized as the etymon of *isolated, exclamatory da*, though there are very few examples of such use of *da*, the form *dea* being more common in this context) and concentrating on the bound morpheme *da* in *oui-da* and *nenni-da*, one may contend that the earlier, attested form *dea* is the clue to the etymology we seek. Both formal similarity and presumed semantic similarity then lead us to find a common origin to our French particle *da* and Italian preposition *da*.

Several scholars agree that the etymon of Italian *da* is DE AB, and Italian *da* has indeed kept the meaning of provenience, whereas ital. *di* < DE has specialized in genitivity. Interestingly enough, here again there is an aura of mystery. Thus Elcock says that "A certain mystery surrounds the much-used Italian *da*, attested in inscriptions since the seventh century: for some scholars it is Latin DE AB, while others see in it a Vulgar Latin borrowing from Oscan DAT (cf. Rheto-Rom. *dad*)." [19] Again it would seem as if, on semantic grounds alone, the DE AB etymology were the more likely one, since it contains the idea of origin or provenience which Oscan DAT (i.e. Latin DE AD) *a priori* would seem not to. And yet Gartner glosses Rheto-Rom. *dad* as follows: "da... regelmässig dad, für den Ausgangspunkt in Ort und Zeit, von;..." [20] This would point to Oscan rather than Latin, though there is a possibility of confusion, in Vulgar Latin, between DE AB and DE AD, of which more presently.

---

[19] W. D. Elcock, *The Romance Languages* (London, 1960), p. 149.
[20] Th. Gartner, *Ladinische Wörter aus den Dolomitentälern* (Halle, 1923), under "da".

Among authorities opting for DE AB, we find Pei,[21] Väänänen,[22] and Migliorini.[23] The latter states: "Nel sistema delle preposizioni italiane, ha acquistato una propria fisionomia *da*, che nel suo principale significato, quello di provinienza, risale a *de ab*. Il primo esempio nei documenti è (per ora) un passo di una carta lucchese dell' anno 700: 'neque subtagendum *da* vos hoc ipse ecclesie' (Cod. dipl. Long., I, p. 31)²."[24] And in footnote 2, Migliorini adds: "Le forme *de ab* e *dab* sono attestate non di rado: citiamo solo *de ab unam partem* delle *Casae Litterarum*, V.5, cod. C..."[25] It is perhaps of interest to note that in both examples, *da* or *de ab*, though carrying a clear meaning of provenience, are followed not by the expected ablatives VOBIS or UNA PARTE, but by accusative forms. Grammatically, then, it is as if one had DE AD, though semantically an ablative would be called for. Perhaps both forms were used concurrently, DE AD originating in Oscan DAT and keeping the ablative meaning but governing an accusative by phonological and grammatical analogy with the Latin AD.

It is surprising that Migliorini should not have adduced the earlier attestation which Pei gives us among his selected Christian inscriptions, found in Rome and dated as between the fourth and the sixth centuries: "...et si aliquis sepulcrum istum biolare bolueri, abea anathema da patre et filiu et scm spm."[26] Again, *da* clearly means "from," not "to," but the *m* of *scm* and *spm* suggests an accusative SANCTUM SPIRITUM rather than an ablative C.L. SANCTO SPIRITU, or V.L. SPIRITO. The coexistence of these accusative inflections with *patre* and *filiu*, where they have already disappeared, is also noteworthy. It suggests ecclesiastical conservatism, since *patre* and *filiu* were also, and primarily, used of humans. At any rate, for Pei there seems little

---

[21] Mario Pei, *The Italian Language*, 2nd edition (New York, 1954), p. 116.

[22] Veikko Väänänen, *Introduction au latin vulgaire*, rev. ed. (Paris, 1967), p. 99.

[23] Bruno Migliorini, *Storia della lingua italiana*, 3rd ed. (Florence, 1961), p. 70.

[24] *Loc. cit.*

[25] *Loc. cit.*

[26] *The Italian language*, p. 175.

doubt that the etymology of It. *da* is DE AB: "The only final labial appearing in Latin (*b*)falls: de ab > da." [27] "Italian *da* (< de ab, or, less probably, < de ad)² is a growth peculiar to Italian soil..." [28] And in footnote 2, Pei gives convincing evidence: "*De ab* seems favored by Old Sardinian *daba* and by *da b enitiu* of the Ritmo Cassinese." [29]

The only amendment we would suggest to the above· is precisely that *da* is not uniquely indigenous to Italy. We find, it, for instance, in Old Spanish: "Certas nacido es en tirra aquel qui en pace i en guera senior a a seer da oriente..." [30] Ford explains it as *de a* "from in" and adds "cf. Ital. *da*" but he concedes that it might be "erroneous for *de*." It seems difficult to see how "da oriente" could be translated as "from in the east," which is what Ford's Glossary suggests. Pure provenience, i.e. simply "from the east," seems more likely since Latin AD, if it is taken as the etymon of O.Sp. *a* in *de a*, would mean "direction away from the speaker" or simply "towards." The further context of the *Auto* confirms this: "...de todos hata in occidente." [31] Since the *Auto* expresses the idea of "in the west" by means of "in occidente," why should one not consider that, had the author wished to say "from in the east," he would have said "de in" or "de en"? Besides, the Auto, written in Spain with an Hispanocentric outlook, would most probably indeed differentiate, in this context, between the faraway East and the immediate West, by means of the contrast *a* < AB versus *en* < IN.

Mohl had also derived both It. and O.Sp. *da* "from the Oscan *da, dat* and from a southern Latin **dabi,* *dabe." [32] This point of view was endorsed by Grandgent. [33] While the latter appears

---

[27] *Ibid.,* p. 61.
[28] *Ibid.* p. 116.
[29] *Loc. cit.*
[30] From the *Auto de los Reyes Magos,* scene I, line 25, in J. D. M. Ford, *Old Spanish Readings, selected on the basis of critically edited texts* (Boston, 1939). Ford uses Menéndez-Pidal's text of the *Auto.*
[31] *Ibid.,* scene I, line 26.
[32] Quoted and paraphrased by C. H. Grandgent, *An Introduction to Vulgar Latin* (Boston, 1907), p. 29.
[33] *Loc. cit.* Grandgent himself favored DE AD, but has it preceded by an asterisk. In a footnote on that same page, he makes this somewhat bizarre statement: "Romance *da, dad* may be the result of a fusion rather

openminded on the subject, Mohl had been quite dogmatic and rigid in rejecting DE AB: "On explique généralement la préposition italienne *da* par *dē ad*, et au point de vue du sens et de la syntaxe il n'y a effectivement rien à objecter contre cette dérivation. En particulier l'objection de Hamp ALL V 365 que *dē-ad* ne pourrait guère signifier que "von - nach," c'est-à-dire "hin" n'a pas de valeur, puisque *ad* en latin vulgaire et déjà fréquemment dans la langue classique confond ses significations avec celles d'*apud*." [34] This, as we have seen, must have been due to confusion with Oscan DAT. If this be true, then Hamp's objection is justified, since it appears to be concerned with Latin only. Elsewhere, Mohl calls "le prototype *dē ab* tout à fait improbable, puisque *ab* a succombé en latin vulgaire dès une époque très ancienne" [35] but he himself adduces ABANTE OCULIS which he lightly dismisses, however, as an example of "locutions composées" and adds that "la plupart de ces formes n'ont qu'une valeur graphique." [36] These forms must have been quite alive in the language to yield, e.g., It. *avanti* and Fr. *avant*. Fr. *devant* < DE AB ANTE would seem to prove that the combination DE AB must have been a Vulgar Latin reality, even if one concedes to Mohl that "Comme préposition indépendante, *ab* est à rayer impitoyablement du lexique vulgaire;...". [37] Should one object that DE AB ANTE might be a fortuitous encounter, one might adduce Fr. "de devant," traceable to V.L. DE DE AB ANTE, which would seem to demonstrate the separate existence of the combination DE AB. The variant *davant* is already attested in *Alexis* (eleventh century). At any rate, Mohl did mitigate his previous statements: "...pour l'Italie tout au moins, la seule forme réellement attestée... est *da* sans qu'on puisse a priori rien préjuger sur la nature complexe ou simple de cette forme." [38] Coming

---

than a combination of *de* and *ad*. In any case it is probably a late product." One wonders what the distinction may be between "fusion" and "combination." Grandgent adds that "some have thought it came from *de* + *ab*."

[34] F. G. Mohl, *Les origines romanes, Etudes sur le Lexique du latin vulgaire, in Sitzungsberichte der königl. böhmischen Gesellschaft der Wissenschaften* (Prag, 1901), pp. 38-47.

[35] *Loc. cit.*
[36] *Loc. cit.*
[37] *Loc. cit.*
[38] *Loc. cit.*

back to Spanish *da*, Mohl states that "il est impossible de séparer de l'italien *da* le vieil espagnol *da* employé toujours comme ablatif local au sens de 'desde' " [39] and that "*da* ou *da* lui-même a pénétré dans la plus ancienne province après la Sardaigne, c'est-à-dire en Espagne." [40] But Mohl mentions no specific instance of Sp. *da*. Svennung mentions the presence of *da* in Isidore of Seville's *Etymologiae*, but is very cautious about accepting it: "DACI AUTEM GOTHORUM SOBOLES FUERUNT, ET DICTOS PUTANT "DACOS" QUASI "DA-GOS" QUIA DE GOTHORUM STIRPE CREATI SUNT... Puisque Isidore mourut en 636 il ne me semble pas absurde de conclure de ses paroles que *d(e)a* a existé comme préposition pendant la première moitié du 7e siècle." [41]

Thus the case for an Old Spanish *da* is a bit weak, but not to be dismissed. Far more important is the evidence for a Gallo-Romance *da*, adduced by Väänänen and Svennung: "Les mots accessoires sont particulièrement sujets à l'usure. Pour y remédier, la langue populaire a recours à leur accumulation. Aussi les adverbes romans sont-ils en bonne partie des juxtaposés latins. Cette tendance remonte au vieux latin: ...*de ab, da* (l'un et l'autre dans les documents mérovingiens et lombards, cf. Svennung, dans ALMA 21, p. 55 sqq.; it. *da*);..." [42] Thus, in addition to inclining towards DE AB as the etymon, Väänänen endorses Svennung's findings which prove the existence of *da* in early times, long before *diva*, on Gaulish soil: the Merovingian dynasty reigned from about 450 to 750 A.D. Moreover, Väänänen appears to endorse the concept of a link between Italian *da* and a Gallo-Romance *da*.

The evidence presented by Svennung is as follows: "...l'exemple *de ab* d'après *Formulae Andecavenses* 4, p. 6, 15 *de ab odiernum diae*: 'depuis le jour d'aujourd'hui'...." [43] These "formules d'Angers" are dated as of the second half of the seventh

---

[39] *Loc. cit.*
[40] *Loc. cit.*
[41] J. Svennung, *L'évolution de la préposition italienne DA à partir de DE AB dans le latin*, in *Bulletin Du Cange, Archivum Latinitatis Medii Aevi*, Volume XXI (1951), pp. 55-85.
[42] Väänänen, *Introduction*, p. 99.
[43] Svennung, *loc. cit.*

century. Clearly *de ab* in this instance was not part of a "locution composée," but functioned independently. Its later phonological outcome could only have become *da*, the very *da* we submit survived in *oui-da*. Svennung quotes an example of the intermediate step in this postulated process: "De l'année 715 environ, on trouve *de a*, qui se présente dans un document venant du cloître de Wissembourg en Alsace méridionale: PARDESSUS II, addit. 36 *quidquid... visus fuit tenuisse tam de a paterna vel materna seo de comparato.*" [44] Svennung's contention that there is a link between the Italian and the French in this respect is clear from the following: "Comme nous le voyons, les exemples proviennent d'Italie ou semblent au moins pouvoir être mis en relation avec les parties occidentales de la Gaule." [45] And so *da*, while prospering on Italian soil, seems to have been present throughout Western Romania.

Assuming, then, that French *da* < *dea* or *dia* < DE AB, just as Italian *da*, and that it originally carried the same ablative meaning of origin; assuming further that this origin was explicit in a complementary expression denoting a wide choice of elements or persons out of which a selection was made deictically by means of HOC ILLE or HOC ILLUD (with or without a verb such as FECIT), we suggest the following possibilities for its Vulgar Latin use and the key to the meaning of later *da*:

1. HOC ILLUD (FECIT) DE AB (HIS, EIS, ILLIS, ECCE ILLIS etc.) plus any ablative plural noun if demonstratives are used as adjectives.
   Hypothetical example: HOC ILLUD DILEXIT DE AB ILLIS TEMPLIS "out of all these available temples, he selected this one."

2. HOC ILLE (or ILLUD) DE AB plus ablative plural demonstrative pronouns (without a verb).
   Thus the situation described in (1) above, if sufficiently clear to the speakers, could have been shortened to, say, HOC ILLUD DE AB ILLIS, "this one

---

[44] *Loc. cit.*
[45] *Loc. cit.*

out of all the available ones," quite a plausible response in answer to a question such as "Which temple did he choose?," if the answering speaker wished to emphasize the fact that he found the choice a bizarre one and would have done much better than the chooser.

All of the postulated reinforcing demonstratives begin with a vowel or an *H*, a fact which in Classical Latin would fully justify AB rather than A, but this consideration is not even necessary. DE AB before consonant is amply documented in Vulgar Latin, e.g. DE AB MURO, DE AB PORTA in Pei [46] or Migliorini's example *supra* "DA VOS." We are apparently dealing with a recurrent phenomenon in the history of Latin: an original AB was reduced to A before consonant in Classical Latin, but must have persisted in Vulgar Latin until it too was reduced, but only after it had fused with DE, unlike AD which was reduced to Romance *a* on its own, irrespective of its use in *DE AD.

Let it again be emphasized that the hypothetical complement *DE AB + its following demonstratives in the ablative plural* must have been optional, and that such an option would have been exercised only for emphasis or reinforcement. In due time, HOC ILLUD or HOC ILLE condensed into *oïl > oui*, DE AB into *dea* or *dia > da*, and the supplementary demonstratives disappeared altogether through ellipsis. The original meaning of *da* was then obscured, and only its emphatic character was still felt as a reinforcer for *oui*. Both *oui* and *oui-da* continued their coexistence in French, with the latter losing ground steadily until it is today confined mostly to rural areas and to older speakers, though this could be qualified by considering that all Frenchmen know of the expression for having met it in literary texts at least, as did this writer as a Parisian schoolboy. Throughout its entire history *oui-da* < *HOC ILLUD DE AB... has kept an emphatic

---

[46] *The Italian language*, pp. 69-70.

character which plain *oui* does not have (unless it is pronounced very loud or with an *accent d'insistance*).

As for *diva*, originating in Old French *dis + va*, and thus a comparatively recent form *not directly* traceable to Vulgar Latin, it continued its existence as an interjection and we submit that only a coincidence of phonological development caused it to be confused with the *other, presumed dea* and *da*. In keeping with this interjectional character, is it any wonder that it was used alone for a long time, without latching on to any other expression the way we surmise DE AB > *da* had to? *Diva* was semantically self-sufficient. It has died out in modern French, though Godefroy reports that in some peripheral districts such as Britanny, the aboriginal form *diva* was still being used in his time, significantly enough as an interjection. This, however, is not pointed out by other authorities.

We would also point out that the steady erosion of *oui-da* in the contemporary tongue has been compensated by the presence of *ouais* for irony or surprise, *ah oui!?* for reinforcement or astonishment, and *ah oui vraiment!* and *mais oui,* *oh oui!* for varying degrees of reinforced affirmation.

Our theory of *da* may be synoptically summarized as follows:

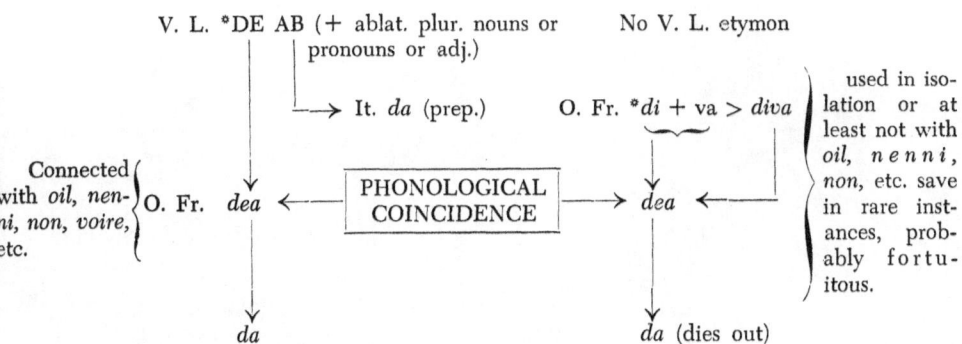

Survives in *oui-da*, preserving emphatic character and exhibiting lack of independent existence in discourse.

It is believed that the above theory is semantically sound, phonologically and grammatically possible, and that it provides a hypothesis at least to explain the definite *malaise* authorities in the field seem to have felt concerning this form. It is suggested that the statistical-semantic approach used in this article would have given rise to a twin-meaning/twin-theory of *da* earlier had it been used instead of what appears to be an exclusively formal approach, coupled with monolingual considerations, which scholars have indulged in.

THE FLOWER IN THE BOWER: *GARRIS* IN *AUCASSIN ET NICOLETTE*

By Eugene Dorfman
University of Alberta

The bower, or *loge*, which Nicolette constructs near the crossroads of the forest into which she has entered, following her escape from her prison chamber, is designed as a test of Aucassin's love:

> A porpenser or se prist
> qu'esprovera son ami
> s'i l'aime si com il dist (XIX, 9-11). [1]

The penalty for failure would be drastic. If Aucassin does not recognize the bower as her handiwork and pause there briefly, he will no longer be her beloved, nor she his:

> Jure Diu qui ne menti,
> se par la vient Aucasins
> et il por l'amor de li
> ne s'i repose un petit,
> ja ne sera ses amis,
> n'ele s'amie (XIX, 17-22)

---

[1] *Aucassin et Nicolette: Chantefable du Moyen Age*, ed. Mario Roques, 2nd ed. rev. (Paris, 1929); *idem.*, photographic copy with "Note Additionnelle" (Paris, 1962). Various Hebraic aspects of the text were discussed in "A Narremic Analysis of Aucassin et Nicolette," The Guild for Medieval and Renaissance Studies, University of Alberta, October, 1969, and "Hebraic Afinities in Aucassin et Nicolette," Western Canadian Modern Language Association, February, 1970. See the author's "Tora Lore in Torelore: A Parastructural Analysis," in *Memorial Volume for Ruth Hirsch Weir* (Mouton,

Since Aucassin has been given no visible hint of the projected test, success for him must depend on his ability to associate the components of the bower with Nicolette, with himself, or with their relationship to each other. The principal components of the bower, upon which recognition depends, are carefully enumerated:

> Ele prist des flors de lis
> et de l'erbe du garris
> et de le foille autresi,
> une bele loge en fist ...(XIX, 12-15).

The narrator repeats that the main components are flowers and leaves:

> Nicolete eut faite le loge, ... molt bele et mout gente, si l'ot bien forree dehors et dedens de flors et de foilles ... (XX, 1-3).

When Aucassin comes riding by in pursuit of her, one quietly beautiful night, it is plainly — there is a break in the text at this point, but the facts are evident — the flowers which catch his eye:

> ... Aucassins si cevauce. La nuis fu bele et quoie, et il erra tant qu'il vin .... defors et dedens et par deseure et devant de flors, et estoit si bele que plus ne pooit estre. Quant Aucassins le perçut, si s'aresta tot a un fais ... (XXIV, 71-76).

Aucassin recognizes in a flash ("tot a un fais") that his beloved has set him a signal, if not a test, and "for love of her," he decides to pause there a while:

> "... ci fu Nicolete me douce amie, et ce fist ele a ses beles mains; por le douçour de li et por s'amor me descenderai je ore ci et m'i reposerai anuit mais" (XXIV, 78-81).

---

forthcoming), and *Parody and Parable in Aucassin et Nicolette: A Narremic and Parastructural Analysis* (in preparation).

Wayne Conner has summarized the attempts to clarify the meaning of the unknown *garris* among the list of materials decorating the bower:

> The omission of *branches* from the list of materials has disturbed some readers, notably Suchier: how can you build a bower without branches? A solution has been sought by interpreting the troublesome *garris* as a Provençal term (*garric*, etc.) 'kind of oak or holly.' As the setting is Southern France, it is indeed tempting to accept *garris* as Provençal; and even some of those who prefer 'moor' to Suchier's translation are nevertheless convinced that *garris* offers a touch of local color if not an indication that the author had been to the South of France. However, the suffix of *garris* (-icius), spelling inconsistencies (*g-* might still represent *j-*), and the fact that *garris* would be the normal Picard form for Fr. *jarris* are factors that practically rule out a Provençal origin.²

Taking *erbe* necessarily into account, Conner continues:

> Perhaps the biggest stumbling-block to Suchier's rendering is that *erbe* can hardly mean 'foliage.' It clearly means 'grass'³ just as it does in the passage — with the same sequence: *fleurs-herbe(s)-feuille(s)* — where Nicolette bandages Aucassin's shoulder: "et puis si prist des flors et de l'erbe fresce et des fuelles verdes, si le loia sus au pan de sa cemisse" (XXVI, 12-14). Accordingly most critics and editors have been content with the pronouncement made by Gaston Paris in reviewing Suchier's first edition — "*De l'erbe du garris* ne peut signifier 'des branches de houx'; *garris* veut dire ici 'lande';" — though this meaning 'lande,' common for the fem. *jarrie* (Prov. *garriga*), is not clearly attested for the masc. form *garris* (*jarris*). From his rich resources Von Wartburg has apparently been able to find for the masc. type *jarris* ... only one example with the sense 'lande,' that of our text.

Conner, in order to maintain the translation "grass of the moor," suggests the possibility of a scribal error which substituted

---

² "The *Loge* in *Aucassin et Nocolette*," *Romanic Review*, 46 (1955), 81-89; see pp. 82-83.

³ There is another meaning of *erbe* which will be shown to be more relevant in this case.

garris for *larris* "so well attested in the sense 'lande,' 'terrain en friche'" (p. 83). Even if this were so, however, it is difficult to see in what way "grass of the moor" could serve as a recognition signal in the love test. The critic is on firmer ground when he insists that the "trimmings" — though he selects only the lilies for this purpose — function as "an unmistakable marker" in the test:

> It is not the essentials, but the trimmings that are mentioned, all that is characteristic of Nicolette and will make the bower an unmistakable marker for her lover. For it is something more than 'divination instinctive'[4] that reveals to Aucassin who has constructed the bower: it is bedecked with lilies, which I take to be Nicolette's signature-flower (p. 84).

If Aucassin can conclude instantaneously that Nicolette's "lovely hands" have fashioned the bower, it is (partly) because — as Conner realizes (his reasoning, though not based on specific evidence, comes close to the mark) — the lilies serve to identify[5] her as a person:

> The lily is the only[6] flower named in the description of the *loge* .... When the term is used of Nicolette, it is not the author describing, using similes, as in 'lé levretes vremelletes plus que n'est cerisse ne *rose* el tans d'esté' (XII, 21-22), or 'et les flors des *margerites* qu'ele ronpoit as ortex de ses piés ...' (XII, 25-28). It is Aucassin addressing his sweetheart, at moments when a name or pet name would come naturally to his lips: 'Nicolete, flors de lis ...' and (after relating how she cured the pilgrim, he resumes) 'Doce amie, flors de lis ....' In my view then,

---

[4] The reference is to n. 22, Myrrha Lot-Borodine, *Le Roman idyllique au mogen âge* (Paris, 1913), p. 115.

[5] Conner assesses Rogger's contribution on this point: "Rogger has the merit of realizing that the lilies must have a special meaning. But to make this flower the symbol of Woman [See his important study 'Etude descriptive de la chantefable *Aucassin et Nicolette,*' ZRP, LXVII (1951), 409-457 and LXX (1954), 1-58] (page 422), rather than of one particular woman, seems to me wide of the mark" (p. 85).

[6] The lily is, in fact, the only flower *named* in the list of materials but not necessarily the only one there in the bower; the precise nature of *l'erbe du garris* remains to be determined.

fleur de lis as used here is more than a conventional term. It is also a nickname or pet name — something, say, like the modern 'Honey' or 'Baby' (also conventional!) — which Aucassin must have been in the habit of using when alone with Nicolette. When, therefore, she wished clearly but discreetly to indicate to Aucassin that she was near, she could not do better than use, as a kind of signature, the flower that was also her name (p. 85).

The immortal heroine in world literature for whom — in her own words — the lily is a signature is the beloved of Solomon,[7] the Shulamite, in the Song of Songs:

> I am a rose [8] of Sharon,
> A lily of the valleys (2: 1).

This is the designation which Solomon himself uses in describing his love:

---

[7] For considerable additional evidence linking Aucassin with Solomon, see forthcoming publications listed above, n. 1. The first scholar to note a general resemblance between the Song of Songs and *Aucassin et Nicolette* was Ernest Renan, "Etude sur le Cantique des Cantiques," (1860); see *Œuvres Complètes*, ed. Henriette Psichari (Paris, 1955), VII, 431-525. After a briefly detailed comparison of the former with *Le Jeu de Robin et Marion*, Renan adds (p. 474): "Le poème d'*Aucassin et Nicolette*, qui a dans les manuscrits la forme d'un roman parsemé d'ariettes, semble ausis avoir eu à l'origine une disposition dramatique analogue à celle que nous essayons d'expliquer." Kaspar Rogger, "Etude descriptive de la chantefable *Aucassin et Nicolette*, II," *Zeitschrift für romanische Philologie*, 70 (1954) 1-58, checked this promising lead, but could discover only a single analogy ("l'unique correspondance de détail," p. 16, n. 1) in the watchmen of the city ("les *escargaites* (XIV/23) qui *venoient tote une rue*,") and the *mantel* (XVI/5) in which Nicolette wraps herself ("que, pourtant, elle n'avait pas mis en s'évadant de la tour"). It is now apparent that the abandonment of this line of research was premature but understandable, since the first threads of discovery, needed to unravel the rest, depended on the recognition of carefully camouflaged clues.

[8] The Hebrew reads: *ani chavatseles ha-Sharon shoshanas ha-amakim* [the transliteration of Heb. *sof* as *s*, following the Ashkenazic pronunciation, rather than the Sephardic or current Israeli style of *t*, is required by linguistic evidence in the text; see Parody and Parable in *Aucassin et Nicolette*]; *chavatseles*, rendered above as 'rose,' is usually translated as 'lily, crocus,' while *shoshana* may normally be either 'lily' or 'rose.' Biblical citations are from *The Holy Scriptures*, according to the Masoretic text (Philadelphia, 1965); and Norman Henry Snaith, *Sefer Tora Neviyim u-Ketuvim* (London, 1965).

> As a lily among thorns,
> So is my love among the daughters (2: 2).

These lines directly follow a description significantly reminiscent of Nicolette's bower:

> Behold, thou art fair, my beloved,
>   yea, pleasant;
> Also our couch is leafy.
> The beams of our houses are cedars,
> And our panels are cypresses (1: 16-17).

The inversions in *Aucassin et Nicolette*, discussed in previous studies, find an additional example here; where Aucassin lies inside the bower, peering out at the stars ("... si se torna sor costé tant qu'il vint tos souvins en le loge; et il garda par mi un trau de le loge, si vit les estoiles el ciel...," XXIV, 86-88), Solomon stands outside, peering in:

> Behold, he standeth behind our wall,
> He looketh in through the windows,
> He peereth through the lattice (2: 9).

There are other indications that the author of *Aucassin et Nicolette* found direct inspiration — and details, which he used in his own way — in the Song of Songs. When Solomon peers through the lattice, he speaks to his love:

> My beloved spoke, and said unto me:
> 'Rise up, my love, my fair one, and come away.
> For, lo, the winter is past,
> The rain is over and gone;
> The flowers appear on the earth;
> The time of singing is come ...' (2: 10-12).

These are the words that Nicolette "hears" in her prison chamber; the season described is the same:

> Ce fu el tans d'esté, el mois de mai que li jor sont caut, lonc et cler, et les nuis coies et series (XII, 2-4).

As Nicolette languishes one night on her prison bed, she observes that "the time of singing is come," and remembers Aucassin, her beloved:

> Nicolete jut une nuit en son lit, si vit la lune luire cler par une fenestre et si oï le lorseilnol center en garding, se li sovint d'Aucassin sen ami qu'ele tant amoit (XII, 5-7).

The Shulamite likewise lies on her bed, longing for the lover who has called upon her to "rise up and come away":

> By night on my bed I sought him whom my soul loveth;
> I sought him, but I found him not.
> 'I will rise now, and go about the city,
> In the streets and in the broad ways,
> I will seek him whom my soul loveth.'
> I sought him, but I found him not.
> The watchmen that go about the city found me:
> 'Saw ye him whom my soul loveth?'
> Scarce had I passed from them,
> When I found him whom my soul loveth:
> I held him, and would not let him go ... (3: 1-4).

Nicolette, making good her escape from prison, "goes about the city [of Beaucaire], in the streets and in the broad ways," "...si s'en isci par mi les rues de Biaucaire" (XII, 29-30), until she finds Aucassin in his prison. Fearing for her life, Nicolette takes great care *not* to be found by "the watchmen of the city," *les escargaites de le vile* (XIV, 23-24), who enter the scene after she has spoken to Aucassin rather than before (as in the case of the Shulamite). In a series of inversions, not without rich comic effect, Nicolette transforms the Shulamite's tender "I held him, and would not let him go" into a lovers' quarrel,[9] insulting her lover (for the purpose of the narrative) with the accusation that he does not love her as much as he says he does, or as much as she loves him:

---

[9] For the functional role of the lovers' quarrel and the insult in the medieval romance, see Dorfman, *The Narreme in the Medieval Romance Epic: An Introduction to Narrative Structures* (Toronto, 1969), Chapter Four, *passim*.

—A! fait ele, je ne quit mie que vous m'amés tant con vos dites; mais je vos aim plus que vos ne faciés mie (XIV, 15-16).

This is a challenge which Aucassin accepts. The model which he inverts is Solomon's passionate declaration of love:

'Arise, my love, my fair one, and come away.
O my dove, that art in the clefts of the rock,
   in the covert of the cliff,
Let me see thy countenance, let me hear thy voice;
For sweet is thy voice, and thy countenance is comely' (2: 13-14).

Coolly, without heat, anger, or passion, Aucassin goes Nicolette's insult one better. In calm debate, he "reasons" with her, carefully explaining the difference between the physical nature of woman's love and that of man, rooted in the heart:

—Avoi! fait Aucassins, bele douce amie, ce ne porroit estre que vos m'amissiés tant que je fac vos. Fenme ne puet amer l'oume con li hom fait le fenme; car li amors de le fenme est en son oeul et en son le cateron de sa mamele et en son l'orteil del pié; mais li amors de l'oume est ens el cué plantee, dont ele ne puet iscir" (XIV, 17-22).

It does not take much imagination to realize how much more appropriate are Solomon's words for Aucassin's situation, but then the humor would be lost.

The debate is interrupted by a friendly guard who sings a warning that the watchmen who seek her death are on their way. With the same coolness displayed by Aucassin, Nicolette finds it easy "to let him go," or rather, by inversion, to leave him, "...ele prent congié a Aucassin, si s'en va..." (XVI, 6-7). On her flight, she encounters some shepherds whom she pays to deliver a message to Aucassin, should he come their way; they are to inform him that he must hunt a beast in the forest with the power to cure him of his malady. While awaiting his arrival, Nicolette plans the love test and the necessary signals.

We recall that Nicolette has stated negatively that if Aucassin does not pause at her bower, he will not be her beloved nor she his:

>   ja ne sera ses amis,
>   n'ele s'amie (XIX, 21-22).

Not unexpectedly, the Shulamite makes the same remark, but affirmatively:

>   My beloved is mine, and I am his,
>   That feedeth among the lilies (2: 16).

The Shulamite repeats this later, with additions significant for the signals:

>   'My beloved is gone down to his garden,
>   To the beds of spices,
>   To feed in the gardens,
>   And to gather lilies.
>   I am my beloved's, and my beloved is mine,
>   That feedeth among the lilies' (6: 1-3).

The two items in Solomon's garden, mentioned by the Shulamite in the "I am his, he is mine" passage clearly relevant to Nicolette's love test, are spices and lilies. The presumption is strong that spices form a part of the recognition signal, suggesting that the "troublesome" *garris* refers in some manner to spices of one kind or another. An attractive solution, in this regard, may be found in Meyer-Lübke, under item 7594a: "*ša'rā* (arab.) 'ein mit Büschen bewachsener Ort,'" where appear the Romance forms: "sp. *jara*, pg. *xara* 'wilder Rosmarin,' 'kretische Ciste' ... . —Ablt.: sp. *jaral*, pg. *xaral* 'mit Rosmarin bewachsenes Feld.'[10]

Rosmarin is 'rosemary,' defined as: "... an evergreen shrub of the mint family, native to the Mediterranean region, with clusters of small, light-blue flowers and leaves that yield a fragrant essential oil ... : rosemary is conventionally a symbol of remembrance and constancy."[11] Since *herbe* is normally 'herb, plant, or weed,' and 'mint' is defined as: "... any of various aromatic plants whose leaves are used for flavoring and in medicine ...," *l'erbe du garris* may be construed as 'the (aromatic, or spicy) plant of

---

[10] *Romanisches etymologisches Wörterbuch*, 3rd ed. (Heidelberg, 1935).
[11] *Webster's New World Dictionary of the American Language* (Cleveland and New York, 1968), for English definitions.

the rosemary.' This would satisfy several conditions of the text: 1) it adds "light-blue flowers and leaves" ("... et de l'erbe du garris, et de le foille autresi ...," XIX, 13-14, and "... si l'ot bien forree dehors et dedens de *flors* et de *foilles* ...," XX, 2-3) to the lilies; 2) the soothing oil and the medicinal properties of the mint (rosemary) serve far better than "grass of the moor" to explain the healing of Aucassin's shoulder (XXVI, 12-14); 3) the fact that rosemary is in itself a symbol of "remembrance and constancy" adds to its likelihood as a lover's signal — in preference to grass.

Kretische Ciste, or *Ziste,* appears to refer to 'rock rose,' defined as: "... any of a number of related plants with large, roselike flowers of white, purple, or red." This could show a relationship between *Aucassin et Nicolette* and the Song of Songs in two ways: 1) the Shulamite calls herself "a *rose* of Sharon (rock rose?), a *lily* of the valleys," and these may be the two components, besides the leaves, in the bower; 2) if the rock rose was known to the poet as a specifically "Kretisch," or Cretan, flower, it is significant that Hebrew *Kreti* means both 'Cretans' and 'Philistines,' [12] since, in addition to the Solomon-Shulamite analogue, in the early part of the story a similar analogy is made between Aucassin-Nicolette and Samson-Delilah [13] (or Samson's Philistine wife). In the same vein, the poet indulges in word-play on placenames, e.g. *baal*-Valence and *Kreti*-Carthage; since Nicolette turns

---

[12] Marchand-Ennery, *Lexique hébreu-français*, 6th ed. (Paris, 1947).

[13] The anonymous author of *Aucassin et Nicolette,* composing his parody of the contemporary epics and romances most likely in the aftermath of the Albigensian Crusade — one of the darker periods of the Dark Ages, in which unauthorized study of the Bible was subject to severe penalties and Talmudical scholarship to frenzied harassment — peppered his work with a considerable number of linguistic clues in Old French, Judeo-French, and Hebrew, pointing to more or less specific portions of the Old Testament, or Tora. This secret, or *parastructural* aspect, which re-inverts the inversions, e. g., the active role of Nicolette as against Aucassin's apparent passivity, or the seemingly absurd *couvade* of the King of Torelore compared with his Amazonian queen, etc., is a profoundly serious study of the Bible. Behind the mask of fantasy, frivolity, and burlesque — inaccessible to Church and government spies as well as all who lack the linguistic keys — is the story of the Education of a Jewish Prince, being trained to become the kind of man needed to lead his dispersed and persecuted people back to Israel. Nothing comparable in purpose and format is known to the present writer to exist in any language; see above, n. 1.

out to be a Carthaginian (Cretan or Philistine?) princess, the rock rose may be intended as a signature-flower linking her with the Shulamite. On balance, the combination "spices and lilies," supported by the medicinal virtues of mint, favor the translation of *garris* as 'rosemary.' In either case, the result is another flower in the bower.

THE EVOLUTION OF THE STRESSED VOWEL SYSTEM OF VEGLIOTE

By Thaddeus Ferguson
Columbia University

1.0. Vegliote, generally considered to be representative of an extinct Dalmatian variety of Romance speech, was spoken on the island of Veglia, or Krk, off the northwestern coast of Yugoslavia, until the latter part of the nineteenth century. The language was described by Matteo Giulio Bàrtoli,[1] whose informant, Antonio Udina, was supposedly the last living speaker of Vegliote. The historical stages of the Vegliote stressed vowel system will be abstracted here primarily through internal reconstruction.

An examination of the Vegliote vowel system along historical lines must take into account two phenomena instrumental in obscuring the Proto-Romance basis of the system. First, there was a bifurcation of the entire vowel system, originally conditioned by a difference in syllabic structure which was later neutralized. This difference in syllabic structure is therefore not *directly* reflected in the final stage of the language. The second and more striking of the factors altering the system was patterned falling diphthongization (and triphthongization), with remonophthongization in some instances.

These modifying forces operated upon the Vegliote stressed vowel paradigm with nearly complete consistency, so that the symmetrical nature of Romance vocalic evolution was fully preserved. Consequently, by comparing the final stage of the

---

[1] Matteo Giulio Bàrtoli, *Das Dalmatische*, 2 vols. (Vienna, 1906).

Vegliote stressed vowel system with the Proto-Romance source and by analyzing many of the vocalic units of this system as reflexes of falling diphthongs, one can recover the intermediate stages of the vowel paradigm with reasonable confidence.

Although the Proto-Romance vowel structuring was indeed preserved in Vegliote, the phonetic reshaping was drastic. As a result, an analysis of the vowel system outside the proper structural framework can lead to any number of highly debatable theories. It is for this reason, for instance, that investigators have been tempted to assert, erroneously, that the underlying Proto-Romance structure of the vowel system of Vegliote had been fundamentally altered through external interference, especially from contact with Slavic speech.[2] In fact, as I shall attempt to demonstrate in the following pages, the entire evolution of the vowel system of Vegliote can be traced in a linear progression from Proto-Romance.

I shall proceed on the principle that in diachronic studies the vowel paradigm must be plotted so as to correlate with that of the proto-language, irrespective of the phonetic — or phonemic — changes which have occurred during the history of a language.

Of utmost importance is the fact that every Proto-Romance stressed vowel regularly yielded *two* different reflexes in Vegliote, depending on whether the proto-phoneme *originally* occurred in open or in closed syllable.

1.1. In Vegliote the reflexes of */i̯/ (Ĭ) and of */e̯/ (Ē) are identical, evolving to /ay/ when in originally open syllable and to /a/ when in originally closed syllable:

Open syllable: /payl/ < */'pe̯ lu̯/ < */'pi̯ lu̯/ (PĬLŬM)
"hair"

/playn/ < */'ple̯ nu̯/ (PLĒNŬM)
"full"

---

[2] See, for example, Roger L. Hadlich, *The Phonological History of Vegliote* (Chapel Hill, 1965).

Closed syllable: /pask/ < */'pęs ke/ < */'pi̯s ke/ (PĬSCĔM)
"fish"

/'sta la/ < */'stęl :a/ (STĒLLĂ)
"star"

1.2. There is a complication, however, in that Proto-Romance */i̯/ (Ĭ) in originally open syllable also evolved to /ay/, merging with the reflexes of open-syllable */i̯/ and /ę/:

/a 'mayk/ < */a 'mi̯ ku̯/ (ĂMĪCVM)
"friend"

But there is good reason to suspect from the start that this merger was relatively late, inasmuch as reflexes of */i̯/ remain distinct from those of */ę/ when in originally *closed* syllable:

/mel/ < */'mi̯l :e/ (MĪLLĔ)
"a thousand"

but: /pask/ < */'pęs ke/ < */'pi̯s ke/ (PĬSCĔM)
"fish"

/'sta la/ < */'stęl :a/ (STĒLLĂ)
"star"

It will be necessary to reserve judgment on this development until later in the analysis (see below, § 3.2.5).

1.3. Since */u̯/ (Ŭ) was lost in all Romance languages through merger with either */u̯/ (Ū) or */ǫ/ (Ō), every Romance vowel system must be examined separately to determine the nature of the merger in that particular language. In Vegliote the reflexes of */u̯/ coincide with those of */ǫ/:

Open syllable: /krawk/ < */'krǫ ke/ < */kru̯ ke/ (CRŬCĔM)
"cross"

/bawd/ < */'vǫ ke/ (VŌCĔM)
"voice"

Closed syllable:³ /'bu ka/ < */'bok̦ :a/ < /'buk̦ :a/ (BŬCCĂ)
"mouth"

The reflexes of */u̦/, by contrast, are distinct from those of */u/ (> */o̦/):

Open syllable: /'loy na/ < */'lu̦ na/ (LŪNĂ)
"moon"

Closed syllable: /'no l'a/ < */'nul' :a/ (NŪLLIĂ)
"nothing"

2.0. From this point I shall follow procedures which, it is hoped, might prove equally practicable in recovering the intermediate stages of any modern Romance stressed vowel system, especially when, as in the case of Vegliote, the earlier stages of the language are insufficiently documented.

2.1. First of all, it is necessary to determine whether or not the phonemic distinction between the mid-open and mid-close levels of the Proto-Romance vocalism is still reflected in Vegliote as recorded. And, indeed, it is clear that the reflexes of */e/ (and */i̦/) remain distinct from those of */e̦/ (Ĕ) in originally open and originally closed syllable alike:

Open syllable: /playn/ < */'ple nu̦/ (PLĒNŬM)
"full"

but: /'pi tra/ < */'pe̦ tra/ (PĔTRĂ)
"stone"

Closed syllable: /'sta la/ < */'ste̦l :a/ (STĒLLĂ)
"star"

but: /'fyas ta/ < */fe̦s ta/ (FĔSTĂ)
"holiday"

---

³ Bàrtoli's data contain no truly reliable examples of reflexes in Vegliote of original Proto-Romance */o̦/ (Ō) — as opposed to */o/ < */u̦/ (Ŭ) — in closed syllable; see Bàrtoli, vol. II, p. 335 (§ 295).

2.2. Similarly, the original phonemic distinction is reflected by the differing reflexes of Proto-Romance */o̦/ (including */o̦/ < */u̦/) and */o̧/ (Ŏ):

Open syllable: /ˈbawd/ < */ˈvo̦ ke/ (VŌCĚM)
"voice"

but: /fuk/ < */ˈfo̧ ku̦/ (FŎCǓM)
"fire"

Closed syllable: /ˈbu ka/ < */ˈbo̦k :a/ (< */ˈbu̦k :a/) (BǓCCĂ)
"mouth"

but: /fwart/ < */ˈfo̧r te/ (FŎRTĚM)
"strong"

It will be noted that */o̧/ in originally open syllable and */o̦/ (< */u̦/) in originally closed syllable both yield /u/ as the reflex in Vegliote; e.g.:

*/ˈfo̧ ku̦/ > /fuk/ "fire"
*/ˈbu̦k :a/ > */ˈbo̦k :a/ > /ˈbu ka/ "mouth"

Merger did not take place, however, until the syllabic structure had been altered as a result of (1) shortening of long consonants and reduction of medial consonant clusters and (2) loss of final unstressed vowels; above, § 1.0.

2.3. Accordingly, one concludes that the stressed vowel system of Vegliote resisted the merger of */ȩ/ with */e̦/ and that of */o̧/ with */o̦/ which occurred in certain Romance languages and dialects, such as Sardinian, some Southern Italian dialects, as well as in the *back* series of the Rumanian stressed vowel system.

2.4. Bàrtoli indicates a partial merger of Proto-Romance */a/ (Ā and Ă) with */o̧/ when in originally open syllable:

/pun/ < */ˈpa ne/ (PĀNĚM)
"bread"

/rur/ < */'ra ru̯/ (RĀRŬM)
"rare"

Compare: /fuk/ < */'fǫ ku̯/ (FŎCŬM)
"fire"

/bun/ < */'bǫ nu̯/ (BŎNŬM)
"good"

This attests to a highly velarized articulation of */a/ (= *[ɑ]).

In some lexical items open-syllable */a/ produced a separate reflex in Vegliote:

/'lu͡ǫ na/ < */'la na/ (LĀNĂ)
"wool"

/'ku͡ǫ sa/ < */'ka sa/ (CĂSĀ)
"house"

I retain Bàrtoli's transcription for /u͡ǫ/. The actual pronunciation is uncertain.

The merger of */a/ with */ǫ/ seems to have been consistent when */a/ was in originally *closed* syllable:

/'bwar ba/ < */'bar ba/ (BARBĂ)
"beard"

/lwarg/ < */'lar gu̯/ (LARGŬM)
"broad, wide"

Compare: /fwart/ < */'fǫr te/ (FŎRTĒM)
"strong"

/mwart/ < */'mǫr te/ (MŎRTĒM)
"death"

3.0. It is now possible to correlate the Vegliote stressed vowel system with the four-degree post-Proto-Romance prototype: [4]

---

[4] Level */ẹ ——— ọ/ of the four-degree post-Proto-Romance prototype reflects the merger of the members of Proto-Romance level */i̯ ——— u̯/ (Ĭ and Ŭ) with (in the case of Vegliote) the original members of Proto-Romance level */ẹ ——— ọ/ (Ē and Ō); see above, §§ 1.1 and 1.3.

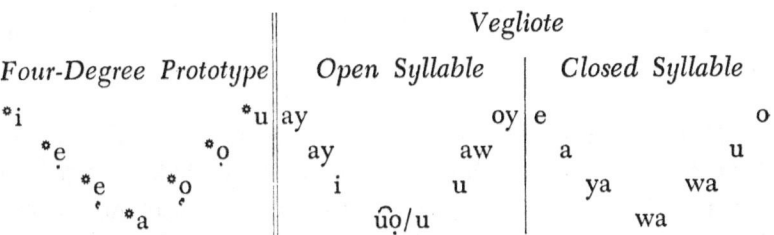

The open-syllable and closed-syllable resolutions will be analyzed independently.

CLOSED SYLLABLE

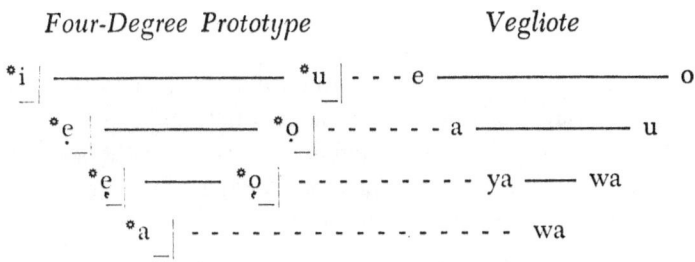

3.1. In some Romance vowel systems, such as those of Spanish and the Rhaeto-Romance dialects, as well as the *front* vowel series of Rumanian, rising diphthongization affected all occurrences of the stressed vowel phonemes of the mid-open level, that is, stressed */ę ——— ǫ/ > */ye ——— wo/ in all phonological contexts. Turning first to the vowels in originally closed syllable (where the vocalic development seems somewhat less complicated), one finds that this likewise holds true for the Vegliote vowel system. Accordingly, a closed syllable did not impede rising diphthongization of the vowels of the mid-open level. One may reasonably deduce that Proto-Romance */ę ——— ǫ/ in closed syllable evolved to Vegliote /ya ——— wa/ through the intermediate stage */ye ——— wo/, followed by opening of the syllabic nuclei to the maximum degree of aperture. Ironically, while diphthongization in certain languages was impeded by a closed syllable, in Vegliote diphthongization of the reflexes of members of */ę ——— ǫ/ is readily perceptible *only* where the vowels were originally in closed syllable. Although diphthongization was just as much a factor in open syllable as in closed, its presence in open syllable must be recovered indirectly, as will be shown below (§ 3.2.4).

3.1.1. It must be assumed that */a/ acquired the articulation indicated by Bàrtoli (/u̯ǫ/) as soon as */ǫ/ diphthongized to */wo/. This is the only phonetically plausible way to account for the complete merger of */a/ with */ǫ/ in closed syllable:

$$*/ǫ/ > */wo/$$
$$*/a/ (= *[α]) > */u̯ǫ/ > */wo/.$$

3.1.2. The fate of the mid-open vowels in turn provides a key to the development of the other vowels in closed syllable, for it is evident that after diphthongization (/ę —— ǫ/ > */ye — wo/), the syllabic nuclei opened one degree (*/ye—wo/ > /ya —— wa/) and the development was terminated. Similarly, the other vowels in originally closed syllable — with one exception — evidence an opening of one degree. The exception is */ǫ/, which closed to /u/. Otherwise:

$$*/i/ > /e/ \qquad */u/ > /o/$$
$$*/ę/ > /a/ \qquad (*/ǫ/ > /u/)$$
$$*/ye/ > /ya/ \qquad */wo/ > /wa_1/$$
$$\qquad\qquad\qquad */u̯ǫ/ > /wa_2/$$

3.1.3. It is not hard to explain why original */ǫ/ closed to /u/ instead of opening in a manner parallel to that of the other syllabic nuclei. Original */ę/ opened to /a/, and the front ~ back opposition was neutralized for this phoneme. A completely symmetrical development of */ǫ/, with similar neutralization of the front ~ back opposition, would have had as a consequence the change of both */ę/ and */ǫ/ into /a/, with the resulting merger of these two phonemes. On the other hand, had original */ǫ/ not shifted at all, it would have merged with secondary /o/ (< */u/).

In fact, as soon as original */u/ began to shift to /o/, *original* */ǫ/ must have preserved distinctive contrast through phonetic modification of some sort. Finally, it closed to /u/.

OPEN SYLLABLE

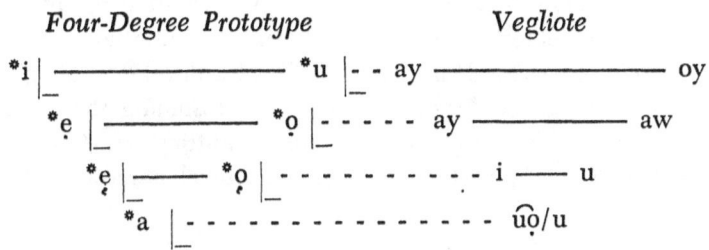

3.2. The vocalism in originally open syllable is more complex, but the over-all pattern is not hard to discern.

3.2.1. It should be noted here that once those members of */a/ which resisted merger with */ǫ/ had assumed the phonetic shape [u̯ǫ], they seem to have undergone no significant alteration, at least on the basis of Bàrtoli's data. However that may be, it is clear that a good proportion of the allophones of */a/ merged with the reflexes of */ǫ/ and underwent the same evolution as the latter, yielding /u/ in originally open syllable.

3.2.2. Members of /i ——— u/ are the reflexes of Proto-Romance */ę ——— ǫ/ in originally open syllable. On the basis of my analysis of the vowels in closed syllable, I shall set up */ye ——— wo/ as the tentative reconstruction of this vocalic level in Proto-Vegliote in open as well as closed syllable, even though this might seem to be of dubious phonetic plausibility.

3.2.3. All other vocoids in originally open syllable are found to have acquired off-glides (except /u̯ǫ/, which remained unchanged). Accordingly, I shall reconstruct the initial stage of Proto-Vegliote stressed vowel development in open syllable as follows:

$$\begin{array}{ccc} {}^*i \text{———} {}^*u & & {}^*iy \text{———} {}^*uw \\ & > & \\ {}^*\text{ę} \text{———} {}^*\text{ǫ} & & {}^*ey \text{———} {}^*ow \end{array}$$

Adhering to phonetic plausibility as a criterion, I have posited /y/ as the original off-glide for front vowels and /w/ for back vowels in *all* cases; hence, */u/ > */uw/.

3.2.4. On the principle that the trend towards the formation of off-glides reflects the pressure of pattern congruity, one may justifiably entertain the possibility that the diphthongs posited for the mid-open vowels in open syllable also developed off-glides, */ye —— wo/ > */yey —— wow/, assuming shapes transitional to their final forms. Therefore, omitting /u̯ǫ/ < */a/ (above), one may plot the open-syllable vowel paradigm at this stage as

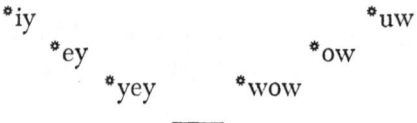

The triphthongs */yey —— wow/ most plausibly monophthongized through the intermediate stage */yiy —— wuw/, resolving in /i —— u/ and terminating the evolution.

The tentative reconstruction of */ye —— wo/ as the source of Vegliote /i —— u/ (above, § 3.2.2) gains in credibility when one considers that */yey —— wow/ is a phonetically plausible intermediate stage between the reconstructed and the actually attested forms. There are, in fact, parallel developments in the vocalism of other Romance languages. In Catalan the reflexes of Proto-Romance level */ę —— ǫ/ are members of /i —— u/ if the stressed vocoid is followed immediately by the reflex of a palatal: */'lęk' tu̯/ (LĒCTV̆M) > /l'it/ "bed"; */'fǫl' :a/ (FŎ-LIĂ) > /'fu l'ə/ "leaf". Similarly, in Northern French members of */ę —— ǫ/ yielded /i —— u/ when the vocoid was followed by a palatal: */'lęk' tu̯/ > /li/ "bed"; */'nǫk' te/ (NŎC-TĔM) > /nẅi/ (< */nuy/) "night". In Castilian the reflex of Proto-Romance */ę/ is /i/ when the vowel is followed by /-y-/ (or /-l'-/) < */-l:-/ (-LL-); e.g., */'sęl :a/ (SĔLLĂ) > /'si ya/ "chair"; */kul 'tęl:u̯/ (CV̆LTĔLLV̆M) > /ku 'či yo/ "knife"; */kas 'tęl :u̯/ (CASTĔLLV̆M) > /kas 'ti yo/ "castle". For all the reflexes cited above the most plausible intermediate stages are */ye —— wo/ > */yey —— wow/ > */yiy —— wuw/, as posited here for Vegliote. However, unlike the situation in Vegliote, where members of /i —— u/ are the regular reflexes of the phonemes of level */ę —— ǫ/ in open syllable, the French and Castilian reflexes are purely the result of contextual phonetic conditioning, while the Catalan forms reflect contextual conditioning in co-ordination with structural pressures.[5] Of these four languages Vegliote is the only one in which */ę/ evolved to /i/ and */ǫ/ to /u/ *without special phonetic conditioning*, but in open syllable only. Conversely, in Catalan, French, and Castilian the following palatal which conditioned the change also blocked the syllabic nucleus of the vocoid; hence, in the latter three languages the development took place in *closed* syllable only. Therefore, no sound correspondences can be set up illustrating the phenomenon for cognate items in all four languages.

3.2.5. If one compares the remaining Proto-Vegliote diphthongs posited here with their modern reflexes:

$$*iy \longrightarrow *uw \dashrightarrow ay \longrightarrow oy$$
$$*ey \longrightarrow *ow \dashrightarrow ay \longrightarrow aw$$

it becomes obvious that the syllabic nuclei of these diphthongs opened in a manner similar to that of the monophthongal reflexes in originally closed syllable:

$$*iy > *ey_2 \qquad *uw > *ow$$
$$*ey_1 > ay_1 \qquad *ow > aw$$

Finally, the reflex of */i/ opened one more degree, ultimately merging with the reflex of */ę/ (see above, § 1.2):

$$*/i/ > */iy/ > */ey_2/ > /ay_2/$$
$$*/ę/ > */ey_1/ > /ay_1/$$

---

[5] In those Romance stressed vowel systems in which the phonemes of level */ę ——— ǫ/ resisted merger with the phonemes of level */ẹ ——— ọ/, the members of level */ę ——— ǫ/ underwent rising diphthongization in at least some of their occurrences. In Catalan a following palatal served as a catalyst for this diphthongization.

The phonetic shape of the final reflex of */u/ in Vegliote is best interpreted as reflecting dissimilation of the off-glide from the (back rounded) syllabic nucleus:

$$*/u/ > */uw/ > */ow/ > /oy/ .$$

This is to some extent paralleled in Portuguese. The reflex of Proto-Romance */aw/ (AV) is /ow/ in Northern Portuguese dialects, while in the standard language the reflex can be /o/, reflecting monophthongization, or /oy/, reflecting dissimilation of the off-glide in a manner similar to that posited here for Vegliote /oy/ < */ow/; e.g., Pr.-Rom. */'aw rụ/ (AVRŬM) > Pr.-Port. */'ow ro/ > mod. Port. /'oy ru/ "gold".

The result is the final stage in the evolution of Vegliote stressed vowels in originally open syllable:

$$\begin{array}{ccc} ay_2 & & oy \\ ay_1 & & aw \\ i & u & \\ \widehat{ou}/u & & \end{array} ,$$

and there is no need to posit hypothetical external influences, Slavic or otherwise, in order to understand the outcome.

THE VEGLIOTE-SARDINIAN LEXICAL AFFILIATIONS

By JOHN FISHER
Fairleigh Dickinson University

In a previous study entitled "The Lexical Affiliations of Vegliote" (to be published in 1971), an attempt was made to compare the basic Latin vocabulary of Vegliote found in the *REW* with cognates in Rumanian, Italian, French, Spanish, and Portuguese with a view to determining the degree of lexical affiliation among these national languages. Compared with the 483 Vegliote entries found in the *REW*, there were 427 Vegliote-Italian, 380 Vegliote-French, 365 Vegliote-Spanish, 344 Vegliote-Portuguese, and 298 Vegliote-Rumanian. In addition, the Pan-Romance (Rumanian, Italian, French, Spanish, Portuguese) total came to 208 cognates. (In a paper on glottochronology, István Fodor[1] proposed that the word material be increased to about 500 items.) It is merely a coincidence that Meyer-Lübke's dictionary lists only 483 lexical items.

In the above study it was found that there was not really any very deep cleavage in the Latin cognates that were investigated. This is not too surprising when the high degree of Roman civilization is considered, as well as the fact that a common background and ease of communication often tend to maintain greater stability due to centripetal forces exerted by a centralized state and a conservative linguistic tradition.

---

[1] István Fodor, *The Rate of Linguistic Change* (The Hague: Mouton & Co., 1965), p. 57.

At the conclusion of the Vegliote study it was suggested that the method employed could be applied to determine the degree of lexical affiliation of any known group of languages or dialects. It should be emphasized that the suggestion implies that there be no artificial word list made up beforehand. This is one of the shortcomings of the theoreticians of lexicostatistics.

For the purpose of this study of Vegliote and Sardinian cognates, the Sardinian reflexes of Latin etyma found in the *REW* [2] were compared with those listed in the *DES*. [3] Since the *DES* is a later and much more detailed work, it was not surprising that there were more Sardinian reflexes in Wagner's work — 349 in the *REW* as compared with 366 in the *DES*. When the total Vegliote lexical items found both in Bartoli and Meyer-Lübke were compared with their cognates in Sardinian (Vegliote 483 and Sardinian 366), it was again found that there was no great cleavage as is sometimes supposed. While this study does shed some light on the problem of Romance lexical affiliation, a much more detailed work (a comparison of the approximately 2,800 Latin etyma of Sardinian reflexes found in the *DES* will be compared with cognates in Rumanian, Italian, Rheto-Romance, French, Provençal, Catalan, Spanish, and Portuguese) is now in preparation.

Some of the needless controversy in Romance linguistics could be avoided if more precise studies of vocabulary were made. As a single instance, the statement concerning the retention rates of cognates [4] made by A. L. Kroeber

> We are assuming that rates of change are reasonably constant in all languages and in all circumstances. This assumption may be roughly true, but it seems unlikely to hold rigorously. If true it is highly important, and should therefore be tested as often as possible.

is based more on assumption than fact. In a subsequent article, A. L. Kroeber compared three quantitative classifications of Ro-

---

[2] Wilhelm Meyer-Lübke, *Romanisches etymologisches Wörterbuch* (Heidelberg: Carl Winter, 1968).

[3] M. L. Wagner, *Dizionario etimologico sardo*, 3 vols. (Heidelberg: Carl Winter, 1960-1964).

[4] A. L. Kroeber, "Romance History and Glottochronology," *Language*, 34, 4 (October-December 1958), 455.

mance.[5] Concerning the Grimes-Agard[6] study, Kroeber infers the following results:[7]

> Sardinian and French are found to be at opposite poles. This suggests a deep cleavage into a Western group (Catalan, Spanish, Portuguese, French) and a non-Western (Italian, Rumanian, Sardinian).

As can be seen from the statistical count cited above, the retention rate of Sardinian (366) and French (380) cognates evidently does not suggest any deep cleavage or that these two Romance vocabularies are to be found at opposite poles.

While Kroeber's article cited above discusses three quantitative classifications of Romance, it is only Rea's study that concerns vocabulary. The Grimes-Agard study is based on 169 sets of phonological correspondences. In addition to a synchronic comparison of basic components of Romance phonology, it contains ranking as well as calculated coefficients. The Pei study is a diachronic approach via phonology. It tabulates the divergence of Romance from Latin stressed vowels.

---

[5] A. L. Kroeber, "Three Quantitative Classifications of Romance," *Romance Philology*, XIV, 3 (February 1961), 189-195.
[6] Joseph E. Grimes and Frederick B. Agard, "Linguistic Divergence in Romance," *Language*, 35, 4 (October-December 1959), 598-604.
[7] A. L. Kroeber, *Ibid.*, p. 190.

THE PLURAL *i*-ENDING OF THIRD DECLENSION MASCULINE NOUNS IN ITALIAN

By PAUL A. GAENG
University of Virginia

Discussing the *i cani* plural type, Gerhard Rohlfs states that "Aus lat. CANES wäre in der Toskana und in vielen anderen Teilen der Halbinsel normal die Form *cane* zu erwarten." [1] The *e* ending, as a matter of fact, is frequently found in medieval Italian texts and Rohlfs notes that even today forms like *i ordene* and *i rovere* are still in current use, as in the patois of Vicenza, for instance. He finds it difficult to decide, however, whether the final *e* in these forms is a reflex of the Latin ending or "(eine) sekundäre Analogieerscheinung" due to the plural *le chiave* (<CLAVĒS) type, which is also quite widespread in medieval literary texts, in general, and in Old Tuscan texts, in particular. [2] On the other hand, Latin *-ēs* normally gives *-i* in southern Italian speech (e. g., Sicilian *cani* (<CANĒS), *munti* (<MONTĒS), and *pisci* (<PISCĒS). The eventual change from *i cane* to *i cani* in literary Italian would be due, according to this scholar, to the analogical pull exerted by plurals of the *o*-declension masculine nouns (as in *il gallo* versus *i galli*), aided by the need to differentiate between singular *cane* and plural *cane*, that is, the need for a distinctive plural ending. A further contributing factor influencing the change of final *-e* to *-i* may have been the masculine

---

[1] *Historische Grammatik der italienischen Sprache und ihrer Mundarten* (Bern, 1949), II, p. 49.
[2] *Ibid.*, pp. 49-50.
[3] *Ibid.*, p. 49.

plural article form in *i* and the unconscious desire to bring about the same kind of harmony between article and plural ending (namely *i cane* < *i cani*) that exists within the *i galli* and *le capre* class of nouns.[3] The same desire to differentiate singular from plural, incidentally, may also have contributed to the eventual change from plural *chiave* to *chiavi*.[4]

This hypothesis of Rohlf's concerning the final *i*-plural outcome of Latin nouns of the CANĒS type may be conveniently referred to as the theory of analogy.[5]

Another explanation to acount for the form *cani* is based on the fact that Latin $\bar{e}$, $\breve{e}$, $\breve{\imath}$, and the diphthong *ae* in unstressed final syllable frequently show an *i*- rather than *e*-outcome in present-day Italian, e. g. *dieci* (< DECĔM), *avanti* (< AB ANTĔ), *lungi* (< LUNGĒ), *domani* (< DE MANĒ), etc. (for older *diece, avante, longe,* and *domane*), as against *sette* (< SEPTĔM), *bene* (< BENĔ), *corre* (< CURRĬT), *ove* (< UBĬ), *pure* (< PURĒ), and many others.[6]

Then there is the well-known theory advanced by Wilhelm Meyer-Lübke to the effect that final Latin -$\bar{e}$ becomes -*i* in Italian (e. g., FLORĒS < *fiori*, VIDĒ < *vedi*, etc.),[7] subsequently modified and restated in the form of a phonetic "law" which states that Latin -*ās* and -*ēs* become -*i* in Italian.[8]

Another possibility that has been envisaged to explain the *i*-outcome of third declension masculine plural nouns in modern

---

[4] *Ibid.*, p. 52.

[5] Rohlfs is by no means the first one to propose an analogical explanation for the change of Latin -$\bar{e}s$ to Italian -*i* in third declension plurals. Among earlier scholars working on this problem, C. H. Grandgent claimed that "the masculines of the third patterned themselves on the second, the great masculine declension." See his *From Latin to Italian* (Cambridg, Mass., 1927), p. 49. In a special study specifically devoted to this question entitled "Unaccented Final Vowels in Italian," in *Mélanges de philologie et d'histoire offerts à Antoine Thomas* (Paris, 1927), 187-193, this scholar draws a parallel between the Italian development, on the one hand, and French, Provençal, and Rumanian, on the other, "which languages early adapted the masculines of the 3d declension to the type of the 2nd" (p. 192).

[6] See Mario Pei, "Latin and Italian Final Front Vowels," *Modern Language Notes*, 58, No. 2 (1943), 116-120.

[7] *Italienische Grammatik* (Leipzig, 1890), p. 60.

[8] F. D'Ovidio and W. Meyer-Lübke, *Grammatica storica della lingua e dei dialetti italiani* (Milano, 1932), p. 90.

Italian is that it is a reflex of the Latin *i*-stem accusative plural endings in -*īs*. Accordingly, Italian *cani* could be considered as the historical continuation of Latin CANĪS rather than CANĒS. [9] This theory presupposes the extension of -*īs* to the nominative plural form which even for *i*-stem nouns and adjectives ended in -*ēs*. As a matter of fact, Ferdinand Sommer records a number of instances in which -*īs* is used for -*ēs* in this grammatical function already in Republican times. [10]

There seems to be ample evidence in late Latin texts and documents from the Italian area that the -*īs* ending came to be increasingly used in the plurals of third declension nouns, regardless of their stem, although it has been deemed unlikely that "in current speech this type was sufficiently common to affect materially the Italian development." [11] In his study of the *Codice Paleografico Lombardo*, Robert L. Politzer finds that in the plurals of the third declension the change of -*ēs* > -*is* occurs in nearly 43 % of all cases, noting particularly that in the nominative endings -*es* and -*is* are about evenly divided, while in the accusative -*es* appears more frequently than -*is*. [12] In a subsequent analysis of the *Codice Diplomatico Longobardo* the authors (Mr. and Mrs. Politzer) conclude that "In the nominative plural of the third declension, the distribution of -*es* and -*is* follows no pattern and seems to indicate that the endings were completely interchangeable. [13] This same use of -*is* for Latin -*ēs* is also observed by Bengt Löfstedt in his study of the language of the *Edictus Ro-*

---

[9] This fact was forcefully pointed out by the Rumanian romanist Sextil Puşcariu in his "Une survivance du latin archaïque dans les langues roumaine et italienne," in *Mélanges de philologie et d'histoire offerts à Antoine Thomas* (Paris, 1927), 359-365, where he concluded "Je crois qu'il faut voir dans cet -*i* des pluriels de la troisième décl., la terminaison latine -*īs*, que nous trouvons souvent chez les écrivains latins (OMNĪS, CIVĪS, PARTĪS, etc.) et que la grammaire latine désigne comme "archaïque" (p. 362). See also Édouard Bourciez, *Éléments de linguistique romane*, 4th. ed. rev. (Paris, 1956), p. 229; Mario Pei, *The Italian Language*, 2nd ed. (New York, 1954), p. 73.

[10] *Handbuch der lateinischen Laut- und Formenlehre*, 2nd and 3d eds. (Heidelberg, 1914), p. 382.

[11] Grandgent, *From Latin to Italian*, p. 50.

[12] See his *A Study of the Language of Eighth Century Lombardic Documents* (New York, 1949), p. 26.

[13] Frieda N. Politzer and Robert L. Politzer, *Romance Trends in 7th and 8th Century Latin Documents* (Chapel Hill, 1953), p. 28.

tharii, with the further comment that "in den ältesten Hss. *-is* ebenso häufig im Nom. wie im Akk. *-es* ersetzt und ebensooft bei Kon.-Stämmen wie bei *i*- Stämmen eintritt." [14]

The facts speak for themselves; there is a concurrent use of two endings in the third declension plurals. The question, it would seem, that we must address ourselves to is whether these instances of *-is* for *-es* spelling are to be interpreted as (a) an orthographic confusion reflecting a change of pronunciation, namely the closing of Latin [e] to [i] under the influence of the following [s] perhaps, [15] that is, a change of a *phonological* nature, or (b) an extension of the old *i*-stem ending resulting in the free variation of two expression-elements on the *morphological* level.

Todate, adherents of a phonological explanation of this phenomenon have been in the majority. In his examination of the development of Latin *-ēs* to Italian *-i*, for instance, Politzer argues in favor of it [16] and, more recently, Löfstedt concludes, after reviewing the various theories proposed to account for this development, that the *-is* for *-es* spelling in late Latin texts from Italy probably reflects a very close pronunciation of [e] or possibly even an [i] pronunciation of the vowel in the ending and that the *i* grapheme is to be interpreted as a "link" between Latin *-ēs* and Italian *-i*. [17] At the same time, he rejects the possibility

---

[14] *Studien über die Sprache der langobardischen Gesetze* (Uppsala, 1961), p. 39.

[15] The theory of the alleged closing influence of final *-s* has been sharply taken exception to by both Grandgent (in his article on "Final Vowels in Italian") and Puşcariu. The former calls it "a conjectural phonetic principle at variance with familiar linguistic experience" (*art. cit.*, p. 193) totally unsupported by direct evidence, wondering, at the same time, "Why should *-s*, which was always feeble in Latin, work such a miracle?" (p. 188). In a similar vein, the Rumanian scholar declares "il m'a toujours paru étrange que *s* final ait pu avoir en tombant une autre influence sur l'*e* précédent que *m* final" (*art. cit.*, p. 361).

[16] See his "Vulgar Latin -es > Italian -i," *Italica*, 28 No. 1 (March 1951), 1-5. What Politzer suggests is that in the final syllable there was a neutralization of the front vowels in late Vulgar Latin, resulting in a single /e/ phoneme in that position, with an [i] allophone occurring before final [s]. With the eventual fall of the latter, however, the /i/ — /e/ opposition was reintroduced as a necessary morphological distinction, with /i/ as the characteristic vowel of the third declension masculine plurals (p. 3).

[17] Löfstedt, p. 46.

of an extension of the -*īs* ending of old *i*-stems to non-*i*-stem nouns and adjectives, that is, a morphological explanation.

The striking fact that supporters of the phonological theory do not seem to have sufficiently underscored is that this constant interchange of -*es* and -*is* occurs only in morphological endings, suggesting a free variation on the level of form rather than a neutralization of the front vowels in final syllable and a consequent orthographic confusion of the kind that can frequently be observed in late Latin texts, as a result of the merger of Latin ē and ĭ and ō and ŭ in the stressed syllable.[18]

Except for passing reference to inscriptional material in the matter of determining whether the classical Latin -*is* ending survived in later Latin or not, inscriptional resources have remained largely untapped. It is the purpose of this investigation to show, by drawing on evidence from inscriptions exclusively, that not only did this ending survive but that in this particular context Latin -*ēs* and -*īs* in postclassical texts may be looked upon as variants of the third declension plural morpheme.

The corpus that we have chosen for our demonstration is made up of Latin Christian inscriptions published in Ernst Diehl's *Inscriptiones Christianae Latinae Veteres*.[19] The advantage of working with this material is that a significant number of Christian epitaphs is precisely dated which means that, in some cases at least, it is possible to pinpoint certain linguistic trends within a specific time limit and to establish a chronology of changes. Out of about 3,000 prose inscriptions chosen for this study, spreading throughout the Italian area all the way from Milan in northern Italy to Syracuse in southern Sicily, 1216 items are dated, or better than 40 percent.[20]

---

[18] Although Politzer (*Study*, p. 26) does point out that the change of unstressed ē > *i* occurs "in the final syllable before *s* in the plurals of the third declension" and that it does not occur "in the final syllable in cases where *e* is not followed by *s*," still he invokes a phonetic criterion for the change in question. Löfstedt (p. 39) also finds that this change occurs only in third declension plurals. Yet, neither of these scholars is willing to recognize the morpohlogical nature of this phenomenon.

[19] 3 volumes, Berlin 1924-1931.

[20] These figures are taken from our study, *An Inquiry Into Local Variations in Vulgar Latin As Reflected in the Vocalism of Christian Inscriptions* (Chapel Hill, 1968), pp. 32-33.

In order to arrive at meaningful results, it seemed to us that the most reliable method of analyzing this material would be to count all occurrences of the plural ending in accordance with classical Lain standards (in this case the -ēs ending of consonant-stems) and then to tabulate all deviations (i.e., the -is ending) and establish a numerical ratio thereby, which could, at the same time, indicate some kind of trend concerning the use of -is for the expected -es. (Since neither inscriptions nor late Latin documents show vowel quantity, we shall henceforth also dispense with it, unless specific reference is made to classical Latin.) Deviations from the classical norm in non-dated inscriptions have not been tabulated; however, non-dated material has been used to further illustrate the phenomenon under study and to support our observations in dated material. To make the tabulation as nearly precise and significant as possible, and in order to attempt establishing both a chronology of the phenomenon and the likelihood of a greater frequency of "mistakes" in one area as against another (possibly pointing to dialectal variations), the inscriptions are grouped into centuries and the whole Italian area subdivided into a *Northern, Central,* and *Southern* region (corresponding to volumes V, IX, X, XI, and XIV of the *Corpus*) with *Rome* as an independent area.[21] Inscriptions found in *northern Italy* are grouped into the fifth and sixth centuries, while those found in *central, southern Italy,* and *Rome* cover three centuries, namely the fourth, fifth, and sixth.[22]

Our findings may be summarized as follows:

1. In the *accusative* plural the change from -es to -is occurs in the following ratios:

		-es	-is
(a) *Northern Italy*	(fifth)	6	3
	(sixth)	4	2

---

[21] The treatment of Rome as a separate area seems justified by the wealth of inscriptional material found there. A separate volume has been devoted to it by G. B. Rossi, *Inscriptiones christianae urbis Romae septimo saeculo antiquiores,* Rome, 1861-1888.

[22] For the sake of simplicity, the few inscriptions from the third century have been grouped with fourth century material and the handful from the seventh century are counted with those of the sixth.

		-es	-is
(b) *Central Italy*	(fourth)	16	1
	(fifth)	4	0
	(sixth)	3	2
(c) *Southern Italy*	(fourth)	2	2
	(fifth)	3	1
	(sixth)	7	3
(d) *Rome*	(fourth)	39	19
	(fifth)	20	3
	(sixth)	2	2

Most of the changes in dated material involve the form *mensis* (for classical Latin MENSĒS), although *nominis sui* (Diehl 849) (with the shift of the neuter *nomina* to the masculine gender, as evidenced by *sui*) and *sedis* (Diehl 39) are also attested in the North. The form *mensis* is also very frequent in non-dated material, thus supporting the data concerning the interchangeability of *-es* and *-is* in dated inscriptions. Other examples of deviations are *tres fratris cursoris* (Diehl 381B), *inter innocentis* (Diehl 2500B), *sororis suas* (Diehl 808An), and *ad laris* (Diehl 4715). An interesting instance of an accusative absolute reads *presentis omnis fossores* (Diehl 3761), in which the *-is* and *-es* endings are used concurrently.

It has been suggested that in the numerous instances in which *mensis* is preceded by *annis*, e.g., *vixit annis LIII mesis VIII* (Diehl 3252A), the *-is* spelling may be due to orthographic assimilation to the form *annis*.[23] A count, however, has revealed that in more than one half of all instances recorded the form *mensis* (also spelled *mesis* or *messis*) is preceded by *annum* and *annos* (sometimes spelled *annus*). As a matter of fact, there are also cases where *annis* is followed by *menses*, e.g., *vixit annis L menses sex* (Diehl 1329). Without meaning to deny the likelihood of such an analogical influence, the evidence does not seem to suggest it; in any event, it does not weaken our contention that

---

[23] Löfstedt, p. 41. For the use of the ablative case to express duration of time, i. e., the use of *annis* for *annos*, cf. Allen and Greenough's *New Latin Grammar*, rev. ed. (New York, 1903), p. 266.

the apparently interchangeable use of -*es* and -*is* in the final syllable is to be interpreted as a free morphological variation. The concurrent use of *menses* and *mensis* in the same inscription (Diehl 3761n) — both times preceded by *annos*, incidentally — is but another scrap of evidence in support of this theory.

2. There are relatively few occurrences of the *nominative* plural in our inscriptional material. However, where this case does occur, it also frequently ends in -*is* rather than -*es*. Deviations in dated material are only attested in *Rome* in the following ratio:

	-es	-is
fourth cent.	12	3
fifth "	1	1
sixth "	1	1

While it would be hardly justified to draw positive conclusions on the basis of so few occurrences, our feeling that the -*is* ending was extended to the nominative is supported by the frequent appearance of *parentis* in non-dated material, outweighing the classical PARENTĒS, in addition to forms like *fratris* (Diehl 4146Fn), *consulis* (Diehl 2139), and *superstitis* (Diehl 2372).

Except for a single example of *parentis* (Diehl 4616) found in *southern Italy*, both the Central and Southern regions appear to be rather conservative, since in the dozen or so occurrences of the nominative plural, this case is always spelled with -*es*.

In *northern Italy*, on the other hand, the form *parentis* (and even *patris* (Diehl 1499) in the meaning of 'parents') is not infrequent in non-dated material, e.g., *parentis dolientis....ficierunt* (Diehl 1366), also pointing to the extension of -*is* to the nominative. There are only two occurrences in dated material, both times spelled -*es*.

On the basis of this evidence, there seems to be little doubt as to the survival of the classical Latin -*īs* ending of old *i*-stem nouns in Vulgar Latin and its extension to both the nominative and accusative plurals of all third declension nouns. The evidence would further seem to suggest that the area of *Rome* may have been the focal point of this development. This latter conclusion, however, must remain quite tentative in view of the disproportion of material found in this area with respect to those to the North and to the South.

Researchers who have concerned themselves with this problem todate have limited their investigations to instances where the classical Latin -ēs ending changes to -is in late Latin documents; hence, they have based their conclusions on this one-way development. It occurred to us that the above findings could be verified from a different direction, namely by establishing a correlation between the -es > -is change and the reverse substitution of -es for classical Latin -īs of the plural accusative of i-stems. For, should the evidence show that this substitution is just as frequent as the -is spelling for -es, the allomorphic nature of these grammatical endings would, indeed, be clearly confirmed.

In conformity with the rules of Latin grammar, the characteristic mark of i-stem nouns and adjectives is that the ablative singular ends in -ī, the genitive plural in -ium, and the accusative plural regularly in -īs. [24] Accordingly, the substantivized adjectives *Aprilis, September, October, November,* and *December* should have an -is ending in the accusative plural, although there seems to be considerable hesitation in the use of -īs and -ēs already in classical authors, with perhaps a preference for -ēs. [25] It is a moot point, therefore, whether to consider a form like *Decembris* to be a deviation from the classical norm. [26] By the same token, and because these original adjectives conform to the pattern of i-stems, there seems to be justification to treat them as such and to consider a form like *Decembres* not to be in accord with the rules of Latin grammar.

These names of the month occur in both dated and non-dated material with some frequency. (In fact, these are just about the only i-stems in our material.) Our tabulation based on dated material shows the following ratios:

---

[24] Allen and Greenough, p. 31.

[25] Thus, one finds *tertio Idus Septembris* and *Kalendas Aprilis* in one author, while another writes *Apriles Idus* and *Kalendas Decembres.* See *Andrew's Latin Dictionary,* rev. by Charlton T. Lewis and Charles Short (Oxford, 1958), under the entries *Aprilis* (p. 145), *December* (p. 517), *October* (p. 1254), and *September* (p. 1674).

[26] Sommer, p. 385.

			-is	-es
(a) *Northern Italy*	(fifth)		8	4
	(sixth)		5	1
(b) *Central Italy*	(fourth)		1	10
	(fifth)		2	2
	(sixth)		4	0
(c) *Southern Italy*	(fourth)		2	0
	(fifth)		2	4
	(sixth)		15	3
(d) *Rome*	(fourth)		20	18
	(fifth)		11	8
	(sixth)		9	0

Once again, the data indicate a frequent interchange between the two endings. But there is more than that. The figures show a definite decrease in deviations, so that if we now compare this table with the one showing the reverse phenomenon, i.e., the change of *-es* to *-is* in the plural accusative of non-*i*-stems, we are struck by the fact that during the same period of time the *-is* spelling is on the increase. Though the available material is far from abundant, it is nevertheless permissible to assume, we believe, that the nominative was also drawn into this trend which would explain why both Politzer and Löfstedt have found constant interchange of *-es* and *-is* in their respective studies. [27]

In conclusion, the evidence presented here seems to suggest not only the survival of what seems to have already been a free variation of *-ēs* and *-īs* in the plural of *i*-stems in classical Latin, but also a considerable extension of the *-is* ending in Vulgar Latin. Is it not possible, therefore, that these variant endings existed side by side for a long period of time, even *after* the fall of final *-s*, until the eventual choice of /i/ as the characteristic plural morpheme, a choice aided by the kind of analogy suggested by Rohlfs? The data culled from inscriptions from the Italian area seem to lend strong support to the theory that the final *-i* outcome of third declension Italian nouns is a survival of the classical *-īs* ending of old Latin *i*-stems and that we are faced with a *morphological* rather than a *phonological* phenomenon.

---

[27] See footnotes 12, 13, and 14.

THE CONCEPTS 'DIFFICULT' AND 'EASY' IN MEDIEVAL FRENCH

By Ralph de Gorog
University of Georgia

When one reads in the *Französisches etymologisches Wörterbuch* that the word *difficile* is attested for the first time in 1330 and that *facile* appears in French texts more than a century later, one may well ask how these concepts were expressed in Old French before these dates. As is well known, these words are learned, a fact that is shown by their phonological shape (cf. FRAGILIS > *frêle* for example), by the intellectual character of the words (it can be mentioned in passing that the maps of the *Atlas linguistique de la France* do not include any patois words meaning 'difficult' and 'easy') and by the history of the various Romance languages.

W. Meyer-Lübke, *Romanisches etymologisches Wörterbuch*, 3rd. ed. (Heidelberg, 1935: Carl Winter) has no article on the Romance reflexes of DIFFICILIS and FACILIS because of the lack of popular forms derived from these roots. The failure to include cross-references to Latin synonyms of given words, some of which did not survive in Romance, is a weakness of the *REW*; cf. the observation made by Mgr. P. Gardette, *Lexicologie et lexicographie françaises et romanes*, Orientations et exigences actuelles, Colloques internationaux du Centre National de la Recherche Scientifique, Sciences Humaines (Paris, 1961), p. 232. Gerhard Rohlfs, *Die lexikalische Differenzierung der romanischen Sprachen* (München, 1954) represents an attempt, on a limited scale, to come to grips with the results in Romance of synonymy in Latin and fills in some of the gaps found in the *REW*.

Note also the absence in Sardinian of reflexes of DIFFICILIS and FACILIS, which have been replaced respectively by *ingúrdu* and *laðinu;* see Max L. Wagner, *Dizionario etimologico sardo* (Heidelberg, 1964: Carl Winter), p. 193 and p. 202. In Roumanian, *dificil* and *facil* are learned words. It is to be noted that bilingual dictionaries tend to give *greu* and *obositor* for 'difficult' and *uşor, comod, liniştit,* etc. for 'easy'.

When one examines the new *Concordance to the Divine Comedy,* edited by Ernest H. Wilkins and Thomas G. Bergin (Cambridge, Mass., 1965: The Belknap Press of Harvard University Press), it is obvious that *difficile* and *facile* were not part of Dante's vocabulary. Professor Pei was kind enough to call to my attention Dante's use of *duro* and *oscuro* in the sense 'difficult to understand'; cf. "il senso m'è duro" and "queste parole di colore oscuro." The absence of a modern Italian index to the new concordance makes it difficult to see at a glance whether the concept 'easy' occurs in Dante, and if so, how it was expressed. It. *difficile* and *facile* are first attested in the works of Domenico Cavalca (ca. 1270-1342).[1]

In addition to DIFFICILIS, Classical Latin had such words as ARDUUS, IMPEDITUS, LABORIOSUS and the expression MAGNI NEGOTII. The concept 'easy' was expressed by FACILIS, EXPEDITUS or NULLIUS NEGOTII. In the *Vulgate* we find DIFFICILIS as the translation of Gk. *dýskolos:* "quam difficile est confidentes in pecuniis in regnum Dei introire" (Mark x.24), "numquid Deo quidquam est difficile" (Gen. xviii.14), "si difficile et ambiguum apud te judicium esse perspexeris...." (Deut. xvii.8), "rem difficilem postulasti" (IV Kings ii,10), "non erit tibi difficile erit omne verbum" (Jer. xxxii.27), and

---

[1] Sp. *fácil* and *difícil* are not attested until 1438. For the concept 'difficult' Gonzalo de Berceo uses *aspero, asperiello, aviesso, bravo, contrario, duro, ençerrado (ençerrado latin* for example), and *oscuro* in the sense of 'difficult to understand'. Berceo's words for 'easy' are *rehez, l(i)eve* and *conocido.* For the date of the first appearance of the reflexes of DIFFICILIS and FACILIS in Spanish and Italian, see J. Corominas, *Diccionario crítico etimológico de la lengua castellana* (Berne, 1954-1957), and S. Battaglia, *Grande dizionario della lingua italiana* (Torino, 1961-   ). See also R. de Gorog, "La Sinonimia en las obras de Gonzalo de Berceo," *Boletín de la Real Academia Española,* 46, Cuaderno 178 (1966), 205-276. I have not yet seen A. Alsdorf-Bollée, *Rückläufiger Stichwortindex zum Romanisches etymologisches Wörterbuch* (Heidelberg, 1969).

several other examples. There is an occasional use of DURUS: "operibus duris" (Ex. i.14) and "durus est hic sermo" (John vi.60), the latter example of DURUS translating Gk. *sklirós* and meaning 'harsh' rather than 'difficult'.

In the Vulgate the concept 'easy' is expressed by FACILIS, translating Gk. *eukopos:* "quid est facilius dicere" (Math. ix.5), "facilius est camelum per foramen acus transire quam divitem intrare in regnum caelorum" (Math. xix.24, Mark x,25, Luke xviii.25), and by LEVIS: "leviusque sit tibi, partito in alios onere" (Ex. xviii.22); cf. also "iugum enim meum suave est, et onus meum leve est" (Math. xi.30) where the original Greek has *elafrós*. [2]

Before taking up the means of expression which Old French had at its disposal to express the concept 'difficult' it would be well to consider the language of one particular author. [3] If we examine the works of Wace we find that the following words are used with the meaning which interests us here:

aspre: "aspre metier a en chevalerie" (*Rou* II, 3913). [4]

engres: "Me combatrai par la grant presse / Ou la bataille iert plus engresse" (*Rou* III, 7687).

fort: "Trop aveit gent en Engleterre, / Et mult esteit fort a conquerre" (*Rou* III, 1292). [5]

---

[2] Work is now being done on a concordance of the *Vulgate*. See *Computers and the Humanities,* 4 (1969), 127.

[3] Meyer-Lübke was skeptical about Brunot's lists of Old French synonyms since he did not see how words used in different periods and in different parts of France could rightly be called synonyms. Recently, however, A. Stefenelli has demonstrated conclusively that surprisingly large numbers of synonyms for the same concept are often attested in the same author. See A. Stefanelli, *Der Synonymenreichtum der altfranzösischen Dichtersprache* (Wien, 1967), p. 16.

[4] The quotations from Wace are taken from H. E. Keller, *Étude descriptive sur le vocabulaire de Wace,* Deutsche Akademie der Wissenschaften zu Berlin, Veröffentlichungen des Instituts für Romanische Sprachwissenschaften Nr. 7 (Berlin, 1953). The abbreviation *N = La vie Saint Nicolas.*

[5] F. Godefroy, *Dictionnaire de l'ancienne langue française et de tous ses dialectes* (Paris, 1881-1902) also gives examples of *fort* in this meaning from *L'Empereur Constant,* a 13th century work: "Ciertes, dist le Empereres, forte chose est de çou croire." Cf. "fors a servir" in *Le Chasteau de labour,* published in 1499, to mention just a few of his examples. The word also appears in this meaning in the *Bible de Macé de la Charité,* edited by J. R. Smeets (Leiden, 1967: Universitaire Pers Leiden), I, 21: "...Ne les fors moz de l'escripture, / Qui lor semble estre trop oscure."

grief: "Gref me serreit a reconter / E gref a vus a esculter / Les granz miracles e les bens / Qu'il fist a plusurs cristiens" (*N* 195-196); "...grefs a prendre" (*Brut* 4679); "Swein ala par Engleterre, / Ne fu mie grieve a conquerre" (*Rou* III, 1292). [6]

lait: "La parole est mult grieve e laide a abaissier" (*Rou* II, 2210).

At a later period we find that Brunetto Latini, *Li Livres dou Tresor,* ed. Francis J. Carmody (Berkeley and Los Angeles, 1948: Univ. of California Press) uses the following synonyms: *grevable:* "certes itex devisemens est grevables, car il a trop de choses" III, 49; *lait:* "car ce seroit laide chose a recomencier .i. autre plet aprés la fin de son parlement," ibid.; *grief;* "Nature est mout grief chose a descrire son estre," III, 52; *oscur:* "Oscur est çou que cil ki le doit oïr ne puet entendre legierement," III, 17; "La ou la matire est oscure a entendre," III, 23; *dur:* "Patience s'esjoist es dures choses," II, 88.

In addition to the words used by Wace and by Brunetto Latini, we find throughout the Old French and Middle French period a number of words used to express the concept 'difficult'. In what follows, each of these forms will be listed with the work in which it appears, and enough of the context in which it appears to make the meaning clear.

agu: "Je forme apres sur les escriptz / Une question bien ague," Guillaume Coquillart, *Les nouveaux Droitz,* I, 113 (Godefroy).

costos (*Roman de Renart* VI, 677); see Gunnar Tilander, *Lexique du Roman de Renart* (Paris et Göteborg, 1924). The word does not seem to be in the Mario Roques edition based on the Cangé manuscript.

destroit: "...Et le .vi. l'ont mise sour trois / Par l'afaire fu destrois," *Chronique rimée de Philippe Mouskes* (Bruxelles, 1836-1838), 20305.

difficile: J. de Vignay, *Le Miroir historial,* published in 1327 (see A. Dauzat, Jean Dubois, Henri Mitterand, *Nouveau dictionnaire étymologique* (Paris, 1964). Cf. *difficile ou grief* as the

---

[6] Godefroy gives an example of the word in this meaning from the *Roman de Troie.*

gloss of *difficilis, Aalma* I, *Recueil général des lexiques français du moyen âge* (XII-XVᵉ siècle), ed. M. Roques (Paris, 1936-38).

divers: "En unne sente la meimes / Qui maine droit hors du bocage,/ Mes molt y a divers passage," *Roman du Comte d'Anjou,* ed. Mario Roques (Paris, 1931), 5218-20.

eschif: "...mais la rive / Roiste lur ert e escive," *St. Brandan,* 1508 ed. Michel; cf. Godefroy; "La droitement si est li lius / Ki n'est oribles ne eskius / U St Jehans fu et sa mere," *Chronique de Philippe Mousket,* 10780.

felon: "Felon le voit pour entamer," *Balaham und Josephas,* ed. C. Appel (Halle, 1907), 6081; "Molt i ot voie felenesse, / de ronces et d'espines plainne," *Chevalier au lyon,* ed. Roques (Paris, 1960), 180-181.

fort a feyre: gloss of *difficile, Abavus,* Roques, *Recueil général.*

grevain: "les choses ke après sevent sunt plus plainiere[s] et moins grevaines (planiora et minus difficilis)," *Altburgundische Übersetzung der Predigten Gregors über Ezekiel,* ed. Konrad Hofmann (München, 1881), 76, 34, quoted by Tobler-Lommatzsch.

grevos: "Ki de vice se voelt entendre / Estudier deit e entendre / A grevose ovre comencier," *Lais de Marie de France,* ed. Jean Rychner (Paris, 1966), Prologue, 23-25. For examples of the word in *Floire et Blancheflore, la Vie de Saint Thomas, Chronique des ducs de Normandie,* etc., see Godefroy.

infacille: "Y nous ont icy dit exemple, / Chose comme a croire infacille," *Mystère du siege d'Orléans,* 9930, cited by Godefroy; cf. *inficille* in Froissart, *Poésies,* ed. Scheler, II, 241, 201: "Car ce seroit fais inficilles."

mal: "Dure bataille i out e male," *Chronique des ducs de Normandie,* ed. Michel, II, 7594; "...maus a acointer," *Roum. d'Alex.,* fº 59ᶜ Michelant; cf. Godefroy for a large number of other examples.

malaisible: "C'est uns feus qui frissonne, qui est legiers a esprendre et malaisivlez a estaindre," Froissart, *Chroniques* II, 339, Luce ms. Amiens.

mal possible: J. Bonnard and A. Salmon, *Lexique de l'ancien français* (Paris-Leipzig, 1901) give this expression with no literary source, and Godefroy does not list it.

malaisiet: "Bien est uoir que li psaultier qui est obscurs en son senz et malaisiet a entendre en maint et plusour psaulmes,"

Lothringischer Psalter, Altfranzösische Übersetzung des XIV. Jahrhunderts, ed. F. Apfelstedt (Wiesbaden, 1881, reprinted 1968), Prologue, 4, 11.

noellos: "Dont il sourdra mainte doubrance / Envers plusieurs, et rioteuse / Par mainte question noilleuse," *La Vieille*, I, III, 5198.

penable: "montagne ... penable a monter," example from 1395-96 (Godefroy).

pesant: "Li latins vos est mult pesanz," *Vie de sainte Juliane* 36, in *Li ver del juise* ... afhandling af Hugo von Fellitzen (Upsala, 1883), quoted by Tobler-Lommatzsch, *Altfranzösisches Wörterbuch* (Berlin, 1925-   ).

scalabreux: listed by Bonnard and Salmon with no literary source available.

li est peine de: this construction is used to express the concept 'difficult' in *Erec et Enide*, ed. M. Roques (Paris, 1953), 6190: "mes n'an fu pas tres bien certainne, / ne d'anquerre ne li fu painne / dom ele estoit, de quel païs, / et dom ses sires ert naïs." Cf. Tobler-Lommatzsch, where the W. Foerster edition, v. 6242 is quoted.

For 'difficile, capricieux' used with reference to persons, we find the following Old French words:

anglos: "Mesmement que ledit trespasse estoit homme engleux, noiseux et rioteux" in a document from 1419 (Godefroy); "Jean Vincent, le plus opiniastre et le plus angleux de ceux du costé de Saint-Marc" in an example from 1617 (Godefroy).

dongereus: "...si est dongereuse et a envie des choses estranges et nouvelles," *Les .XV. Joies de Mariage*, ed. Jean Rychner (Genève-Paris, 1963), 3, 15; "e se tu l'autre refusoies, / Qui n'est mie moins doucereus, / Tu seroies mout dangerus," *Roman de la Rose* 2668-70, ed. E. Langlois (Paris, 1924).

grevable: "bestes non grevables," *Métamorphoses d'Ovide moralisées*, ed. Tarbé (Reims, 1850), p. 115; "femme ... grevable," *La Vieille*, 377.

entulle: "Moult legier suy a courroucier / Dur et entulle a appaisier," *Prière à Notre-Dame*, ms. Chartres 411, quoted by Godefroy.

potieux: "Vieillard, poutieus, morose et difficile," La Porte, *Epith.*, published in 1581 (Godefroy); "Homme potieux, qui a mal de coeur de toute chose...; Tu es trop potieux, il te faut trop de chose," Nicot, *Thrésor*, quoted by Godefroy.

Before the appearance of the adverb *difficilement* in 1539 in the works of Robert Estienne (cf. Dauzat, s. v. *difficile*) the concept was expressed by a number of different words and expressions:

a destroit, G. Cohen, *Recueil de farces françaises inédites du xve siècle* (Boston, 1949: Mediaeval Academy of America), XXXVI, 64.

a grant dur: "mes ce fu a grant dur," Froissart, *Chroniques*, ed. Luce, IV, 163.

a envis: "Biau foz, ce dit la dame, de vos part a envis," J. Bodel, *Saisnes*, ed. Michel, LIII (Godefroy).

maisement: "vous pourries maisement mangier char de cheval," *Le Livre des Mestiers, dialogues français-flamands*, ed. H. Michelant (Paris, 1875), quoted by Godefroy, with other examples from *Perce-forest* and the fifteenth century *Quatrains moraux*.

a peines: "En grant piece ne fut delivre / La dame, ainçois guarit a peines," Jean Renart, *Galeran de Bretagne*, ed. L. Foulet (Paris, 1925: Champion), 680-81.

povrement: "Or me sui ça venu com tafur poverement," *Horn et Rimenhild*, ed. F. Michel (Paris, 1845), 4290, quoted by Godefroy.

soufraitosement: "Le texte de Aristote en cest probleume est moult obscur souffraiteusement translates, ou il est corrompu par le mal entendant," Evrart de Conty, *Problèmes d'Aristote*, quoted by Godefroy.

Although *difficulté* is attested in French as early as the thirteenth century (cf. Dauzat), a large number of words are found with that meaning, many of which are figurative uses of words with other meanings. In the following examples given by Godefroy, only the author or work will be given for reasons of economy:

ademise, f. (G. de Coinci); *argu*, m. *(Mistere du viel testament)*; *arguance*, f. (Christine de Pisan); *berele*, f. *(Vie des anciens pères)*; Rutebeuf, *(La Vie sainte Marie l'Egyptienne)*; *contrebat*, m. (Cartulary from 1277); *dangier (Roman de Troie, Roman de Renart*, etc.); *defois*, m. *(Floire et Blancheflore)*; *destroit*, m.

(*Chanson de Roland, Roman de Brut,* etc.); *encombrance,* f. (Charles d'Orléans); *encombrage,* m. (*Chevalier au cygne); encombrement,* m. (*Les Loherains;* Marie de France; St. Bernard, etc.); [7] *essoine,* f. (*Eneas; Chroniques des ducs de Normandie*); *grief,* m. (Cartularies from 1264, 1284, 1332, and also *L'Atre périlleux*); *grieté,* f. (*Le Roman du Saint-Graal,* Cartulary from 1290, etc.); *hoingne,* f. (*Li Dialogue de Saint Grégoire*); *malaisance,* f. (Amyot); *malaisibleté,* f. (*Dialoge Gregoire lo Pape); obicion,* f. (document from 1367); *porsoin* (document from 1421); *ravoire* (*Mistere du siège d'Orléans*); *reboutement* (Jean Molinet); *revel* (*Le Jugement d'Amours*).

Tobler-Lommatzsch gives an example of *dif(f)iculté* from the thirteenth century glossary in the Bibliothèque royale of Brussels published by Baron de Reiffenberg, as well as an example of *fort* 'difficulty, distress' in Béroul, *Le Roman de Tristan,* 2457: "Molt par est mis Tristran en fort"; cf. v. 2459 in A. Ewert, *The Romance of Tristran* (Oxford, 1958: Basil Blackwell). In texts which have been edited recently, there are additional examples of words glossed as 'difficulté': *achaisun,* f.: "Pais li doinst en sa regiun / Que pris n'i seit a achaisun, / Ne damage n'i ait ne hunte / Par chamberlens ne par vescunte," Thomas, *Roman de Tristan,* ed. Bartina H. Wind (Paris-Genève, 1960: Droz), 1404; *chose,* f.: "Mais il y a une chose, car ilz prennent celles paines pour joyes et liesses," *Les .XV. Joies de Mariage,* ed. Jean Rychner (Paris-Genève, 1963: Droz), Prologue 131; *contraire,* m.: "S'en vont souffrant mal et contraire," *Galeran de Bretagne,* 1332; *melencolie,* f.: "...de tant lui fera el plus de melencolies pour lui donner soussy," *Les .XV. Joies de Mariage,* VI, 47; *rongne,* f.: "Il y a bien eu de la rongne a jugier Jhesus," G. Cohen, *Le Livre de conduite du régisseur et le compte des dépenses pour le Mystère de la Passion* (Strasbourg, 1924: Publications de la Faculté des Lettres de l'Université de Strasbourg), p. 339.

Compared to the number of Old French words used to denote the concept 'difficult', the words designating 'easy' were small in number. Whereas Wace uses a number of synonyms for 'difficult',

---

[7] Godefroy gives *esploit* with the meaning 'difficulté, affaire, querelle' but A. J. Greimas, *Dictionnaire de l'ancien français* (Paris, 1969: Larousse) does not include this meaning.

he appears to use only *legier* to designate its opposite. In the Old French and Middle French periods the following words with the meaning 'easy' are attested:

aise: "de la ville on trouvoit tres mal aise maniere d'avoir une piece de bois pour traverser l'arche du pont," Cousinot, *Chronique de la Pucelle*, 48 (Godefroy), a rather late example; Godefroy's other examples of *aise* clearly mean 'content'; note that Greimas gives *aise* 'qui est à l'aise, content' and 'facilement'.

aisé: "Ne lui furent pas aisees a porter [les armes], *Le saint voyage de Jherusalem du seigneur d'Anglure*, ed. F. Bonnardot et A. Longnon (Paris, 1878), 17, quoted by Tobler-Lommatzsch.

aisible: "...la ou la riviere estoit plus aisieule a passer," Froissart, *Chroniques* I, 61, Luce (cited by Godefroy); Greimas gives an example from 1220 in Gautier de Coincy.

aisif: "C'est asive chose a prover," *La Voie de Paradis*, 14th century (Godefroy); "je cuit qu'il en seroit aisieus a conseiller," *Guiteclin de Sassoigne* (quoted by Godefroy). [8]

faisable: Li Remèdes d'Amors, ed. G. Körting (Leipzig, 1871), 181; *Poésies de Gilles li Muisis*, ed. Kervyn de Lettenhove (Louvain, 1882), II, 114 (Tobler-Lommatzsch).

legeret: "...armes / Qu'il ot faites apareillier / Legerietes por tornoier," *Partonopeus de Blois*, ed. Crapelet, 9607 (Godefroy).

legier: "n'est pas legiers a estre ocis / Tant cum jo seie sains e vis," Wace, *Brut* 4799; "Rome est trop loing e en forte terre, / N'est mie legere a conquerre," *Chronique des ducs de Normandie*, ed. Michel, I, 1813 (quoted by Godefroy); "N'est pas legier a alentir / Langue puis k ele est escapee," Renclus de Moiliens, *Miserere* CXVII, 2, ed. Van Hamel (Godefroy); "Moult legier suy a courrocier," *Prière à Notre-Dame* 411 (Godefroy); *legiers* as gloss of *facilis*, *Abavus*, Roques, *Recueil général*.

legier a fere: gloss of *facilis*, *Abavus* IV-V, Roques, *Recueil général*; cf. *ce qui est sens difficulté* as gloss of *facilis*, *Aalma* I, ibid.

passable: "Or pensez de demander donques, et s'il est a moy passable saichiez que ja n'en serés esconduit," *Renaut de Montau-*

---

[8] It was considered unnecessary to give details concerning the manuscript and folio of unpublished works since these can be found in Godefroy under the word in question.

ban, ca. 1200, quoted by Greimas; Godefroy gives a sixteenth-century example from Garasse: "Il est aysé ou passable de disputer de la destinee." This probably represents a semantic shift from an earlier 'guéable', 'facile à traverser' to 'facile'.

planier: "Li viers si dist en teil maniere, / La sentence en est moult planiere," *Dits et Contes de Baudouin de Condé et de son fils Jean de Condé,* ed. A. Scheler (Bruxelles, 1866-67), I, 357, 76, quoted by Tobler-Lommatzsch, who glosses the word 'leicht zugänglich'. Cf. also *plus plainiere[s]* as a translation of *planiora,* above s.v. *grevain.*

Before the appearance of *facilement* in 1475, the concept expressed by that adverb was found in a number of words and phrases. Godefroy gives the following, which are scattered through the different volumes of the *Dictionnaire: a delivre* (Gautier de Coinci, Marie de France, etc.); *a peu de fait* (Froissart, *Chroniques*); *de legier* (Guiot de Provins; *Roman de la Rose* 3540, *Girart de Rossillon,* Ronsard, Regnier); *por un petit d'escroe* (*Dit des Mais*); *aisiblement,* 1370 (Godefroy); *aisieument* (Guillaume de Machaut), with another example in *Les Livres du Roy Modus et de la Royne Ratio,* ed. Gunnar Tilander (Paris, 1932: S.A.T.F.) 120, 94M; *alligiement (la tresample et vraye expos. de la reigle); apareilleement (Folque de Candie; Mort Artu;* Froissart, *Chroniques,* etc.); *delivranment (Fregus); delivrement (Li Romans de Dolopathos;* Froissart, *Chroniques); expediement* (Jean Golein, *Rational du devin office); faisablement (Catholicon latin-français,* mentioned by Ducange s.v. *agibilis); legierement (Troilus; Lancelot; Fierabras;* St. Bernard, *Sermons; Chronique de Turpin),* with further examples in Wace, *Brut* 175, *Rou* III, 7469 and 11245; *La Chirurgie de Maître Henri de Mondeville,* ed. A. Bos (Paris, 1898: Firmin Didot) 26, 989, 1342, 1622, 1624, etc.; Brunetto Latini, III, 17; *soef (Partenopeus de Blois,* quoted by Greimas) and an example from a fifteenth-century proverb in Godefroy.[9]

Tobler-Lommatzsch gives the following expressions not found in Godefroy: *de poi* (13th century); *de petit* (Gautier de Dargies); *bien (Roman de la Rose,* 3100, etc.); *de plaine main (Le Dit du*

---

[9] Godefroy gives an example of *a faict* 'facilement' used by Montaigne.

Courtois Donneur). In addition to these, the editors of several texts have glossed certain words as 'facilement': *bel, Chronique des ducs de Normandie par Benoît*, ed. Carin Fahlin (Uppsala-Lund 1951-1954: Bibliotheca Ekmaniana) 502 etc.; *simplement, La Geste de Monglane*, ed. David M. Dougherty and E. B. Barnes (Eugene, 1966: Univ. of Oregon Books) G 1440; Judeo-French *volenteirs*, Raphael Levy, *Trésor de la langue des Juifs Français au moyen âge* (Austin, 1964: University of Texas Press).

As for the concept 'facilité', Godefroy gives the following words with that meaning: *adition:* "Quar s'il ne se confesse comme il a toutes ses aditions, il ne puet plaire a nostre segneur." *Compos. de la s. escripture*, ms. Monm.; *aisine:* "Armes et homme tient en seure saysine, / Et tost apres quant eut temps et aysine / Au la poincte de sa lance il travaille / De transpercer le harnoys et la maille," Octovien de Saint-Gelais, *Eneide; aisibleté:* "Considerer la faculté ou aisibleté de executer l'office," Gilles de Rome, *Gouvernement des rois et des princes; covenableté:* "Pource qu'il ha une maniere de inclination et alcune convenableté naturelle a vivre civillement," ibid.; *copie:* "S'il hont copie dou faire si se abstiegnent de vin," *Cont. des Chartreux*, ms. Dijon, included, like the preceding word, in Greimas.

From the preceding, one may conclude that at some time between the late Latin period and the appearance of the first Romance texts the words DIFFICILIS and FACILIS ceased to be part of the vernacular. Indeed St. Jerome may have been using them as literary forms which were no longer part of the spoken language. There was probably a tendency to favor more concrete terms such as DURUS and LEVIS, just as the disappearance of DIFFICILIS and FACILIS throughout Romania would seem to be traceable to their abstract nature; one may recall that the latter were reintroduced into the Romance languages through literary channels. The large number of words used to express the concepts 'difficult' and its opposite attest to the fact that there always was a need to express such fundamental notions; one must realize, on the other hand, that such a concept as 'interesting' was not part of ancient or medieval man's scheme of things; the concept does not appear in the Bible, judging by its absence from any of the Bible concordances, and Godefroy and Tobler-Lommatzsch have included no Old French words with this meaning, except perhaps *vaillant* 'qui attache, qui intéresse puissament'. Until the appearance of *intéressant* in the early eighteenth century there apparently was no word to express this notion; what is more, the introduction of the French word into German, Dutch, and the Scandinavian languages demonstrates that there was no native Germanic word with this meaning either.

The words used in Old French and Middle French to make up for the loss of DIFFICILIS and FACILIS had the disadvantage of polysemy; such words as *grevable, grief, fort, agu, pesant,* etc. all had other meanings, and 'difficult' was indeed not the primary meaning of any of these words. Even after the introduction of *difficile* and *facile* into French, a few other words continued to compete with them; but as stated, it was probably the polysemy of these partial synonyms which militated against their retention, whereas *difficile* and *facile* had the advantage of being more specific and less ambiguous than any of the competing terms. [10]

---

[10] Cf. S. Ullman, *Précis de sémantique française* (Berne, 1959: A. Francke), p. 317: "*La fréquence de la polysémie et de l'homonymie augmente le risque d'ambiguïté et d'association fâcheuses.* La langue réagit contre ce danger avec une vigueur particulière. Les collisions polysémiques et homonymiques constituent en français une cause importante de désuétude." See also Jules Gilliéron, *Généalogie des mots qui désignent l'abeille* (Paris, 1918) for a similar view.

THE CONCEPT OF EUPHONY IN TRADITIONAL FRENCH GRAMMAR: MYTH OR REALITY?

By Jesse Levitt
University of Bridgeport

French grammarians and writers have traditionally attributed enormous importance to the factor of "euphony" not only in creative writing, but also in some of the basic grammatical forms of the language. The *Larousse du dix-neuvième siècle* (1866), for example, defines *euphonie* as "harmonie des mots, que l'on produit par quelque changement apporté à leur forme régulière ou à leur arrangement indiqué par les règles ordinaires." It distinguishes between "l'euphonie poétique," in which the taste of the author alone must serve as a guide, and "l'euphonie grammaticale," which is obtained "par l'intercalation de certaines lettres ayant pour effet d'adoucir la prononciation des mots ou d'éviter certaines rencontres désagréables à l'oreille." As examples, the encyclopedia cites the intercalation of *d* in *tendre* (from Latin *tener*), *s* in *vas-y*, and *l* in *si l'on veut*, as well as elision of the article and the use of *mon* before a feminine singular noun starting with a vowel.[1]

The significance of euphony is stressed by many of the leading *grammairiens philosophes* of the eighteenth century. Dumarsais notes: "S'il y a des occasions où il semble que l'Euphonie fasse aller contre l'analogie grammaticale, on doit se souvenir de cette réflexion de Cicéron, que l'usage nous autorise à préférer

---

[1] Pierre Larousse, *Grand Dictionnaire universel du dix-neuvième siècle* (Paris, Larousse, 1866) under *euphonie*.

l'Euphonie à l'exactitude rigoureuse des règles." [2] Jean-Jacques Rousseau, speculating on the nature of the first language, says that this language "négligeroit l'analogie grammaticale pour s'attacher à l'euphonie, au nombre et à l'harmonie des sons." [3] Diderot stresses the notion of economy of effort; if certain sounds or their combinations produce great fatigue in the organs of speech, they are eliminated by "l'euphonie, cette loi puissante qui agit continuellement et universellement sans égard pour l'étymologie et ses défenseurs..." [4]

According to Nicolas Beauzée, "on voit le principe de l'Euphonie adopté partout parce que c'est une suggestion de la nature; mais l'application s'en fait, comme celle de tous les autres principes généraux, selon le goût particulier de chaque nation..." He finds euphony in French rational and in accord with grammatical analogy. He refers to three euphonic consonants — *n*, *t*, and *s*, as in *on apprend*, *souffre-t-il*, and *vas-y*, whose main function is to prevent hiatus. [5]

Traditional notions of grammatical euphony have continued into the twentieth century among men of letters and the general public. Thus Paul Robert's *Dictionnaire alphabétique* notes: "Par euphonie et pour éviter un hiatus, on intercale une lettre entre deux mots: 'Qu'a-t-il dit?'" Georges Duhamel repeats the doctrines of the eighteenth-century *grammairiens philosophes* when he writes: "C'est que la langue française est fort exigeante en matière d'euphonie. Pour satisfaire à la musique, elle enfreint des règles, altère des mots, ajoute des lettres, consent toutes sortes de sacrifices." [6]

The *Grammaire des Grammaires* of Girault-Duvivier — the most "authoritative" of the traditional nineteenth-century grammars — considers *s*, *t*, and *l* as "lettres euphoniques." In an

---

[2] *Encyclopédie méthodique* (Paris, Panckoucke, 1789), *Grammaire et littérature*, II, 42-43.

[3] Jean-Jacques Rousseau, *Œuvres complètes* (Paris, 1792) vol. XIX, *Essai sur l'origine des langues*, p. 233.

[4] Denis Diderot, *Œuvres complètes* (Paris, Garnier, 1876), vol. XIV, *Encyclopédie*, p. 441.

[5] *Enc. méth.*, *Gram. et lit.*, II, 43 under *euphonique*.

[6] Paul Robert, *Dictionnaire alphabétique et analogique de la langue française* (Paris, Presses Universitaires, 1951 ff.), under *euphonie*.

imperative like *mènes-y-moi*, *s* is said to be inserted "pour éviter la rencontre de deux voyelles qui se choqueroient désagréablement pour l'oreille." [7] The Bescherelle brothers (1867) maintain that in *songes-y* and *penses-y*, *s* is added "pour cause d'euphonie." [8] Yet it is perfectly obvious that the intercalation of /z/ makes pronunciation more, not less, difficult. It is easier to say **songe-y* [sɔ̃ʒi] than *songes-y* [sɔ̃ʒzi], **mène-y-moi* [mɛnimwa] than *mènes-y-moi* [mɛnzimwa]; besides, there would be no hiatus in **songe-y* or **mène-y-moi*. A more plausible explanation for the /z/ is the analogy of forms like *finis*, *rends*, or *viens*, which contain an "etymological *s*," i.e., a latent /z/ that reappears in liaison, or else the possible analogy of the second person present indicative which contains a similar latent /z/. Only in forms like *vas-y* can the /z/ be regarded as preventing hiatus; and it is not added if *y* or *en* is followed by an infinitive: "*Va* y chercher ta mère." [9]

Euphonic *t*, according to Girault-Duvivier, is placed after a verb ending in a vowel (i.e., a written vowel) when the verb is followed by *il*, *elle*, or *on*, as in *m'aime-t-elle*; the euphonic *t*, "ne servant qu'à empêcher la rencontre de deux voyelles," is not used if the verb ends with a *t*, as in *craint-on*. [10]

Traditional notions of euphony are thus strongly influenced by spelling; the *t* of *m'aime-t-elle* is "euphonic," that of *craint-on* is not. Yet the analogy of *on craint* to *craint-on* is exactly the same as that of *on a* to *a-t-on* or of *elle m'aime* to *m'aime-t-elle*. When the subject pronoun precedes the verb, there is no /t/, but when the verb precedes a subject pronoun starting with a vowel phoneme, the latent /t/ reappears; /t/ is simply the third person singular verb morpheme, which is reduced to zero in final position or before a consonant, but which reappears in certain cases before a vowel.

---

[7] Charles-Pierre Girault-Duvivier, *Grammaire des Grammaires* (Brussels, Établissement Encyclographique, 1837), I, 196.

[8] Louis N. Bescherelle, *Grammaire nationale* (Paris, Garnier, 1867), p. 637.

[9] Maurice Grevisse, *Le Bon Usage* (Gembloux, Belgium, Duculot, 1964), p. 569.

[10] Girault-Duvivier (1837), II, 664.

Historically, the Latin /t/ in *amat* and *habet* disappeared during the Middle Ages, but was restored as a liaison consonant by analogy with *vient-on* or *dort-on,* where the /t/ survived. Sixteenth-century grammarians write *aime-elle,* but note that an unwritten *t* is pronounced between the two words. In the seventeenth century, the *t* began to be written. [11]

Thus the /t/ in *m'aime-t-elle* or *a-t-on* is clearly analogical. It may prevent hiatus, as in *a-t-on,* but that is purely incidental. No hiatus would be produced in hypothetical forms like *parle-il [parlil] or **m'aime-elle* [mɛmɛl]. The preposition *à* may be followed by *elle* or *eux,* despite hiatus, and no "euphonic *t*" is intercalated because the *t* is a verb ending.

According to Girault-Duvivier, the "euphonic *l*" is placed "pour la douceur de la prononciation" before *on* when *on* is preceded by *et, si, ou, que,* or *qui (et l'on, si l'on,* etc.). [12] Girault-Duvivier draws no distinction between prose and verse; in fact, this rule is obligatory only in classical verse, but has never been fully observed in prose. [13] Literary usage sometimes replaces *qu'on* (which contains no hiatus) with *que l'on,* especially when it is a question of avoiding the alliterative combination [kɔ̃kɔ̃], as in Boileau's verse: "Ce que l'on conçoit bien s'énonce clairement."[14]

Traditional grammar assumes that all hiatus is necessarily cacophony. [15] For Beauzée, hiatus is "l'espèce de cacophonie qui résulte de l'ouverture continuée de la bouche dans l'émission consécutive de plusieurs voix qui ne sont distinguées l'une de l'autre par aucune articulation." Avoidance of hiatus, he says, is "une loi qui paroît universelle et fondée en nature." [16]

It has been said even by recent linguists that hiatus is contrary to the phonetic "genius" of the French language because historically, vowels in hiatus within a word were reduced to monophthongs, as in the case of *reine, âge* (originally *eage*) and *mûr* (originally *meür*), and because hiatus between words was

---

[11] Édouard Bourciez, *Précis historique de phonétique française,* 9th edition (Paris, Klincksieck, 1958), p. 150.
[12] Girault-Duvivier (1837), I, 249.
[13] Grevisse, pp. 503-504.
[14] Girault-Duvivier (1837), I, 249.
[15] Girault-Duvivier (1837), I, 51.
[16] *Enc. méth., Gram. et lit.,* II, 244-246.

eliminated by elision and liaison.[17] But this process was never completed. At most, it represents a general tendency of the language, which still permits hiatus internally in such common words as *réussir, obéir, trahir,* and *haïr,* and between words in ordinary constructions like *j'ai été, il a eu, tu as, qui êtes-vous* and *à eux.* The elimination of /h/ (the aspirate *h*) has increased hiatus within the last three centuries. Even Girault-Duvivier is forced to admit that it would be pedantic to try to avoid hiatus in conversation: "...La prononciation de la conversation souffre une infinité d'hiatus pourvu qu'ils ne soient pas trop rudes; ils contribuent à donner au discours un air naturel."[18] Littré notes that though poets reject the sequence of *et* plus a vowel, "cette rencontre n'a rien de dur à l'oreille."[19]

For eighteenth- and early nineteenth-century grammarians, however, norms of linguistic "purity" and "correctness" were set by verse rather than prose.[20] In classical verse, hiatus between words is banned as "cacophonous," but within a word it is accepted; *tu as* is "uneuphonic," but *tua* is acceptable. Even between words, classical verse permits vowel sequences when the first word ends with an orthographic *e muet* and the second starts with a vowel, as in *année entière* and *joie extrême,* or when the second starts with a so-called aspirate *h,* as in *au haut.*

Thus, considerations of spelling and word division, rather than purely acoustical impressions, affect the entire notion of hiatus and euphony. Though most of the older grammarians remain silent on these contradictions, Marmontel finds some forms of hiatus pleasant and attacks the rule banning hiatus in verse as "une règle capricieuse et aussi peu d'accord avec elle-même qu'avec l'oreille qu'elle prive d'une infinité de douces liaisons."[21]

The notion of what constitutes a pleasant or unpleasant sound or succession of sounds must always remain subjective to a very

---

[17] Pierre Guiraud, *La Versification* (Paris, Presses Universitaires, 1970), p. 92.

[18] Girault-Duvivier (1837), I, 54.

[19] Émile Littré, *Dictionnaire de la langue française* (Paris, Hachette, 1863-73) under *et.*

[20] Girault-Duvivier (1837), I, 92; II, 521-522; Alexis François, *La Grammaire du purisme et l'Académie française au dix-huitième siècle* (Paris, Société Nouvelle de Librairie et d'Édition, 1905), p. 189.

[21] *Enc. méth., Gram. et lit.,* II, 247.

large extent. Voltaire goes so far as to declare that words ending in *-oin*, like *coin* and *soin*, represent "le plus insupportable reste de la barbarie welche et gauloise" and that such words "tiennent moins de l'homme que de la plus degoûtante espèce d'animaux." He also finds a lack of harmony in the words *oncle, ongle, perdre, longue, dieu, feu, bleu, peuple, nuque,* and *plaque*. [22] Remarks of this type illustrate the highly capricious attitudes of the grammarians on questions of euphony.

It is an unfounded assumption to regard all hiatus as cacophony. Besides, many of the vowel combinations traditionally regarded as producing hiatus need not really do so. When the first vowel is an unstressed /i/, /u/, or /y/, it may become a semi-consonant, as in *il y a* [ilja], *si elle* [sjɛl], *ou il* [wil] or *tu as* [tɥa], and hiatus is thereby eliminated. When the two vowels are identical and unstressed, they may become one prolonged vowel, as in *j'ai ete* [ʒe·te]. [23]

According to Maurice Grammont, if there is a difference in the pitch and the acoustical impression of the vowels in contact, the transition produces an extremely pleasant effect, as in: "Cette soirée a eu un succès énorme." The ease of such vocalic liaison, he maintains, explains the decline of consonantal liaison. [24] He finds hiatus unpleasant only when the two vowels in contact are identical, as in "Il va à Avignon" or "sa vie innocente." Even in this case a poet may use hiatus to suggest a prolonged or a brusque and repeated motion, as in La Fontaine's verse: "Après bien du travail le coche arrive *au haut*." [25] The language of ordinary conversation, according to Frei, contains many words with internal hiatus used for onomatopoeic effect and suggesting prolonged noise or confusion — *brouhaha, chahut, cohue, huée*. [26]

For Girault-Duvivier alliteration is uneuphonic, and he defines cacophony in part as the effect produced by "la répétition trop

---

[22] Voltaire, *Œuvres complètes*, (Paris, Garnier, 1877), vol. XIX (*Dictionnaire philosophique*), p. 188.
[23] Maurice Grammont, *Traité pratique de prononciation française* (Paris, Delagrave, 1930), p. 136; Henri Frei, *La Grammaire des fautes* (Bellegarde, Ain, Société Anonyme des Arts Graphiques de France, 1929), p. 104.
[24] Grammont, *Prononc.*, p. 136.
[25] Maurice Grammont, *Le Vers français* (Paris, Champion, 1913), p. 338; J. Marouzeau, *Précis de stylistique française* (Paris, Masson, 1950), p. 21.
[26] Frei, pp. 282-283.

fréquente des mêmes lettres et des mêmes syllabes." As an example, he cites Voltaire's verse: "Non, il n'est rien que sa vertu n'honore." [27] Voltaire criticizes Corneille for *faire fondre* and *car contre*, Louis Racine objects to his father's verse: "Banissez-le loin d'elle," [28] and Paul Claudel finds fault with "d'imprononçables bouillies" like "Je pars pour Paris." [29] Grammont explains that one says *un pot au lait* and *le pot aux roses* with liaison of the *t*, but *un pot à tabac* without linking to avoid repetition of the syllable *ta*. [30]

Alliteration tends to be regarded with disfavor in French. The French word, unlike the English, often loses its accent within the word group. Repetition of initial consonants is either less noticeable than in English, or else may distort the normal accentuation of the word group. Alliteration may be used humorously, as in "Pauvre pêcheur partant pêcher pour prendre petits poissons," or in an advertising slogan, as in "Petit Parisien partout présent." [31] But it is also used for emphasis in proverbs and traditional expressions: *à tort et à travers, qui vivra verra, sain et sauf, bel et bien*. Poets use it for imitative harmony and onomatopoeic effect, as in the case of Racine in *Andromaque*: "Pour qui sont ces serpents qui sifflent sur vos têtes?" or Victor Hugo in "Booz endormi": "Un frais parfum sortait des touffes d'asphodèle." [32]

In one basic feature of its syntax, the use of two consecutive third person object pronouns (*le lui, les leur*, etc.) modern French insists on alliterative combinations, contrary to the old French custom of eliminating *le, la*, or *les* before *lui* or *leur*. Vaugelas (1647) insists that, regardless of the cacophony produced, the direct object pronoun must be used with the indirect, "car il vaut bien

---

[27] Girault-Duvivier (1837), II, "Remarques détachées," p. 21.
[28] Ferdinand Brunot, *Histoire de la langue française des origines à 1900* (Paris, Colin), vol. VI, part II, fascicule 2, pp. 2079-2080.
[29] Paul Claudel, *Œuvres complètes* (Paris, Gallimard, 1959), vol. XV, *Positions et Propositions*, p. 53.
[30] Grammont, *Prononc.*, p. 131.
[31] Marouzeau, pp. 28-29.
[32] Kr. Nyrop, *Grammaire historique de la langue française* (Copenhagen, Gyldendalske Boghandel, 1899-1930), I, 453-454; Marouzeau, p. 29; Alexis François, *Histoire de la langue française cultivée* (Geneva, Jullien, 1959), II, 280.

mieux satisfaire l'entendement que l'oreille, et il ne faut jamais avoir esgard à celle-cy, qu'on n'ayt premièrement satisfait l'autre." [33] In a recent investigation of the order of preposed adjectives in twentieth-century French, it was found that the wording "la jolie grande grille" was preferred to "la grande jolie grille." "The wording *la grande jolie grille,* which would break the usually unfavored alliterative sequence *grande grille,* was rejected by all but four persons, who regarded the adjectival order as optional." [34]

It is therefore doubtful that avoidance of alliteration plays any significant role in ordinary speech forms or syntactic constructions. Even on the literary level, alliteration may be cacophony to one writer, but imitative harmony to another. A blanket condemnation of alliteration as cacophony is unwarranted.

Traditionally, monosyllabic interrogative forms like *dors-je, mens-je,* and *furent-ce,* have been regarded as uneuphonic. [35] Among modern linguists, von Wartburg and Zumthor consider the inversion of *je* "cacophonique," [36] while de Boer considers avoidance of such forms a "simple question d'euphonie." [37] Yet *dors-je* is homonymous with *d'orge, mens-je* with *mange, sers-je* with *serge.* There is nothing in any of these forms or their homonyms that is contrary to the French phonemic system. The French avoid *dors-je, mens-je,* or *furent-ce* because they are unlike *dors-tu* or *dort-il,* where the stress falls on the pronoun. *Dors-je,* with an unstressed pronoun consisting of one consonant phoneme that fuses with the verb into an unrecognizable form, sounds strange to the French speaker, and he therefore avoids it. [38]

The forms of the imperfect subjunctive containing /s/ have frequently been regarded as uneuphonic, though traditionally the

---

[33] Claude Favre de Vaugelas, *Remarques sur la langue françoise,* edited by Jeanne Streicher (Paris, Droz, 1934), p. 33.

[34] Reine Cardaillac Kelly, "The Order of Preposed Adjectives in French," *French Review,* XLIII (April 1970), 788.

[35] Girault-Duvivier (1837), I, 195.

[36] Walter von Wartburg and Paul Zumthor, *Précis de syntaxe du français contemporain* (Bern, Francke, 1958), p. 28.

[37] Cornelis de Boer, *Syntaxe du français moderne* (Leiden, Universitaire Pers Leiden, 1947), p. 229.

[38] Albert Dauzat, *Le Génie de la langue française* (Paris, Payot, 1944), p. 234.

grammarians have insisted that they be used in the interests of "correctness." The abbé Sicard (1801) objects to *On voudrait que j'aille:* "On fait cette faute parce qu'on trouveroit désagréable et dur d'employer *j'allasse*... Mais faut-il préférer un contre-sens à des sons un peu durs?" [39] A recent grammar refers to the substitution of the present subjunctive for the imperfect "par souci d'euphonie." [40]

The seventeenth century found nothing unpleasant or amusing about the imperfect subjunctive. By the end of the eighteenth century, Marmontel refers to the disagreeable sound of *qu'ils commandassent* and *que nous confondissions*. [41] In 1807 Domergue, the leading grammarian of the First Empire, declared in an address: "Plût à Dieu, messieurs, que vous vous enthousiasmassiez comme moi de l'imparfait du subjonctif en *asse!* L'emploi de ce temps est aussi nécessaire à l'harmonie qu'à la correction." Domergue's remarks were received with wild laughter; [42] the imperative subjunctive had become ridiculous in the spoken language.

Yet it is obvious that the endings of the imperfect subjunctive contain nothing phonetically unpleasant in themselves or contrary to the French phonemic system. *Partissions* is homonymous with the noun *partition, fisse,* with the noun *fils, menassiez* with the imperfect indicative or present subjunctive form *menaciez. Partition, fils,* and *menaciez* are not regarded as uneuphonic.

The disfavor with which the imperfect subjunctive is regarded stems from the fact that its endings are longer than those of other tenses. When these endings are added to a verb with a polysyllabic stem, the form produced seems extremely cumbersome to the French speaker (e. g., *délibérassions, enthousiasmassiez*). In some cases, there is alliteration *(grimaçasse, menaçassions),* in others there are ambiguities which may produce ridiculous misunderstandings; *sussiez* is homonymous with *suciez, vissiez* suggests the verbs *visser* or *vicier.* The development of pejorative

---

[39] R. A. Sicard, *Élémens de grammaire générale* (Paris, Deterville, 1801), II, 251.
[40] Marcel Galliot and Raymond Laubreaux, *Le Français, Langue vivante* (Toulouse and Paris, Privat-Didier, 1966), p. 293.
[41] *Enc. méth., Gram. et lit.,* II, 673.
[42] Larousse, under *Domergue.*

verbs in *-asser*, like *rimasser* and *traînasser*, tends to make endings in *-asse* seem ridiculous. By the end of the eighteenth century the imperfect subjunctive was no longer used in the spoken language. Once the forms of the tense had disappeared from speech, they were considered as sounding strange; thence the notion that the imperfect subjunctive was "uneuphonic." [43]

Many other linguistic forms and phenomena are attributed to euphony by traditional French grammar: sandhi variations of adjectives like *fou, fol* or *beau, bel*, the replacement of *ma, ta*, and *sa* by *mon, ton*, and *son* before a feminine singular noun starting with a vowel, the choice of *de* or *a* between a verb and an infinitive complement. [44] In all these instances euphony is equated with avoidance of hiatus. For Girault-Duvivier euphony plays a part in determining the masculine plural of adjectives ending in *-al* (*-als* or *aux*, i. e., zero or suppletion with /o/), [45] and in the choice of *-teuse* or *-trice* as the feminine of adjectives ending in *-teur*. Just how this supposed euphony operates remains obscure; while Girault-Duvivier accepts forms like *scrutatrice* and *dénonciatriace*, Pierre-August Lemaire, the editor of the posthumous editions of Girault-Duvivier's grammar, finds them "dures à l'oreille." [46] For Girault-Duvivier, a combination like "un goût et une noblesse parfaits" would be unephonic because a masculine-sounding adjective follows a feminine noun; the nouns should be reversed. [47] This is obviously a question of syntactic concord that has nothing to do with phonology.

Dealing finally with the major differences between French and Latin, Girault-Duvivier notes that French uses many small words that are essential for meaning — *avoir, être, que*, the personal pronouns. "De là, pour ne pas déchirer l'oreille par des sons désagréables, on est souvent forcé de préférer l'actif au passif, l'infinitif aux autres modes; de changer, selon les phrases, la place des pronoms personnels; de mettre le verbe entre deux mots négatifs, ... etc. Cette contrainte entraîne un ordre différent dans

---

[43] Nyrop, VI, 336-339.
[44] Girault-Duvivier (1837), I, 10; II, 392; Larousse under *euphonie*.
[45] Girault-Duvivier (1837), I, 147-153.
[46] Charles-Pierre Girault-Duvivier, *Grammaire des Grammaires* (Paris, Cotelle, 1848), I, 234.
[47] Girault-Duvivier (1837), I, 164.

la suite et l'enchaînements des mots, et par conséquent des constructions variées, mais toutes propres à la langue françoise." [48]

Thus the scope of euphony is extended to the entire field of morphology and syntax. Euphony becomes a universal explanation for every grammatical form or construction, an evasive formula for explaining everything, which in reality explains nothing. For the speaker of any language, the usual expressions, constructions, and rhythm patterns "sound" right and can be justified by the supposed appeal to the ear.

For example, the nineteenth-century grammarian and writer Philarète Chasles approves of the sentence: "Vous avez sa parole, fiez-vous-y," but objects to "Vous avez vu M. tel? Vous vous y fiez?" This is obviously a matter of semantics, the meaning of *y*; but for Chasles, it becomes a question of Euphony: "L'oreille, un instinct secret, d'accord avec le sens véritable des mots et le génie du langage vous avertiront que la première des deux [phrases] est excellente; mais qu'il y a dissonance, faute, incorrection dans la seconde." [49]

The use of the term "euphony" in traditional grammar thus seems to us on the whole to be highly subjective, arbitrary, and misleading. The so-called euphonic *s* and *t* have been used to explain linguistic forms that are really the result of analogy. The "euphonic l," confined to the single form *l'on*, is largely a literary convention with little reality in spoken French, which does not fear hiatus. Many of the forms and processes ascribed to euphony (liaison, elision, forms like *mon amie, fol amour, bel homme*) are examples of sandhi. Their net effect is to eliminate hiatus, and they may be regarded as examples of euphony. Nevertheless, the French language tolerates hiatus in some of its commonest words and syntactical constructions, and the equation of hiatus with cacophony is a false assumption. Alliteration, though less common and less acceptable, nevertheless appears in many proverbial expressions and some common syntactical constructions like third person object pronouns used together; it can not be dismissed as entirely alien to the language. On the artistic level, euphony

---

[48] Girault-Duvivier (1837), II, 660.
[49] Bescherelle, p. 7.

seems entirely subjective; what is cacophony to one writer may be imitative harmony to another.

The stereotyped notions of euphony in traditional grammar are both inaccurate and misleading, and it seems advisable to use the term "euphony" with extreme reserve and considerable skepticism in the explanation of grammatical forms and constructions.

GADDA'S "PLURILINGUISMO" IN THE *PASTICCIACCIO*

By JOAN MCCONNELL - MAMMARELLA
Stanford University

After the first few pages of *Quer Pasticciaccio brutto de via Merulana*, the reader is struck by Gadda's skillful and, in certain instances, even unorthodox handling of the Italian language, a fact which immediately distinguishes him from most contemporary Italian authors. Gadda's language is a potpourri of archaic and learned words, dialects, highly specialized terminology and neologisms, all blended together in a framework of standard literary Italian. The result Gadda achieves demonstrates the rich expressive potential of the Italian language in its broadest sense.

It therefore becomes obvious that Gadda's view of language differs from literary Italian. He openly rejects formal linguistic restrictions because such conventions conflict with his definition of language. For Gadda language is a continuum; while, on one hand, it synthesizes human experience from by-gone centuries, it must, on the other, be capable of recording contemporary man's achievements and aspirations. Ideally a language should be able to absorb the old and the new, the popular and the erudite, the general and the specialized, the dialectal and the foreign. When instead language is viewed purely in terms of formalism, Gadda maintains that it cannot fulfill its complex function as a medium of communication and, above all, of artistic expression.

Gadda's language may thus be defined as eclectic. This eclecticism, far from being an isolated example, represents a continuation of what critics term "plurilinguismo," an anti-purist trend that stands in opposition to the more traditional "unilinguismo" or cult of classical linguistic models.[1] In an essay on language in *I Viaggi la morte*, Gadda declares his acceptance of "plurilinguismo" and consequently opposes literary formalism as well as a uniform standard for the spoken and written language: "E' ovvio, per me, che la lingua d'uso non può tener da sola il campo della umana conversazione."[2] In his opinion, an author should not be bound by the inherent limitations of the "lingua d'uso" which tends to minimize the historical function of language in general. Since the "lingua d'uso" reflects man's present experiences and exigencies while it ignores the hereditary tradition, Gadda terms it inadequate for artistic expression. By his definition, language must represent "il lavoro collettivo, storicamente capitalizzato in una massa idiomatica storicamente consequenziato in uno sviluppo."[3]

Gadda's opposition to the "lingua d'uso" represents a protest against the low intellectual level of the petty bourgeoisie or, in his words, against "il desiderio (della piccola borghesia) d'aver tutti inginocchiati al livello della sua zucca."[4] Not only does linguistic standardization strip a language of its wealth but it also restricts an author's creativity. Language instead should enable the author to express his ideas in more than one way: "Non esistono il troppo nè il vano per una lingua."[5] Ideally an author should add his own mark of individuality to the multitude of forces that have created a particular language. It is therefore more than legitimate to employ new words or even those that have fallen into disuse provided they enhance the expressive potential of a language.[6]

In the *Pasticciaccio* we find the best examples of Gadda's rich use of language, a characteristic which appears in his earlier works, although to a lesser degree. The loosely constructed plot confirms the lack of importance Gadda attaches to the narrative. As the reader soon discovers, Gadda never has true narrative

---

[1] Pier Paolo Pasolini, *Passione e ideologia* (Milano: Garzanti, 1960), p. 313.
[2] Carlo Emilio Gadda, *I Viaggi la morte* (Milano: Garzanti, 1958), p. 94.
[3] *Ibid.*, p. 77.
[4] *Ibid.*, p. 99.
[5] *Ibid.*, p. 95.
[6] *Ibid.*, p. 96.

interests in the situations he chooses for his novels, but rather uses them as a springboard for engaging in peripheral discussions which titillate his linguistic fantasy. Although such a technique creates a fragmentary, often confusing narrative, the linguistic variety of these descriptions compensates for the weak plot.

Gadda's language in the *Pasticciaccio* is much more than a generous sprinkling of dialectal, popular, or learned expressions, thrown in for color or effect. It is correct to state that the author has succeeded in adding a new dimension to the Italian language. He creates a complex interplay of standard Italian, dialects, archaic forms, specialized terminology, foreign borrowings, and, many times, his own neologisms sometimes in the same paragraph and, at times, in the same sentence. The result of this vocabulary blending is what Gianfranco Contini calls Gadda's linguistic "calderone."[7] Gadda's skillful mixing of traditionally incongruous words is particularly efficacious when he employs the "style indirect libre." The contrasts between the plebian speech patterns of the majority of the characters in the *Pasticciaccio* and the cultural, often erudite or specialized language of the author add linguistic depths that overshadow the rather flimsy plot.

The vocabulary innovations of the *Pasticciaccio* can be divided into three major categories: archaic and learned words, dialects, and original neologisms. The author's propensity for archaisms and learned expressions confirms his debt to the classical heritage of Italian. The following are just a sampling of some learned words that Gadda uses: *stizzo* (p. 36)[8] "fire-brand" which recalls Dante's use of the same in the episode of Pier della Vigna (*Inferno* XIII); *l'aire* (p. 91) "push" < Latin locution AD IRE; *anguicrinito* (p. 108) "one who has serpents for hair" < Latin ANGUIS + CRINIS; *conquiso* (p. 122) "conquered" < Latin CONQUISUS possibly through Provençal *conquis*; *illecebra* (p. 179) "lure" < Latin ILLECEBRA; *dolco* (p. 235) "muggy" < late Latin DULCARE; *apotropaico* (p. 237) "apotropeic" < Greek ἀπο -τρόπειν; *capillizio* (p. 245) "scalp" < Latin CAPILLUS + -TIO, -ONIS.

---

[7] Carlo Emilio Gadda, *L'Adalgisa*, con saggio introduttivo di Gianfranco Contini (Torino: Einaudi N U E, 1963), p. ix.

[8] All references come from the following: Carlo Emilio Gadda, *Quer Pasticciaccio brutto de via Merulana*, 7th printing (Milano: Garzanti, 1962).

In some instances Gadda shows preference for rare Italian words instead of their more conventional counterparts: *foco* (p. 30) "fire" instead of *fuoco; sitire* (p. 107) "to be thirsty" for *aver sete; ebriaco* (p. 238) "drunk" for *ubbriaco; piova* (p. 306) "rain" for *pioggia*. Furthermore the Manzonian inspired style used for a major portion of the prose narrative is another example of the author's homage to literary Italian.

Sometimes Gadda gleans new words from other languages, classical and modern, although Italian has, in most cases, a legitimate counterpart. For example, in describing a crowd of bystanders, Gadda uses English *vegetables* (with the Italian translation *verdure* in parenthesis) in the middle of a sentence. There appears to be no plausible reason why Gadda chose *vegetables* rather than *verdure* except as a "linguistic" caprice. There are other examples of foreign borrowings that tend to confirm Gadda's delight in adding a touch of affectation to his prose: Latin phrases such as MANU ARMATA (p. 80), NON-CONFITEOR (p. 153), FIAT LUX (p. 244), MOTU PROPRIO (p. 263); French *coûte que coûte* (p. 108) and *loisir* (p. 189); Spanish *desde* (p. 59) and *prensa* (p. 59); Greek δύναμις (p. 15) and ἐξώτερα (p. 177). In συμπανία (p. 126) however, we see an outstanding example of Gadda's sophistication: instead of the correct etymon συμπάθεια, he uses Greek characters to spell *simpatia* Italian-style with the original Θ replaced by τ.

The *Pasticciaccio* is also dotted with words lacking literary tradition. There are copious examples of words from the sciences, specialized fields, and the world of technology, all of which reflect Gadda's long years of contact with the scientific and business world. Sometimes Gadda's vocabulary becomes so specialized that the reader is forced to consult a dictionary for clarification.

If Gadda's linguistic experiments were confined to obsolete, foreign, or highly specialized terms, we could define him a reactionary, a conservative, or the like, but this is not the case. In addition to the literary aspect of his vocabulary, we find a second important division: namely, the use of popular, particularly dialectal words. Since the *Pasticciaccio* is set in Rome, the principal dialect is Romanesco with a liberal admixture of Neapolitan (Dr. Fumi), Abruzzese (Ingravallo), and Venetian (Countess Menegazzi). The various dialects help Gadda describe the political and social climate of Fascist Rome in the late 1920's. The rivalry between the petty bourgeoisie, rising to new economic power, and the socially immobile proletariat, desirous of improving their living conditions, serves as background to the action of the novel.

> L'inchiesta (concerning the murder and the robbery) ha inizio e si allarga in cerchi sociali più vasti e affonda in strati sempre più bassi ed equivoci. Qui l'uso dei vari dialetti, dal romanesco al veneziano al napoletano, ha una funzione essenziale: ed è quella di portare alla luce la istintività schietta dei personaggi borghesi e plebei in una ridda di passioni e di interessi collegati. [9]

By using dialects, Gadda accentuates the social and economic division among his characters in a way that probably would have been impossible had he limited his vocabulary choice to standard Italian. In such cases, Gadda recognizes that the spontaneity and occasionally the vulgarity of many dialectal phrases and expressions produce more forceful effects than literary Italian. For example, the Romanesco in the *Pasticciaccio* captures the flavor of the vulgar, equivocal sub-proletarian world where Inspectors Ingravallo and Fumi, along with the police from the "Castelli romani," hunt Countess Menegazzi's jewels and Liliana Balducci's murderer. The Neapolitan-Abruzzese of Ingravallo reveals how this police officer, despite his lengthy stay in Rome, has retained not only the phonetic peculiarities of his native dialect but also a more "Southern" mentality. The Venetian of the Countess Menegazzi accentuates the isolated world in which she lives, a world of fantasy distant from the more tangible reality of her Roman neighbors.

It is important to point out that Gadda's purpose is not that of writing a novel in dialect. Since his use of dialect is primarily literary, he is not concerned with the philological niceties of exact phonetic transcription and the like. In fact, he adapts standard Italian phonology and orthography to fit the dialects, but is often inconsistent even in that system. But Gadda does not pretend to be a professional philologist. Rather he is concerned

---

[9] Giorgio Pullini, *Narratori italiani del 1900* (Padova: Liviana Editrice, 1959), p. 81.

with the various linguistic effects to be attained by mixing standard literary Italian with the dialects.

In studying Gadda's vocabulary, we must not forget the third and most original division: that of his own neologisms. As we have seen, Gadda's linguistic versatility enables him to cull new words and expressions from learned, specialized, and popular sources. Failing, however, to find words suited to his particular needs, he does not hesitate to create new ones. In many cases, Gadda's neologisms pass almost unnoticed (unless we consult a dictionary) because they blend so well into the structure of Italian. This is especially true in examples of derivation where Gadda uses prefixes and/or suffixes to form his own new words. The following words, for example, although not listed in any Italian dictionary, seem legitimate; in theory they could exist inasmuch as they represent inherent possibilities of the language: *quattrinoso* (p. 27) "very rich" < Italian *quattrino* < Latin QUATTUOR (+ diminuitive suffix *-ino*) + Italian *-oso* < -OSUS; *rubalizio* (p. 36) "ceremony of robbery" < Italian *rubare* < Germanic RAUBON via popular Latin + Italian *-izio* < Latin -ITIO, formed probably on the anaology of *sposalizio* "nuptials"; *chilometrare* (p. 52) "to travel far" (literally "to go 'lots of chilometers'" Italian *chilo* < Greek χίλιοι + Italian *metro* < Latin METRUM < Greek μετρον + verbal suffix *-are;* the obviously obscene *invulvare* (p. 59) formed from the prefix *in* < Latin IN + *vulva* < Latin VOLVA (or less common VULVA) + verbal suffix *are; questurinizzato* (p. 109) "having been made like the police" < Italian *questurino* < Italian *questura* < Latin QUAESTOR + verbal suffix *-izzare* < Latin IZARE < Greek - ιξειν ; *Federzonite* (p. 109) "the disease of Federzoni" [10] < proper name Federzoni + *-ite* < Latin -ITIS < Greek - ιτης ; *stivalista* (p. 175) "booted" with particular reference to the highly centralized, pro-military Fascist regime < Italian *stivale* < Old French *estival* < *estive* < Latin *STIPA < STIPES "hay" + *-ista* < Latin -ISTA < Greek - ιστα; *maltonico* (p. 179) "referring to Rosa Maltoni, Mussolini's mother" < proper name Rosa

---

[10] Luigi Federzoni, Mussolini's Minister of the Interior (1924-26), passed laws for public safety and hygiene, measures for reorganizing the police, laws for the repression of the Mafia.

Maltoni + adjectival suffix -*ico* < Latin -ICUS < Greek - ικος; *detopaziato* (p. 228), the past participle of Gadda's new verb *detopaziare* "to remove the topaz" < prefix *de* < Latin DE + *topazio* < Latin TOPAZIUS < Greek τοπάξιον + verbal suffix -*are; patateria* (p. 280) "the quality of being potato-like" < *patata*, a variant of the native Taino *batata* + -*eria* < Latin -ARIA; the corresponding adjective *patatoso* (p. 297).

Some examples of composition better demonstrate Gadda's consummate skill in manipulating Italian and obtaining original results through the combination of various roots. Take, for example, words like *gravidico* (p. 93) "bureaucratic 'goobledegook' " < Italian *grave* < Latin GRAVIS + Italian *dico* < Latin DICO; *cancheromotrice* (p. 129) "cancer producing" < Italian *cancheroso (cancro)* < Latin CANCER, CANCRI + Italian -*motrice* < Latin MOTUM + TRIX (feminine suffix of agent for -TOR); *domicilio-aggredito* (p. 228) "assaulted at home" < Italian *domicilio* < Latin DOMICILIUM + Italian *aggredito*, past participle of *aggredire* < Latin AGGREDI; *criptorutto* (p. 231) "silent belch" < Italian *cripto* < scientific Latin CRYPTUS < Greek κρυπτός + Italian *rutto* < Latin RUCTUM.

Gadda becomes particularly inspired when he has occasion to attack Mussolini. Although the list of insults is impressively long, we will just mention two efficacious examples: *eredoluetico* (p. 58) "hereditary syphilitic" < Italian *eredo* < Latin HERES, HEREDIS + Italian *luetico* < Latin LUES, LUIS + suffix -ICUS; *predappiofezzo* (p. 159) formed from *Predappiese* or *Predappiense*,[11] a euphemism for Mussolini in 1944 + *fezzo*, probably an example of contamination of *fez*, symbol of Fascist authority, and *fesso* "stupid." The noun *fezzeria* (p. 58) is another instance of the unflattering equation: Fascism and stupidity.

Puttanicizia (p. 250) is an interesting example of contamination: Italian *puttana* "prostitute" < Latin *PUTTA < PUTUS + Italian *pudicizia* "modesty" < Latin PUDICITIA. In *puttanicizia* Gadda fuses two diametrically contrasting concepts to describe one character's excessive "prostitute-like" modesty.

---

[11] Alfredo Panzini, *Dizionario moderno,* con appendice di dodicimila voci di Bruno Migliorini (Milano: Hoepli, 1963).

At this point it might be helpful to say a few words about the source of Gadda's linguistic versatility. The explanations for his vocabulary wealth are many. As we have seen earlier, Gadda's eclectic view of language is proof of his impatience with accepted linguistic convention. For him linguistic taboos do not exist. To satisfy his artistic creativity, he draws on all possible sources, even those considered anti-literary or anti-intellectual.

Another facet of the linguistic richness in the *Pasticciaccio* and Gadda's work in general stems from his tendency to digress. The bulk of his narrative is a series of essays *(I Viaggi la morte)*, short stories *(Accoppiamenti giudiziosi)* or sketches *(L'Adalgisa)*; both the *Pasticciaccio* and *La Cognizione del dolore* [12] are incomplete. This fragmentism confirms Gadda's involvement with language and style rather than plot. Many times Gadda will elaborate on details to such an extent that the reader will forget the main thread of the narrative and have to turn back to remember what is happening. This preoccupation with language, however, explains why Gadda is omnipresent in every page of his narrative.

The other important aspect of Gadda's artistic creativity — and this perhaps is the fundamental explanation for his linguistic richness — results from his cultural formation not only in the traditional academic definition but also in a more general, modern sense. His culture is vast and includes even seemingly contradictory interests; suffice it to say that Gadda's professional training and source of income for many years was engineering, not literature. His professional work took him to various parts of Italy, to Germany, France, Belgium, and even South America. Many of Gadda's experiences and interests noticeably work their way into his narrative: his Lombard background appears in most early works *(L'Adalgisa* and in parts of *La Meccanica)*; his virulent hatred of Fascism can be found in both the *Pasticciaccio* and *Eros e Priapo;* his awareness of the linguistic inadequacies of standard literary Italian appears in various essays of *I Viaggi*

---

[12] Part Three of *La Cognizione del dolore* first appeared in the English translation by William Weaver (C. E. Gadda, *Acquainted with Grief*, trans. William Weaver, New York: G. Braziller, 1969) and then in Italian (*La Cognizione del dolore*, 4th ed., Torino: Einaudi, 1970).

la morte; his South American sojourn provides the background for the fictitious South American nation of Maradàgal *(La Cognizione del dolore)* which nonetheless vividly recalls Lombardy. In the case of Gadda, all these experiences do not simply enrich his viewpoint, but bring in their wake a whole series of linguistic influences that characterize his prose.

It would therefore be absurd to define Gadda a traditionalist because of his literary fonts or even a progressive because of his recourse to the dialects, or an eccentric because of his own linguistic creations. Gadda is no one of these but all three combined. His language is vital, sometimes shocking, sometimes abstruse, sometimes bitter, sometimes comical, but always to the point. Gadda's cult of language is often so extreme that the plot suffers. In many instances, the choice of a foreign, archaic, or highly specialized term in place of a more "direct" everyday word reveals his tendency to "show off." In others, the coarseness of certain dialectal expressions shows his preoccupation with the vulgarity of the people or situation he is describing. In others, his own neologisms fill what he considers a gap in the expressive possibilities of Italian. No matter what Gadda is discussing, no matter how involved he may be in a certain issue, language remains his primary concern. His linguistic virtuosity offers by far one of the most remarkable contemporary examples of what can be done with the Italian language in all its manifestations from the most literary to the most popular.

LINGUISTICS, LANGUAGE TEACHING AND PEDAGOGY[*]

By ROBERT L. POLITZER
Stanford University

Mitis depone colla — magister; adora quod incendisti, incende quod adorasti.

The general history of language teaching and its relation to the development of linguistics in the United States has been traced by various scholars — including the author of this article.[1] A reconsideration of these topics appear to be justified at this point in time, for language teaching is once again in the process of undergoing a reorientation due to changes in the field of linguistics.

The recent history of language teaching in the United States can be quite, roughly of course, divided into the following periods: (1) The "Grammar Translation Method Period" which extended throughout the beginning of the century til perhaps the twenties. (2) A period of uncertainty as to aims and method during which however a reading method and reading aim gained some prominence. This period lasted approximately from 1929 (the date of the so-called Coleman Report[2] which advocated the

---

[*] This article is a revised version of an address delivered August 17, 1970 at the Meeting of the Australian Universities Language and Literature Association.

[1] R. L. Politzer, "The Impact of Linguistics on Language Teaching," *Modern Language Journal*, XLVIII (1964), 146-151. William G. Moulton, "Linguistics and Language Teaching in the United States 1940-1960," in *Trends in European and American Linguistics* (Utrecht: 1962), pp. 82-109.

[2] A. Coleman, *The Teaching of Modern Foreign Languages in the United States* (New York: 1929).

reading proficiency as the goal of instruction) til the onset of World War II. (3) The audio-lingual period which had its origin at the beginning of World War II and which saw the height of its development in the sixties of this century.

During each of these periods language teaching seems to have been influenced chiefly by the following factors: (1) The general educational and political climate. (2) Theories of the nature of learning. (3) Theories of the nature of language. While this article is chiefly concerned with the third of these factors, the others must also be considered in order to explain how and why linguistics could make its impact.

At the beginning of this century one of the main purposes of university and even high school education was to form an intellectual elite. Members of the intellectual elite were thought to have certain qualities which characterized the ideal of an "educated man." One of the characteristics of the educated man was that he knew a foreign language or languages — preferably including at least one of the classical languages. Underlying this view of foreign language being part of the education of any intellectual were fundamental assumptions concerning the nature of language and of the learning process: Grammar was thought of as being identical with or at least containing elements of a universal type of logic. The learning process was identified with the training of special compartimentalized abilities or faculties. Thus training in language or grammar was considered as a lesson in logic, as a sort of mental calisthenics in which the faculty of "logical thinking" received its training.[3]

Linguistics as well as the psychological foundations of the grammar translation method were severely shaken by the beginning of this century. Faculty psychology and the concept of training specific abilities by using them had come under severe attack during the late nineteenth century.[4] The equation of

---

[3] A typical statement of this view is found in Stuart Mill's Rectorial Address at St. Andrews (1867): "Consider for a moment what grammar is. It is the most elementary part of logic. It is the beginning of the analysis of the thinking process." "... The structure of every sentence is a lesson in logic." Quoted by Otto Jespersen, *The Philosophy of Grammar* (New York: 1924), p. 47.

[4] One of the first attacks on faculty psychology was undertaken by William James, *Principles of Psychology* (New York: 1890).

grammar with logical universal had been questioned by nineteen century linguists and by the beginning of this century Ferdinand de Saussure had established the doctrine that a language was a closed system — a structure in which each element received its value by contrasting with other elements within that system.

On the American scene, the change in psychological doctrine was communicated directly to educational thinking by certain key figures in Educational Psychology (e.g., Professor W. Thorndyke at Teacher's College of Columbia University). However the immediate cause for the crisis in Foreign Language Education which characterized the twenties and thirties were general educational and political trends, above all the increasing democratization of secondary education and political isolationism. As a result of the democratization of education the ideal of the educated elite was no longer felt to have any relevance to the goals of education. The political isolationism questioned the practical relevance of foreign language in the U.S.A., a country which the political isolationists of the twenties and thirties liked to think of as a self-sufficient monolythic, monolingual giant.

In spite of the loss of the old justification for foreign language study many public high schools still retained at least a two year Foreign Language Program. The main reason for this was probably that many of the institutions of higher education still adhered to the educated man ideal, and continued to recommend foreign language as preparation for college entrance or insisted on some sort of knowledge of foreign language as a graduation requirement.

The advent of World War II brought an end to the "depression" in Foreign Language Teaching. The involvement in world affairs resulted in a reversal in attitudes toward foreign language teaching. The new emphasis on the practicality of foreign language and their relevance for political goals was maintained throughout the period following the war. The inclusion of provisions for the improvement of Foreign Language Teaching in the so-called National Defense Education Act of 1958 was the culmination of that trend.[5]

---

[5] The classical statement on the relation of foreign language study to national interest was made by William R. Parker. *The National Interest and Foreign Languages* (Washington D. C.: Department of State, Rev. ed., 1957).

The new practical emphasis required a new method. The new method, as well as its linguistic and psychological foundation, was provided by the descriptive structural linguists. It became known as the so-called audio-lingual approach. Perhaps the best single and simple generalization that can be made about the audio-lingual method is that it represented an attempt to convert the discovery procedures employed by descriptive linguists into a classroom method. The initial impact of American structuralism in language teaching was often made in teaching of so-called rare or little known languages. The teaching procedures consisted very often in language being taught by a team made up of a descriptive linguist (quite typically ignorant of the language to be taught) and a native informant. The descriptive linguist went through the process of discovering the structure of the language — this means "learning the language" — and the class "learned" with him.

Of course, "learning a language" through the discovery procedure of descriptive linguistics means "finding out" — not acquiring the ability of using the language. Many descriptive linguists never learn the language or dialects, the structure of which they are describing. This ambiguity of the meaning of learning must be kept in mind when assessing the use of descriptive linguistics in language teaching. This ambiguity was not always clearly spelled out. Leonard Bloomfield's very important and influential pamphlet on how to learn a foreign language [6] leaves at times the reader in doubt whether the publication was addressed to a student of a foreign language or a linguistic field worker.

The discovery procedures of linguistics do not contain any psychological principles of learning. A theory of learning had to be grafted on the discovery procedure of linguistics in order to transform them into a teaching method. For descriptive linguists Behaviorism was the logical choice. Behaviorism was the school of psychology and theory of learning in which structural linguists felt most at home. For paradoxically enough, Bloomfield in his fundamental book *Language* (1933) had fully and uncritically

---

[6] L. Bloomfield, *Outline Guide for the Practical Study of Foreign Languages*, (Baltimore: 1942).

embraced behaviorism in an avowed effort to "free" linguistics from the influence of psychological doctrine.[7] Behaviorism was also the most popular doctrine of psychology in the United States throughout the thirties and forties — reaching perhaps the height of its popularity in the 1950's with the publication of such works as B. F. Skinner's book *Verbal Behavior*.[8]

Most of the salient features of the audio-lingual approach can be derived from the union of descriptive structuralist methodology with Behaviorism.[9] The very emphasis on the audio-lingual aspect of learning can be traced to the descriptionist definition of language as a set of spoken signals and to the fact that the methodology of descriptive linguists is often applied to the description of languages which exist only in spoken form. The procedures of using minimal paris in phonetic training (e.g., contrasting French *roue, rue; doux, du;* etc.) corresponds to the method used to identify phonemes. Substitution drill is derived from the procedures used in establishing substitution classes. The comparative lack of concern with how meaning is applied (most audio-lingual texts simply provide English translations of basic dialogues) can be traced to the field inquiry situation in which meaning is established most easily and conveniently through the use of a bilingual informant. The behaviorist psychology underlying the audio-lingual approach accounts for the emphasis on drill (especially memorization and repetition) and for the concept of practice through reinforcing of correct responses in laboratories.

It is probably fair to say that the audio-lingual method period came to an end in the late sixties. Today foreign language teaching in the United States is again in a period of uncertainty and crisis. It would be an over-simplification to single out the audio-lingual method as the cause of the crisis. The abolishing of language

---

[7] In his preface to *Language* (New York: 1933) L. Bloomfield stated (p. vii) that he wanted to show "that we can pursue the study of language without reference to any one psychological doctrine." In the same book (p. 24), the goal of language is defined by the fact that "language enables one person to make a reaction (R) when another person has the stimulus (S)."

[8] B. F. Skinner, *Verbal Behavior* (New York: 1957).

[9] A concise summary of the major assumptions of the audio-lingual approach is given by W. Rivers *The Psychologist and the Foreign Language Teacher* (Chicago: 1964), Chapter III, pp. 19-22.

requirements by many major institutions and the falling enrollments in foreign languages can be accounted for by various causes. Some deal with the aims rather than the methods of instruction. The concepts "international involvement" and "National Defense" with which the foreign language boom of the fifties and early sixties was associated have changed their connotations and have lost all of their joyous ring. The aim of teaching foreign language for practical reasons must face the fact that most of the students studying foreign language in high school or university are not likely to study the specific language which the practical exigencies of a fast moving world will require. What is perhaps even more important, the democratization of education which affected secondary education in the thirties and forties has now reached the college level. The result is that the training of an elite and the ideal of the educated man seem to have lost their last vestiges of relevance even for Higher Education. If today major American universities are abandoning foreign language requirements, the reason for this seems to lie not so much in the questioning the importance of foreign language *per se* or in the failure of foreign language instruction, but rather in the unwillingness of students to subject themselves to any kind of requirements and the unwillingness of administrators and faculties to enforce them. But this unwillingness to maintain general educational requirements must ultimately be explained by a complete uncertainty — on the part of educators as well as of students — as to what in fact the real purpose of "university education for everybody" may be.

The uncertainty as to general educational objectives is also accompanied by complete uncertainty as to the best method. The psychological and linguistic assumptions underlying the audio-lingual approach have become as questionable as those of the grammar translation approach had been in the thirties, principally as the result of the advent of generative transformational grammar.

Probably the best single name to be associated with the questioning of the premises of the audio-lingual approach is that of Nom Chomsky whose book *Syntactic Structures* appeared in 1957 and whose review of B. T. Skinner's *Verbal Behavior* was printed in the journal *Language* in 1959.[10] At the time the audio-lingual method was most vigorously introduced in the American high schools — namely in the five years following the passage of the National Defense Education Act of 1958 — the theoretical assumptions underlying the method had been already called into question.

The initial impact of transformational grammar on foreign language teaching was probably a negative one. Transformational grammar cast conisderable doubt on two of the basic premises of the audio-lingual method: (1) The behaviorist model of language acquisition and (2) The concept of pattern.

In his famous review of *Verbal Behavior* Chomsky made it clear that the creativity which is an essential characteristic of human language makes it impossible to account for its acquisition by a mechanism of selective reinforcement of responses. Since 1957 the basic epistemological philosophy underlying the attempts to account for the acquisition of language steadily moved from Locke to Descartes. The complete switch is clearly illustrated by a comparison of Skinner's *Verbal Behavior* with Lenneberg's 1967 publication *Biological Foundations of Language*.[11] Skinner had attempted to show how language is created by selective reinforcement of responses occurring from outside the learning organism. Lenneberg stresses the innateness of language. The final section of Lenneberg's book is written by Noam Chomsky — who has himself traced his own intellectual ancestry to Descartes.[12]

The insufficiency of the concept of pattern had been from the very outset one of the main themes of the transformationalist. To quote a simple example that has been used so often that it is likely to give its name to a period of linguistics: The sentences *He is easy to please* and *He is eager to please* have the same pattern, or, to use the transformationalist concept, the same surface structure. The identity of pattern does not help us in accounting

---

[10] N. Chomsky, *Syntactic Structures* (Leyden: 1957); "Review of B. F. Skinner's Verbal Behavior," *Language* XXXV (1959), 26-58.

[11] E. H. Lenneberg, *Biological Foundations of Language* (New York: 1967).

[12] N. Chomsky, *Cartesian Linguistics: A Chapter in the History of Rationalist Thought* (New York: 1966).

for the fact that it is possible to say *It is easy to please him* while it is impossible to formulate **It is eager to please him.* The pattern or surface structure hides the underlying or deep structural facts — namely that *He is easy to please* must be derived from sentences like *It is easy ... Something pleases him* while *He is eager to please* goes back to sentences like *He is eager* and *He pleases,*

Transformational, generative grammar challenged descriptive structuralism not only in questioning its method, but rather attempted to set new goals and aims for linguistis science. Descriptive structural linguistics held that the description of a limited "corpus" was the goal of linguistic inquiry. Transformational grammar set itself the much more ambitious goal of accounting for the underlying competence of speakers that enabled them to produce an infinite number of sentences by observing a limited number of rules. "Rule governed creativity" replaced "structure" as the slogan characterizing language. On the most general level the redefinition of language as "rule governed creativity" has lead some to emphasize again the learning or at least the understanding of rules. The distinction between competence (the set of rules governing language production) and performance (actual production of utterances) which is a crucial one in transformational grammar has been introduced into pedagogical discussion with a plea to make competence (ability to produce new utterances) rather than mere performance (language like behavior consisting in mimicking someone else's language production) the goal of the instructional process. [13] On the more concrete level the introduction of transformationalist thinking to teaching implies a deemphasis of repetition and simple substitution drill, and the advocacy of exercises — usually of a conversion or transformation type — that can reveal deep structures or at least the relationships of structures to each other. [14] Perhaps one of the most specific of

---

[13] See for instance R. J. DiPietro's article *Linguistics* in the *Britannica Review of Foreign Language Education*, Volume I, E. Birkmaier, editor (Chicago: 1968), pp. 31-32 for a statement of the pedagogical implication of "performance vs. competence." For the distinction of "language" vs. "language-like behavior," see B. Spolsky, "A Psycholinguistic Critique of Programmed Foriegn Language Instruction," *International Review of Applied Linguistics in Language Teaching*, IV (1966), 119-129.

[14] See, for instance, S. Belasco, "Developing Linguistic Competence," *Modern Language Journal*, LII (1968), 213-215.

the pedagogical recommendations based on transformational grammar has been the plea not to combine structures which have only surface resemblance in the same drill,[15] for the obvious reason that this procedure may mislead the student to apply identical conversions to unrelated structures on the basis of surface similarities.

That the reorientation of linguistic and psychological thinking which has taken place during the recent years should affect language teaching is neither surprising nor necessarily harmful. What is questionable, however, is the directness with which linguistic and psychological theory appears to make its impact in pedagogical matters. As to theories of first language acquisition, we can only point out that they have in fact very little direct relevance to second language learning. First and second language acquisition are simply different processes. Skinner's attempt (or failure) to account for first language acquisition by a mechanism of response reinforcement has no direct implication for language teaching. Granted that response reinforcement and behavior shaping do not account for first language acquisition, they may still be powerful tools for the reshaping of already existing responses and thus be efficient second language teaching devices. The theory that human language is acquired through the unfolding of innate capacities may also have little direct relevance for second language learning. If the process of first language acquisition is the biologically determined growth of innate capabilities, then it is also a developmental process which can not be repeated in the same form in the same individual. This does not mean that theories concerning first language learning may not be highly suggestive of hypotheses concerning second language learning. But theories concerning one field have to prove their validity in the other. They can not be transferred from one to the other on the basis of speculation alone.

The lack of direct relevance of either descriptive linguistics or transformational grammar to language teachers is even more obvious. Neither the adequate description of a corpus (the aim of descriptive linguistics) nor the description of the total

---

[15] See R. Jacobson, "The Role of Deep Structures in Language Teaching," *Language Learning*, XVI (1967), 153-160.

competence of a speaker (the aim of generative grammar) have any immediate concern with how to teach foreign languages. It is for good reason that some language pedagogues are now rebelling against the direct importation of linguistic theory into language pedagogy. Thus a recent issue of the Journal *Language Learning* contains articles on the "Irrelevance of Linguistic Theory to Second Language Teaching" [16] and "The Failure of Linguistics in Language Teaching." [17] Of course, as the author of the second article recognizes himself, linguistics can "fail" in language teaching only in the sense that it can be misapplied. That linguistics is "irrelevant" to language teaching seems to be an overstatement. There is a relevance, but what does it consist in? In other words — just what is "Applied Linguistics?" I believe that Applied Linguistics in Foreign Language Teaching is simply the total of all the possible ways in which linguistics may be used to give some insights into the process of learning and teaching a second language. These uses or applications can be of different types:

The process of foreign language teaching is a very complex one. It supposes, among others, (1) a subject be taught (the foreign language); (2) teachers who have specific personal characteristics like aptitudes, personalities, etc.; (3) students who have specific characteristics like motivation, aptitude, native language habits, etc.; (4) methods used by the teachers, or methods of learning used by the students; (5) goals and achievements that must be specified and measured.

The main function which linguistics can performs in the analysis of this complex process lies simply in the use of linguistic concepts in the formulation of hypothesis. Several distinct situations and type of hypotheses can be distinguished.

1. *Linguistics can be used in the formulation of general hypotheses about the learning process per se*, e. g., "structures which contrast with those of the native language are more difficult

---

[16] J. T. Lamendella, "On the Irrelevance of Transformational Grammar for Second Language Pedagogy," *Language Learning*, XIX (1969), 255-270.

[17] F. C. Johnson, "The Failure of the Discipline of Linguistics in Language Teaching," *Language Learning*, XIX (1969), 235-244.

to learn than those that parallel native strucure." Hypotheses of this type are often advanced without reference to specific characteristics of individuals, methods used, learning situation etc. For this reason, they are often difficult to prove and are perhaps of limited value.

2. *Linguistics must be used in the statement and measurement of goals and achievements.* Such statements form an essential part of any pedagogical hypothesis, The statement that "Method A is better than Method B" implies some sort of criterion measure of linguistic performance or competence.

3. *Linguistic concepts can be used in the formulation of hypotheses concerning teaching methods.* Under this rubric two types of linguistically based hypotheses must be distinguished.

> A. Linguistics is used in the measurement of specific variables which are used in the hypothesis, e.g., the hypothesis, that "a lesson should proceed from less to more complex structures" implies that linguistic measures of complexity must be found.
> B. Linguistics is applied insofar as certain theories of language seem to make some types of teaching procedure look more promising than others. The general impact of linguistic theory on language teaching discussed in this article was largely based on this type of hypothesis, e.g., the pattern practice approach was based on the hypothesis that "substitution procedures used for identification of word classes can be used effectively as teaching procedures and will result in learning of those patterns."

4. Linguistics can finally be used in the formulation of rules and the description of the material to be presented to the student. Here the use of the latest linguistic formulation should assure maximum accuracy. In addition it can again lead to the formulation of hypotheses: e. g., "formulations based on transformational grammar will be more effective than those based on structural linguistics."

The hypotheses used as examples are quite vague. Some linguistically based hypotheses are perhaps beyond proof. But the very effort of attempting to prove an hypothesis of refining it, of specifying criterion measures can lead to new insights into the process of teaching and learning. The attempt to find the "best" method of teaching which has characterized most of pedagogical discussion seems futile in any case. Even the best experiments can never determine the best method. They can only tell us that, for certain purposes at least, some alternative may be better than some others. The attempt to find the best method should probably be replaced by an effort to find better methods for specific situations and for specific individuals. Teaching is only one of the many variables which affect the complex process of language learning. What may be appropriate for one student may simply not be for another. Improvement of instruction may, above all, necessitate greater individualization.

In this process of improvement, linguistics can perform a vital role simply because it is essential to the conceptualization of the teaching process itself. Especially in a time of uncertainty as to aims and public support of language instruction, language teachers should welcome all new developments in the field of linguistics. Such new developments should be looked at neither as a cause of confusion and uncertainty nor as the sources of new revealed truth or inspiration. To use again an example referred to above, that "structures should not be combined in the same exercise on the basis of surface similarity" is an interesting hypothesis which may be true in certain situations or for certain individuals. It is not an undisputable truth. The contribution of generative grammar illustrated by this hypothesis does not lie in the truth that has been revealed but in the simple fact that without generative grammar the entire hypothesis could never have been formulated, because we lacked the concepts of deep and surface structure.

Hypotheses are not truth. Linguistics is not Pedagogy. If linguistics is to have a positive impact in the field of language teaching we must continuously keep in mind the distinction between truth and hypothesis. We must learn to resist the temptation to convert linguistic theory into pedagogical doctrine — an attempt which has characterized so much of the past and recent history of language teaching. We must learn to interpolate experimentation and above all practical pedagogical experience between the fields of linguistics and language teaching.

THE *CONFRÉRIE DES JONGLEURS ET DES BOURGEOIS* AND THE *PUY D'ARRAS* IN TWELFTH AND THIRTEENTH CENTURY LITERATURE

By Louise Barbara Richardson
Johnson State College

The literary societies of northern France are an interesting feature of medieval life, and those of Arras are particularly significant since many of the members were gifted poets, who made the rich, industrial city of Arras one of the most flourishing literary centers of the twelfth and thirteenth centuries.[1] Two societies in which poets played a leading role are mentioned in the literature of these centuries; they are the *Confrérie des jongleurs et bourgeois* and the *Puy d'Arras*.[2] Several medieval documents provide information on the *confrérie*, but the references made in literature to the *puy*, are only brief, often indefinite, allusions that frequently leave scholars in disagreement as to their interpretation.

---

[1] Cf. Henry Gruy, *Histoire d'Arras* (Arras, 1967), pp. 72-75; J. Lestocquoy, *Les dynasties bourgeoises d'Arras du XIe au XVe siècles*, Mém. de la Comm. dép. des mon. hist. Pas-de-Calais, t. 5, fasc. 1 (Arras: 1945), pp. 31 ff., 125.

[2] The reason for the use of the word *puy* (PODIUM) for a literary society is not clear. Henri Guy, *Essai sur la vie et les œuvres littéraires du Trouvère Adan de le Hale* (Paris: 1898, New York: Burt Franklin Reprint, 1969), pp. xxxiv ff., suggests that it is used in the sense of 'mount of the muses'. Guy also mentions another suggestion: it derives from the name of the city Le Puy-en-Velay, where there was also a literary *puy*, probably founded later than the *puy* at Arras, however, and where there was a celebrated shrine of Notre Dame in whose honor several *confréries* in northern France were founded. M. Rösler, "Die Beziehungen der Puis zu den Gilden," *ZRP*, t. XLVI (1926), pp. 289-91, connects *puy* with the sense of 'support' provided for the members of the society.

A reevaluation of the material would seem in order at the present time, especially since much of the scholarly research on the *puy* and the *confrérie* was done in France over fifty years ago and is not readily available to the contemporary American student. It is the purpose of the present paper, therefore, to reexamine the principal twelfth and thirteenth century literary material referring to these two societies and to point out what information it provides about the foundation, organization and activities of the *Puy d'Arras* and its relation to the *Confrérie des jongleurs et bourgeois*.

Knowledge about the *confrérie* can be gained from MS. 8541 of the Bibliothèque Nationale, a MS of fifty folios, executed in the twelfth, thirteenth, and fourteenth centuries; fols. 3-45 contain a list of the members, inscribed at death, from the years 1194 to 1357; [3] fols 46-49 contain the society's statutes and regulations, [4] many of which are also summarized in the thirteenth century MS, the *Règlement de la Confrérie*. [5]

The origin of the *Confrérie des jongleurs et bourgeois* is explained by the medieval legend that relates how a miraculous candle, *la Sainte Chandelle*, or *le Saint Cierge*, was bestowed by Notre Dame on two jongleurs. The legend is recorded in several sources. There is a Latin version preserved in a seventeenth century MS, the *Registre Thieulaine*, [6] and an Old French poem, attributed to the thirteenth or fourteenth century, but extant only in MSS of the sixteenth and seventeenth, among others the *Regis-*

---

[3] Bibl. Nat. f. fr. 8541, fols. 3-45, ed. Roger Berger, *Le Nécrologe de la Confrérie des jongleurs et des bourgeois d'Arras*, Mém. de la Comm. dép. des mon. hist. du Pas-de-Calais, t. 11, fasc. 2, t. 13, fasc. 2 (Arras: 1963, 1970); cf. t. 13, pp. 31-37.

[4] Bibl. Nat. f. fr. 8541, fols. 46-49, ed. A. Guesnon, *Statuts et règlements de la Confrérie des jongleurs et des bourgeois* (Arras: 1860), and Louis Cavrois, *Cartulaire de Notre-Dame des Ardents* (Arras: Bradier, 1876), pp. 103-113, 167-170, 174-175.

[5] MS of 8 fols. in the archives of the *Conf. de Notre-Dame des Ardents*, now in the *Bibl. Municipale d'Arras*, ed. Cavrois, *Cart.*, pp. 117-126.

[6] *Registre Thieulaine*, fols. liiv°-lxi, ed. Cavrois, *Cart.*, pp. 91-103 and Berger, *Néc*, t. 13, pp. 139-56. The MS is in the *Bibl. Mun.* at Arras.

tre Thieulaine.[7] There is also an Old French prose version of the legend, preserved in a MS of the second half of the thirteenth century.[8] This version, which is enjoyable to read because of its rather lively narrative style and spontaneous use of dialogue, is very important as a source, since it is the only full length account of the legend that is extant in a medieval French document. The legend, in briefer form, is also recorded by Alfonso el Sabio in the *Cantigas de Santa Maria:*

> Dest' un miragre grande foi fazer
> a Virgen, que vos quero retraer,
> de dous jograres que fez ben querer;
> . . . .
> E deu-lles log' hũa candea tal
> con que ssãassen as gentes do mal
> a que chaman fogo de San Marçal.[9]

No scholar of the *Sainte Chandelle* seems to have called attention to this Portuguese version; yet the *Cantiga*, which is preserved in four thirteenth century MSS,[10] is important, for it represents a second account of the legend existing in a medieval source.

The outline of the narrative is essentially the same in all versions. The miraculous bestowal of the candle occurred in the time of Bishop Lambert,[11] when Arras was afflicted with a terrible plague known as *le feu d'enfer*.[12] One night Notre Dame appeared in a vision to two *jugleeurs,* or *menesterieus,* Norman and Itier, who were mortal enemies, and told them to go to the cathedral in Arras where, after being reconciled through the me-

---

[7] *Reg. Thieu.,* fols. xxxix v°-lii. Cf. Berger, *Néc.* t. 13, p. 40, n. 5, who says the poem exists in various MSS but does not identify them. The poem in somewhat different versions has been edited by Cavrois, *Cart.*, pp. 127-154, and Auguste Terninck, *Notre-Dame du Joyel* (Arras. 1853), pp. 73-77.

[8] Bibl. Nat. f. fr. 17229, fols. 352v°357v°; ed. Berger, *Néc.*, t. 13, pp. 137-56

[9] Alfonso X, *Cantiga* 259. 6-8, 31-33, *Cantigas de Santa Maria,* ed. Walter Mettmann, Acta Universitatis Conimbrigensis, 3 vols. (Coimbra: 1959, 1964), III, 24-25.

[10] Mettmann, "Introduction to the Cantigas," I, vii.

[11] Bishop from 1094-1115; cf. Berger, t. 13, pp. 41 ff.

[12] Also called *le mal des ardents, fogo de San Marçal* by Alfonso.

diation of the bishop, they would receive from her a holy candle that would effect the cure of all those in Arras afflicted with the plague. They went at once to Arras where, after being reconciled by Bishop Lambert, they received the candle from Nostre Dame Sainte Marie, whom they saw descend into the choir of the cathedral early in the morning of Pentecost Sunday. She addressed them thus: "'Vos jugleor,' fet ele, 'qui vivez de chant et de vielle, venez ça; ceste chandoile vos baill a garder a tozjorz. Mes parmenablement quiconques crestiens, soit hom, soit fame, aura la choison de ce mal c'on apele feu d'enfer, se on alume cest cierge, et de la cire qi remetra par la force del feu degoute on en eve et de cele eve face son epröement seur le leu ou li malages est espris et bleciez, tantost sera estainz en tel manere que, se il croit, il guerira.'" [13]

After having received the above instructions, the jongleurs followed them carefully and effected the cure. In thanksgiving they formed a *charité* or society. The candle remained in the possession of the society and was under the special surveillance of the jongleurs, two of whom were the heads of the association, Norman and Itier being the first. After their death, however, some of the nobility who had become members, in particular two proud knights, Jehan and Nicolas, resenting the presence of the lowly jongleurs, caused them to be banished from the society. However, the two malefactors soon repented of their pride. They became seriously ill. Mary appeared to them in sleep, and having reprimanded them for conspiring against the minstrels to whom she had entrusted the candle, warned that they would soon suffer death unless they repented. The warning was heeded, and the jongleurs were reinstalled in the society.

The account of the jongleurs' expulsion and subsequent return is given in both the Old French poem and the prose text, but not in the Latin version, [14] which represents an earlier form of the legend composed, apparently, before these events occurred.

---

[13] Bibl. Nat. f. fr. 1'/229, fols. 355v°-356.
[14] Alfonso does not mention the episode.

Berger remarks that they are also referred to in the statutes, in a section written between 1184 and 1203, and therefore, must have taken place sometime before 1203, probably not much before 1184. [15] The date cannot be specified more definitely than this.

The significant point is that there was at some time a split between the jongleurs and the other members of the *confrérie* and that the jongleurs were separated from the group only to return at a later date. We have no information about what they did in the interim; perhaps it was at this time that they formed their own literary association, namely the *Puy d'Arras*, the circumstances of whose origin are unknown. Most scholars see a close connection between the *confrérie* and the *Puy d'Arras*, since many activities performed in one or the other of these societies were performed in a single literary society in other medieval cities of northern France, for example, Amiens or Valenciennes. [16] Some scholars actually regard the *puy* as an outgrowth of the *confrérie*. [17] If this is correct, the episode of the jongleurs' expulsion and later return may explain in legendary form how during a temporary severance from the *confrérie* the jongleurs formed the *puy*, a society dedicated solely to literary pursuits. Their return to the former society can be corroborated by historical fact since many poets whose work indicates that they participated in the *puy* were also, according to the list given in MS 8541, members of the *Confrérie des jongleurs et des bourgeois*. [18] After a temporay split, then, when they formed their own society, the jongleurs would have continued to be active in both the religious and the literary associations. No scholar has given this interpretation to the episode of the quarrel between the jongleurs and knights; it can only rest in the realm of

---

[15] Berger, *Néc.*, t. 13, pp. 41, n. 9, 45-46, 137.

[16] Cf. Edmond Faral, *Les Jongleurs en France au moyen âge*, Bibl. de l'Ecole des hautes études, fasc. 187 (Paris, 1910, 1964), pp. 140; Louis Cavrois, "Le Puy académique d'Arras," *Mém. de l'Acad. d'Arras*, 2ᵉ série, t. 19 (1888), pp. 231-37.

[17] Louis Passy, "Fragments d'histoire littéraire," *Bibl. de l'Ecole des chartes* (Paris, Dumoulin, 1859), 4ᵉ série, t. 5, pp. 491-92; Guy, *Essai sur Adan*, pp. xxxi-xxxiv.

[18] Cf. Guy, *Essai sur Adan*, p. xxxiii.

conjecture but might be considered a possible explanation for the origin of the *Puy d'Arras*, in want of any definite documentary evidence.

The existing documents do not mention any literary activities in which the jongleurs participated as members of the *confrérie*. The statutes indicate that the purpose of this association was primarily charitable and religious. One religious ceremony in which the jongleurs were leaders is described in a most moving passage in literature. This was a special procession, an annual function according to the statutes, when the jongleurs bore the *Sainte Chandelle* from the chapel in the *Place du Petit Marché* of Arras, where it was usually lodged, to the Cathedral of Notre Dame.[19] The poet Baude Fastoul recalled the procession in his moving *Congés*, in which he bade farewell to the citizens of Arras after he had been tragically struck by leprosy; pathetically addressing the *trouvères*, he wrote:

> Trop volentiers fuisse avoec eus,
> Mais li mals que j'ai me conselle
> Que ne doi porter le Candelle,
> Car je sui uns hors menestreus.[20]

Seventy years earlier Jehan Bodel also had spoken of paying honor to the *Sainte Chandelle* in the *Place du Petit Marché*. Struck by leprosy like Fastoul, Bodel likewise said farewell in his *Congés* to the candle and to his confrères, the minstrels. Addressing Our Lady, he wrote:

> Dame, en cui sont tout bien logié,
> A vo Candoille pren congié
> Que donnastes as jougleours;
> . . . .
> Et quant iere ou Petit Marchié,
> De moi iert baisie la tours
> Ou establis est ses sejours,

---

[19] "Statuts," ed. Cavrois. *Cart.*, p. 109.
[20] Baude Fastoul, "Congés," 633-36, éd. Pierre Ruelle, "Les Congés d'Arras," *Travaux de la Fac. de Phil. et Lettres de Bruxelles*, XXVII (1965); Ruelle dates the "Congés," 1272.

> S'avrai cuer mains mesaaisié.
> He! menestrel, douch conpaignon,
> Ami m'avez esté et bon
> Conme tres fin loial confrere. [21]

Thirteenth century literature of Arras contains many references to the *puy*. Although only brief allusions, they do give some indication about the activities of this organization. Many poets refer to the *Puy d'Arras* as a center where their work could be presented to an appreciative audience. Thus the jongleur Andrieu Contredis speaks of sending his song to the *puy:*

> Chançon, vat-en sans nul arestoison,
> Droit à Arras au Pui sans demourée;
> Là fai chanter et le dit et le son,
> Là serés vous oïe et escoutée! [22]

Jehan Bretel, a wealthy merchant and amateur poet of considerable talent, also speaks of his intention to present a song at the *puy:* "Au pui d'Arras, canchon, va tesmougnier/ Que pour ma dame aim mieus amendiier/ Tout mon vivant...." [23] Robert du Chastel expresses a like intention while praising the members: "A la noble compaignie/ Del Pui fais present/ De ma chançon...." [24] A poet sometimes asked another to present his work, Mahieu de Gand: "Bretel, ma cancon envoïe/ Vous ai, por cou que soit oïe/ Au pui..." [25]

Other poets speak of poetic competitions being held in the *puy;* thus Andrieu Douche says:

> Chançon, va t'en tout sans loissir
> Au pui d'Arras te fai oïr
> A ceulz qui sevent chans fournir;

---

[21] Jehan Bodel, "Congés," st. 43, ed. Ruelle.
[22] Andrieu Contredis, "Chançon," ed. Arthur Dinaux, *Trouvères artésiens* (Paris: Téchener, 1843), p. 70.
[23] Jehan Bretel, "Chanson," ed. Gaston Raynaud, "Chansons de Jehan Bretel," *Bibl. de l'Ecole de chartes* (Paris: Picard, 1880), t. XLI, p. 212; cf. 194 ff.
[24] Robert du Chastel, "Chanson," ed. Passy, "Frag. litt.," p. 491.
[25] Mahieu de Gand, ed. Paulin Paris, "Chansonniers," HLF (Paris: Welter, 1895), t. XXIII, p. 658.

> Là sont li bon entendeour
> Qui jugeront bien la meillour
> De nos chançons... [26]

Occasionally a poet complains of an unfair judgment rendered by the judges at these competitions; thus Jean de Renti comments:

> Se ce n'estoit pour ma dame honerer,
> Jamais au pui ne diroie chanson;
> Car j'en voi ciaus souvent l'oneur porter
> Qui de chanter ne sevent un boton. [27]

Robert de le Pierre remarks that some colleagues resent his receiving a prize:

> Cil qi m'ont repris
> De ma kanchon courounée,
> N'ont pas bien enkuis
> Que je senc... [28]

As this poem indicates, the victor seems to have received a crown. Although no definite indications exist as to procedure in the contests at Arras, more precise information is found in the statutes of the *puys* at Valenciennes and Amiens. In these societies a competition of rhetoric was conducted annually, when poets were invited to compose a work in honor of la sainte Vierge; at the end of the competition silver crowns were given as prizes to the two poets whose work was judged the best. [29] We do not know whether some of the competitions at Arras also stipulated religious poetry; however, many poems in honor of Mary were written by poets of Arras like Jacques de Viniers, Guillaume de Viniers and Adam de la Halle. [30]

Quite frequent mention is made in poetry to the literary society's presiding officer who bore the title *Prince du puy*. He

---

[26] Andrieu Douche, "Chanson," ed. Dinaux, *Trouv. art.*, p. 76.
[27] Jean de Renti, ed. Paris, "Chans.," p. 646.
[28] Robert de le Pierre, "Chanson," ed. Passy, "Frag. litt.," p. 320.
[29] Cavrois, "Le puy d'Arras," pp. 231 ff; Grace Frank, *Medieval French Drama* (Oxford: Clarendon, 1954, 1967), p. 116.
[30] Paris, "Chans.," p. 589; François Blondel, "Les Principaux trouvères du XIII siècle," *Mem. de l'Acad. d'Arras*, 2ᵉ série, t. 44 (1913), p. 39.

is mentioned in the *Jeu de la Feuillée,* where Adam's father refers to him:

> Ha! biaus dous fieus, seés vous jus,
> Si vous metés a genoillons,
> Se che non, Robers Sommeillons,
> Ki est nouviaus prinches du pui,
> Vous ferra.

The fool responds:

> Bien kiiét de lui.
> Je sui mieus prinches k'il ne soit.
> A sen pui canchon faire doit
> Par droit maistre Wautiers as Paus. [31]

The well known *Dit artésien*: "Arras est escole de tous biens entendre" mentions *l'ostel le Prince,* saying that it was such a celebrated literary center that God Himself came down from Heaven to meet the fine poets assembled there. [32]

The title of *prince du puy* often appears in the *jeux partis,* or poetic debates. Jehan Bretel is thus addressed in 15 out of 88 *jeux* in which he is a partner. The fact that Bretel was frequently so addressed by his partners in the *jeux* might seem to suggest that these debates were presented in the *puy.* Whether the *jeux partis,* of which so many have been handed down from thirteenth century Arras and whose clever twists of thought and word play exhibit the ready wit so popular in that city, were performed in the *puy,* cannot be stated conclusively. There is no specific statement in the works themselves indicating this, and no judgment of one of the debates or even a mention of one has survived. [33] That many of the poets who participated in the *jeux* contributed poems to the *puy* is indicated by their own statements, and some scholars definitely maintain that the *jeux partis* were presented at the *Puy d'Arras,* or perhaps even prepared in

---

[31] Adam le Bossu, *Jeu de la Feuillée,* 402-409, ed. Ernest Langlois, 2ᵉ éd. rev., CFMA (Paris: Champion, 1923, 1964).

[32] "Dit artésien," ed. A. Jeanroy et H. Guy, *Chansons et dits artésiens du XIII siècle,* Bibl. des Univ. du Midi, fasc. II (Bordeaux: 1898), pp. 33-34.

[33] A. Langfors, A. Jeanroy et L. Brandin, *Recueil général des jeux-partis,* SATF, No. 79 (Paris: Champion, 1926), pp. vi-ix.

the *puy* and then presented in an open meeting which many more people than the members would have attended.³⁴

Dramatic representations were no doubt also held in the *Puy d'Arras*, as they were in similar societies elsewhere. Paulin Paris says that the members of this *puy* gave pastoral and satiric representations such as the *Jeu de la Feuillée*. He gives the following reason as proof this play was performed in the *puy:* many of the play's characters, including the author himself, are historical people and members of the *puy*.³⁵ They probably enacted their own role on the stage and thus, swallowing their pride, would have exposed themselves to the audience's laughter, to gratify their colleagues' taste for raillery,³⁶ a taste so characteristic of thirteenth century Arras.

That dramatic productions formed part of the activities of some *puys*, is known from their statutes; at Amiens on Candlemas Day a dinner was held at which a *jeu de mistère* was represented; at Valenciennes the drama of the Assumption was represented to the crowd by members of the *puy* on the Sunday within the octave of this feast day.³⁷ The celebration at that date calls to mind the Old French poem about the *Sainte Chandelle*.³⁸ The rubric in the *Registre Thieulaine* reads: *Avenement du Sainct Chierge en vers anciens quy se chantent la veille de l'Assomption*. The work is a narrative poem, written in octosyllabic couplets grouped in stanzas of varying lengths, but the directions given in the margins of the MS seem to suggest a semidramatic representation of the work. The indications *chantié haut, chantié bas* keep recurring and seem to indicate that the poem was sung antiphonally and the words *en lisant* appearing at intervals signify that parts were read. Once the gloss reads: *Il faut monstrer le St. Chierge*, which further illustrates the poem's dramatic quality. The poem was perhaps presented in front of

---

³⁴ Lestocquoy, *Dyn. bourg.*, pp. 40-42; Guy, *Essai sur Adan*, pp. liii-lv.
³⁵ Cf. *Jeu de la Feuillée*, 402-409.
³⁶ Paulin Paris, "Adam de la Halle," HLF (Paris: Welter, 1895), XX, 642-43; cf. Frank, *Med. Drama*, pp. 96, 167-8. Langlois, "Introduction," *Jeu de la Feuillée*, p. xvi, asserts that the play was in no way connected with the *Puy d'Arras*.
³⁷ Cavrois, "Le Puy d'Arras," pp. 231-34; Frank, *Med. Drama*, p. 116.
³⁸ *Supra*, p. 162.

the chapel in the *Place du Petit Marché,* where the thirteenth century *Règlement* mentions an annual ceremony with singing taking place the evening of *le mi aoust.* [39] The work would no doubt have been presented under the direction of the jongleurs in the *confrérie,* whose foundation it celebrates.

In conclusion it may be said that the writings of the poets of Arras point to the *puy* as a most active literary society; its members engaged in various activities: poetic competitions, presentions of diverse poetic genres, including *chansons* and *jeux partis,* and dramatic performances. In addition to their activities in the *puy,* the poets of Arras also participated in a religious *confrérie,* where they held a place of honor because of the special favor shown to their profession by Notre Dame.

---

[39] Règlement, ed. Cavrois, *Cartulaire,* p. 124.

VOCALIC ALTERNATION IN THE SURSILVAN ROMANSH VERB

By Kenneth H. Rogers
University of Rhode Island

1.0. The modern Sursilvan literary language spoken in the Grisons canton of Switzerland contains a bewildering variety of vocalic alternations in the present tense of its verbal system. Nowhere do these alternations seem to have been presented in their entirety. Theodor Gartner, in his *Handbuch der rätoromanischen Sprache und Literatur*,[1] discusses "irregular" verbs (pp. 222-248); but he does not deal in detail with vocalic alternations, with the exception of the /u - ó/ alternation of *purtar/porta*. Likewise, Jakob Stürzinger, in his thesis *Ueber die Conjugation im Rätoromanischen*,[2] confines himself to a partial treatment of the Sursilvan alternations. In the present paper I will attempt to present these alternations in as complete a fashion as possible, and to comment upon several salient features of the verbal system represented by such alternations.[3]

Some 3,107 verbs have been examined, for the most part found in the *Vocabulari Romontsch* of R. Vieli and A. Decurtins.[4] This

---

[1] Halle: Niemeyer, 1910.
[2] Winterthur: Buchdruckerei von Bleuler-Hausheer und Cie., 1879.
[3] Included in Josef Huonder's "Der Vokalismus der Mundart von Disentis" (*Romanische Forschungen*, XI /1901/, 431-566), is an enumeration of some fifty-seven vocalic alternations for the verbs of the Disentis (Muster) dialect. I hope to comment on this list and on its implications for literary Sursilvan in a subsequent paper.
[4] Ramun Vieli and Alexi Decurtins, *Vocabulari romonsch: sursilvan-tudestg* (Cuera: Ligia romontscha, 1962).

dictionary purports to be, on the whole, descriptive rather than prescriptive:

> Dapi l'entschatta dall'ovra ein ils redacturs stai en stretg contact cun informaturs e correspondents leuora sin la tiara. La stad 1957 havein nus fatg ina cuorsa tras la Surselva per sclarir ina liunga gliesta da plaids buca diltut clars.[5]

While no dictionary can fix for all time the dynamic corpus of forms, neologisms, and dialect and idiolect variants of any language, least of all a fragmented tongue such as Sursilvan Romansh, the data drawn from the Vieli-Decurtins dictionary will at least afford us an approximate notion of the state of affairs in literary Sursilvan.

1.1. From the outset, certain categories of verbs can be eliminated from our study. There are, to begin with, 557 verbs whose present-tense stems show no vocalic alternation. An example of such verbs is *bandunar* (to abandon):

jeu bandúnel [6]	nus bandunéin
ti bandúnas	vus bandunéis
el bandúna	els bandúnan

Verbs in this category contain stem-vowels in /o/, /u/, /i/, /a̯u/, /(u)e̯i/, and /a̯i/. However, not *all* verbs with the aforementioned stem-vowels fall into the category of nonalternating verbs, a fact which will be apparent from the following paragraphs.

1.2. A second class of verbs to be omitted from our discussion is that of verbs with the /-éš-/ "inchoative" infix in persons 1, 2, 3, and 6 of the present tense. *Causar*[7] (to cause) will illustrate this class of verbs:

jeu causéschel	nus causéin
ti causéschas	vus causéis
el causéscha	els causéschan

---

[5] *Ibid.*, p. x.

[6] I have indicated primary word stress in this paper with the /´/ sign; Sursilvan orthography generally does not reflect stress.

The Vieli-Decurtins dictionary lists 1198 verbs with this infix: 997 whose infinitive ends in *-ar*, 194 in *-ir*, two [8] in *-ér*, and five in *-er*. Removing these and the non-alternating verbs from consideration, then, leaves a total of 1,352 verbs to consider as alternating in the present tense.

2.0. The Sursilvan present tense is characterized by several types of vocalic alternations; all have in common, however, the fact that persons 1, 2, 3, and 6, on the one hand, are opposed to persons 4 and 5 on the other. The most important, from the point of view of sheer numbers of verbs involved, is the type in which one vowel or diphthong appears in the syllable under stress, and a second vowel appears in the same syllable when not under stress. An example of such an alternation type is *fimar/féma* (to smoke):

jeu	fémel	nus	fiméin
ti	fémas	vus	fiméis
el	féma	els	féman

Such an alternation may conveniently be designated /i - é/.

2.1. There are twenty-six different alternations of this type in modern Sursilvan. The following list shows: alternation, example(s) (more than one where orthographic or conjugational differences warrant), and the number of verbs appearing in the Vieli-Decurtins dictionary with each alternation.

(1) Vowel-vowel alternations

/ə - í/	buserar/busíra [9]	(to strain oneself)	3
/u - í/	luar/líua	(to melt)	4
/ə - é/ [10]	fermar/férma	(to close)	448

---

[7] In Sursilvan orthography, teh letter *s* represents the sound /z/.

[8] There is, additionally, a third verb in *-ér* with the /-éš-/ infix, listed as a variant of *nuscher/nóscha* (to damage); I have counted this verb among those alternating in /u - ó/.

[9] The infinitive (or, in the case of verbs in '*-er*, the first person plural) will be used in this paper to represent ending-stressed forms; the third person singular, to represent those stressed on the stem.

[10] It may be possible to analyze the /ə - é/ and /i - é/ alternations as four, and not two, distinct types; such an analysis depends upon one's acceptance of the phonemic status of an /ẹ/ - /ę/ distinction in Sursilvan. I expect to deal more fully with this question in a subsequent article.

	suarar/suéra	(to taste)	
/i - é/	firmar/féma	(to smoke)	128
/ə - á/	caṣar/cáṣa	(to shelter)	287
	smeṣar/smáṣa	(to mangle)	
/i - á/	ditgar/dátga [11]	(to esteem)	11
/u - á/	schuar/scháua	(to water)	1
/i - ó/	tschintschar/tschóntscha	(to speak)	19
/ə - ó/	clamar/clóma	(to call)	26
/u - ó/	purtar/pórta	(to carry)	78
/ə - ú/	scuclanar/scuclúna	(to uncork)	4
	cuglienar/cugliuna	(to cheat)	

(2) Vowel-diphthong alternations

/i - íə/	ríetscher/ritschéin	(to vomit)	1 [12]
/ə - íə/	tgemblar/tgíembla	(to fill, cram)	4
/u - íə/	durmir/díerma	(to sleep)	2
/u - ué̯/	encurir/enquéra	(to seek)	4 [13]
/i - éi̯/	dittar/déita	(to rock, swing)	4
/ə - éi̯/	menar/méina	(to lead)	32 [14]
	zavrar/zéivra	(to divide)	
/u - éi̯/	béiber/buéin	(to drink)	2
/i - ái̯/	plidar/pláida	(to speak)	2
/i - áu̯/	filtschar/fáultscha	(to scythe)	1
/ə - áu̯/	alzar/áulza	(to lift)	14 [15]
/u - áu̯/	ludar/láuda	(to praise)	17
/i - i̯a/	zanistrar/zaniástra	(to turn around)	1

---

[11] Although not central to the topic of this paper, it should be noted that the graphy *tg* represents the voiceless alveolar palatal affricate /ć/, which contrasts in Sursilvan with the voiceless alveopalatal affricate /č/, represented in spelling by *tsch*.

[12] A second alternation for the verb *sittar/sétta* (to shoot, fire) is *sittar/síeta*; for statistical purposes, this verb is counted under the /i - é/ alternation, since the /i - í ə/ is only a variant.

[13] There is, additionally, fifth verb, *burlir/búorla* (to roar, of animals) which has *burlir/bérla* as an alternate form.

[14] Although not counted in the figure of thirty-two, *empalar/empéila* (to lead) appears in Vieli as a variant of *empalar/empála*.

[15] In the case of six of the fourteen verbs of this class, the stem-vowel is followed by a nasal consonant, causing the /áu/ diphthong to be realized phonetically as /ę́u/: *brancar/bráunca*, /ə - ę́u/.

/ə - iá/	serrar/siára	(to close)	16 [16]
	emparar/empiára	(to ask)	
/u - uá/	curclar/cuárcla	(to cover)	6
/u - úə/	mussar/múossa	(to show)	34 [17]

2.2. There are eight classes of verbs where, in addition to the vowel-vowel or vowel-diphthong alternation, the metathesis of the consonant /r/ is involved. These eight classes are as follows:

(3) Vowel-vowel alternations with /r/ metathesis

/ər - rí/	barschar/bríscha [18]	(to burn)	1
/ər - ré/	dertgar/drétga	(to litigate)	24
	sgarflar/sgréfla	(to scratch)	
/ər - rá/	patertgar/patrátga	(to think)	14
	bargir/brágia	(to weep)	
/ər - ró/	tachergnar/tacrógna	(to hesitate)	44 [19]
	sgarmar/sgróma	(to skim)	
/ur - ró/	curdar/cróda	(to fall)	5
/ur - rú/	furschar/frúscha	(to rub, wipe)	4

(4) Vowel-diphthong alternations with /r/ metathesis

/ər - réi/	sferdar/sfréida	(to cool off)	5 [20]
/ər - ríə/	trietscher/tartschéin	(to remove)	2
	endríescher/enderschéin	(to learn)	

---

[16] Pretonic /a/ and /e/ are both realized as /ə/.

[17] An additional alternation — which, if counted, would bring the number of alternations so far discussed to twenty-eight — is that in /o - úə/: transformar/transfúorma. This form, however, is only a variant of transformar/transforméscha, and therefore I have omitted it from the number of alternations.

[18] In the Sursilvan orthography, sch represents the voiced fricative /ž/.

[19] Professor M. A. Borodina, in her recent book Sovremenniĭ literaturniĭ retoromanskiĭ jazyk Svejtsarii (The Contemporary literary Rheto-romance language of Switzerland) (Leningrad: Nauka, 1969), omits the /er - ró/ alternation from her list of the "principal" alternations in Sursilvan (pp. 92-93), mentioning only the /ər - rá/, /ur - ró/, and /ər - ré/ classes. This is curious, in view of the number of verbs in the /ər - ró/ group.

[20] The infinitive of three verbs of this group (crer and its compounds) has a third vowel /e/, actually giving three of the five verbs in the class a triple alternation.

2.3. Six classes of verbs in Sursilvan alternate simultaneously in two syllables of the stem:

/u-ə/ and /ə-ó/	cumandar/camónda	(to command)	11
/u-ə/ and /i-ú/	buntganar/bintgúna	(to nudge, jog)	8
/u-ə/ and /ə-ú/	burschanar/barschúna	(to brush)	27
/u-i/ and /ə-ó/	dumignar/damógna	(to conquer)	1
/u-ə/ and /ə-ú/	tschugalar/tschagúola	(to drivel)	1
/u-i/ and /ə-úi̯/	murtirar/martúira	(to torture)	1

2.4. Finally, six classes of imparisyllabic verbs complete the panorama of alternations in the Sursilvan present tense. Five of these classes show one fewer syllable in the ending-stressed forms than in the stem-stressed forms:

/u/ - /ə-ú/	luvrar/lavúra	(to work)	4 [21]
/ə/ - /ə-ó/	sesmargnar/sesmarógna	(to befoul self)	1
/i/ - /ə-í/	digrar/daghíra	(to trickle)	1
/u/ - /u-íə/	cuvrín/cuvíerer	(to cover)	6
/ə/ - /ə-i̯á/	satrar/satiára	(to bury)	1

The remaining class contains one fewer syllable in the stem-stressed forms than in the ending-stressed forms:

/ə-ə/ - /á/	mascarar/máscra	(to disguise)	2

Additionally, it should be pointed out that the verb *perdegar/prétga* (to preach) offers an alternation pattern which neatly parallels that of *mascarar* and would be eligible for inclusion in our list but for two factors: (1) it is only a variant of *perdegar/perdégia*, and (2) the metathesis of /r/ and the alternation between /g/ and /ć/ as stem-final consonants, render the *perdegar/prétga* alternation too irregular and unstable to count for our purposes.

2.5. The above catalogue of vocalic alternations has intentionally omitted thirty-six verbs which, from the standpoint of

---

[21] The other three verbs of this class are all compounds of *luvrar*.

their stems, can only be classed as "irregular." [22] Verbs such as *ir* (to go) cannot be described as having a stem-vowel alternation parallel to those discussed above, since the stem itself varies so greatly in other respects:

jeu mon	nus mein
ti va*s*	vus meis
el va	els van

3.0. Having seen what alternating classes exist in the modern Sursilvan Romansh verb, it remains for us to comment upon the system as a whole, keeping in mind the state of affairs in the other Romance verbal systems.

3.1. Enumerated above are no less than forty-six classes of verbs, in terms of the vocalic alternation in the present tense. The figure of forty-six classes does not include (1) the "inchoative" verbs, although, as we have seen (Section 1.2 of this paper), these verbs do endeed "alternate" in the presence or absence of the /-éš-/ infix, (2) the "irregular" verbs (see Section 2.5 of this paper), nor (3) the plethora of variants — nearly four hundred in all — mentioned in the Vieli-Decurtins dictionary. On the other hand, it must be conceded that, while the total number of verbs which alternate is 1,316, twenty-eight of the alternation classes are represented by fewer than ten verbs, eleven alternation classes, indeed, consist of no more than a single verb.

3.2. A comparison of the above data with comparable figures compiled for the other Romance languages will show that Sursilvan Romansh has many more alternation classes than its nearest competitor among the five major Romance languages, French, with a total of sixteen alterantion classes. [23] In another respect, however, Sursilvan verbs show a type of distribution which parallels that of the other Romance languages: most of the major Romance languages contain two or three important classes, in terms of the

---

[22] For a detailed treatment of these verbs, see Alexi Decurtins, *Zur Morphologie der unregelmässigen Verben im Bündnerromanischen*, Romania helvetica, 62 (1958).

[23] Kenneth H. Rogers, *Studies in differentiating Analogy in the Evolution of the Romance Present Tense*, unpublished PhD Dissertation, Columbia University, 1970, p. 230.

numbers of verbs involved. Spanish groups most of its alternating verbs, for example, in the /e - ié/ *(sentar/siénta)* and /o - ué/ *(probar/pruéba)* classes; Italian, in the /ę - ę̂ *(cessare/céssa)* and /ǫ - ǫ́/ *(dormire/dórma)* classes;[24] and French, in the /ə - ę́/ *(lever/lève)* and /e - ę́/ *(préférer/préfère)* classes. Sursilvan is comparable on this point to the three languages mentioned above, in that the overwhelming majority of its alternating verbs are found in four large classes: /ə - é/, /ə - á/, /i - é/, and /u - ó/.

3.3. In the type of double-syllable vocalic alternations typified by *cumandar/camónda* (see Section 2.3 of this paper), Sursilvan Romansh may be compared only to Rumanian, where verbs such as *depără/déperi* (to tear out one's hair) occur. The pattern of Rumanian double-alternation verbs is, however, more complex than that of Sursilvan double-alternation verbs, in that vowels of the two syllables are not consistently paired:

deápăr	depărăm
déperi	depăráti
deápără	deápără

Rumanian has three such alternation classes, involving nineteen verbs;[25] Sursilvan Romansh, as we have seen, has six classes, involving forty-nine verbs.

4.0. The evolution of forty-six different types of vocalic alternation in Sursilvan has resulted from, as is to be expected in a highly structured and formally interdependent system such as that of the verb, an extremely complex interplay of phonological changes and analogical interference; this is true both of the changes that have taken place, and of the levelling that has failed to occur. Many pioneering discoveries in this area were presented by G. I. Ascoli in his *Saggi ladini*[26] and in his *Saggio di morfologia e lessicologia soprasilvana*.[27] More recent studies in the field of the Sursilvan Romansh verb, as well as in other areas of Rheto-

---

[24] For the controversial phonemic status of the /ę - ę/ and /ǫ - ǫ/ distinctions in contemporary Italian, see Bertil Malmberg, "A Propos du système phonologique de l'Italien," *Acta linguistica* III, 1940-1941, 39.

[25] Rogers, *op. cit.*, pp. 112-117.

[26] *Archivio glottologico italiano* I, 1873, esp. pp. 9-50.

[27] *Archivio glottologico italiano* VII, 1880-1893, pp. 406-602.

romance phonology and morphology, are Robert von Planta's "Birkicht und Vokalmetathese im Rätischen," [28] and Alexi Decurtins *Zur Morphologie des unregelmässigen verben im Bündnerromanischen.* [29]

Much remains to be done in this field, however. The problem of which verbs retained their intertonic syllables (e. g., *madirar* < MATŪRĀRE) and which verbs lost them (e. g., *luvrar* < LABŌRĀRE), and the unsnarling of the complex forces of phonetic change and analogy, still await thorough examination and analysis.

---

[28] *Festschrift Gauchat*, 1926, esp. p. 213.
[29] See note 22.

FRAY MARTIN SARMIENTO, *AMADIS DE GAULA* AND THE SPANISH CHIVALRIC "GENRE"

By Barton Sholod
Queens College of the City University of New York

By the end of the fifteenth century Castilian prose style had developed sufficiently so as to produce two literary gems, one imbued with such realism as was to characterize much of Spanish letters for posterity, the other textually inflated through the mechanics of euphuism but whose sublime ideals of love and courtesy were to prevail upon Western literature and conventionality for more than two centuries. Certainly Fernando de Rojas' *Tragicomedia de Calisto y Melibea* more than makes up for much of the everlasting human quality lacking in Rodríguez de Montalvo's *Amadís de Gaula* and for this reason, no doubt, the testimonial to an astute go-between, Celestina, has maintained its popularity with Hispanophiles the world over, while the seemingly ever-increasing fantastic adventures of the "virtuoso caballero" have long since become irksome for the modern reader, accustomed as he is to a more realistic and "scientific" literary tradition. Nevertheless, it is significant that our own century has already yielded sixteen versions of this supposedly outworn chivalric tale (only the reprint of the nineteenth century Gayangos edition, the C. O. P. edition, F. Buendía's version and Professor Place's scholarly production can qualify as "editions"), in contrast to the five editions, including one reprint, published in the last century. [1]

---

[1] For a comparative list of nineteenth and twentieth century editions and adaptations of the *Amadís*, readers are directed to *Amadís de Gaula*. Edición y anotación por Edwin B. Place, vol. I (Madrid: CSIC, 1959),

Coupled with the fact that in recent years the *Amadís* has also become the subject of several important scholarly articles and dissertations, admirers of Montalvo's work and of Spanish medieval literature in general may legitimately suppose that, together with what may presently be categorized as "camp" (and why, we facetiously ask, should scholarship be exempted from this contemporary mode?), "neo-Gothic," etc., Spain's most important *libro de caballerías* is undergoing some sort of scholarly (Gothic!) revival.

In a like manner, eighteenth century Spanish historical, literary and linguistic themes have recently attracted the attention of scholars, at once reluctant to enter the crowded field of nineteenth century Spanish studies and eager to unveil the "earliest origins" of that century's neo-classical and romantic attitudes purveying all attempts at cultural self-analysis. [2] Among those figures foreshadowing the more highly-developed critical outlook of the next century is Fray Martín Sarmiento (1695-1771), born Pedro José García Balboa but assuming the name of the saint under whose auspices his Benedictine abbey in Madrid had been founded. Like the celebrated Padre Feijoo (also a Benedictine and a fellow Galician), with whom he colaborated and whose controversial

---

pp. XXVI-XXVIII. I also wish to add the following versions omitted by Prof. Place:

Aventuras del invencible caballero andante Amadis de Gaula, reimpreso literalmente segun el testo de la mas apreciable edicion (Madrid: M. Pita, 1838), 2 vols.

Aventuras de Amadís de Gaula, relatadas a los niños por María Luz Morales. Con ilustraciones de Albert (Barcelona: Araluce, 1930?), 134 pp.

Amadís de Gaula in *Libros de caballerías*. Selección y prólogo por Ramón María Tenreiro; dibujos de F. Marco, 2nd ed. (Madrid: Instituto-Escuela, Junta para Ampliación de Estudios, 1935), pp. 31-224.

Amadís de Gaula. Según el antiguo texto de Garci-Ordóñez de Montalvo. Modernizado y compendiado por E. Pérez Mariluz (Buenos Aires: Atlántida, 1944), 133 pp. [A second edition appeared in 1951.]

[2] Just a few of these outstanding works devoted to the eighteenth century are: J. Sarrailh, *L'Espagne éclairée de la seconde moitiée du XVIII siècle* (Paris, 1954); J. Reglá y Santiago Alcolea, *El siglo XVIII* (Barcelona, 1957); R. Herr, *The Eighteenth-Century Revolution in Spain* (Princeton, 1958); A. Gil Novales, *Las pequeñas atlántidas: Decadencia y regeneración intelectual de España en los siglos XVIII y XIX* (Barcelona, 1959); F. Lázaro Carreter, *Las ideas lingüísticas en España durante el siglo XVIII* (Madrid, 1949).

"scientific" opinions he defended against the rigidity of contemporary ignorance, [3] Sarmiento was one of the gifted Spanish polygraphs of his day whose inquiring, encyclopedic mind embraced a truly colossal range of subjects: natural sciences, especially minerology and botany (he corresponded with the Swede Linnaeus), medicine, mathematics, cosmography, history, philosophy, religion, folklore, paleography, the evolution of languages and dialects, Latin and Greek, the beginnings of literature, particularly poetry, contemporary morality and pedagogy. [4] Small wonder that Padre Feijoo, in his essay *Glorias de España,* calls Sarmiento "un milagro de erudición," and even includes him in a catalogue of "españoles ilustres," knowing that his protégé was still a very young man. [5] Yet unlike Feijoo, Sarmiento refused to have his works published (cf. note 3), never attempting to edit or polish them, insisting: "Yo sólo escribo para mi instrucción y para complacer á cuatro amigos." How very different this attitude from that of the other two indefatigable "publishers" of Sarmiento's own pre-Enlightenment generation, Gregorio Mayáns y Siscar, and Padre Enrique Flórez, who availed themselves of the Benedictine's critical notes and insights in the areas of linguistic evolution and Spanish church history respectively. [6] Instead, Sarmiento, once having left Galicia (he had been raised in Pontevedra, where his father was a civil servant, and had gone on to study humanities at the monastery of Lérez), confined himself to the contemplative and scholarly life (except for an interval in which he served as "cronista de las Indias"), first as abbot of the Catalan monastery at Ripoll, and then as a humble but outwardly

---

[3] Indeed, the only work of Sarmiento's published during his lifetime was his defense of Feijoo's attitudes, entitled *Demostración crítico-apologética del teatro crítico universal* (1732), written in answer to Salvador Mañero's attack (the so-called *Antiteatro crítico*) on Feijoo's *Teatro crítico universal.*

[4] See Antolín López Peláez, *Los escritos de Sarmiento y el siglo de Feijoo* (La Coruña, Andrés Martínez, 1901), p. 135 and Reglá y Santiago Alcolea, *op. cit.,* p. 80.

[5] Cf. José María Chacón y Calvo, "El P. Sarmiento y el 'Poema del Cid,'" *Revista de Filología Española,* XXI (1934), 143.

[6] Cf. Reglá, *op. cit.,* p. 80 and Ángel del Río, *Historia de la literatura española.* Edición revisada. Tomo II (New York, Holt, Rinehart and Winston, 1963), pp. 28-29.

eccentric friar at the abbey of San Martín in Madrid. Here, in an anxiety-ridden, individualistic manner somewhat analogous to that of the twentieth century Unamuno, he wrote "contra esto y lo otro," and, in an unfinished essay entitled *El porqué sí y el porqué no del Padre Sarmiento* (1759), he hoped to defend himself adequately against those cosmopolitan types who criticized him "por no salir de casa, no empeñarse por nadie, rehuir las cofradías literarias y no publicar nunca sus obras." [7] Actually, for Sarmiento the cloister was never a prison-like confinement but rather a spiritual and meditative refuge away from the conformist universities and academies that he so despised, for "si las primeras se fundaron en el tiempo de la barbarie, las segundas en el de la charlatanería." [8]

Sarmiento, though availing himself of the most "creative" literary form of the neo-classical period, the essay (the more "imaginative" genres languished in eighteenth century Spain), really anticipates the subsequent decline of the "classical" taste in letters throughout the last years of his century and the first decade of the next. In all matters philosophical and literary, he was a consummate rebel, always propounding a freedom of thought and expression not consonant with the prevailing restrictive formality of neo-classicism but representative of the "romanticism" already close at hand. His very style of writing, characterized by a complete lack of formality, a simplicity and straightforwardness more typical of oral discourse than writing — that is, an utterly spontaneous or "natural" form of composition — coincides with his project for the creation of a *general*, not *universal*, language that would embrace all the natural phenomena bequeathed man by God and exclude all things fabricated by human caprice and superficiality. [9] Indeed, his writings are filled with such digres-

---

[7] Cf. Reglá, *op. cit.*, p. 80, and Chacón y Calvo, *op. cit.*, p. 142.
[8] Cf. Reglá, *op. cit.*, p. 80.
[9] In his *Tentativa para una lengua general* (ca. 1760), MSS of which are preserved at the Biblioteca Nacional and the Real Academia Española in Madrid, he writes: "... muchos han sido los autores que tentaron la lengua universal... Yo prosigo con mi sistema general de reducirlo todo a lo más sencillo y natural. ...que abrace las cosas que Dios ha criado, dejando las cosas que el capricho humano o fabricó o fingió" (cf. Lázaro Carreter, *op. cit.*, pp. 97, 118-119).

sions and anecdotes suggestive of the medieval chroniclers he admired and whose works he strove to rescue from oblivion; they all partake of the same "cumulative" quality we tend to associate with the Peninsular *crónicas generales* and coincide with Sarmiento's liberal interpretation of what was to be considered literature: "costumbres, etiquetas, ceremonias, juegos, supersticiones, vulgaridades que se practican en diferentes sitios de España: refranes, frases, dichos y hechos que hoy se aplican a otros y de los que hay noticias en autores antiguos." [10]

Nowhere was Sarmiento's interest in oral literature better expressed than in his tireless investigation of Galician music, poetry and dialects which merged to form for him a cultural "whole." Not for nothing has he been called "el primer regionalista gallego," and all his concern for early Galician literature and folklore is initially motivated by a profound interest in the origins of the Galician tongue and its historical development in poetry and prose, a pattern of thought that guides his research in the general area of Peninsular medieval studies. [11] In fact, Sarmiento's *Estudio sobre el origen y formación de la lengua gallega* (finally published by Editorial Nova in Buenos Aires, 1943) probably influenced Mayáns' contemporary studies in Castilian and Valencian, especially his *Diccionario castellano-valenciano*. [12] So emotionally involved was Sarmiento with his Galician heritage that he undertook to compose verses in "Gallego," and sang centuries-old poetry in that language to the accompaniment of the various string instruments that hung in his cell, once again anticipating the attitudes and aesthetic inclinations of the nineteenth century Romantics, especially the creators of the so-called Galician Renaissance. He urged that the Spanish archives be combed for specimens of early medieval lyrics "que están lidiando con la carcoma, y polilla en los rincones," this in his little-known *Memorias para la historia de la poesía y poetas españoles* (his only work published posthumously by his abbey in 1775), the first formal treatise in Spanish to examine the sources of Peninsular poetry and actually written (1745) years before the appearance of Luis Josef Velásquez'

---

[10] Cf. Chacón y Calvo, *op. cit.*, p. 148.
[11] *Ibid.*, p. 119.
[12] Cf. Del Río, *op. cit.*, p. 29.

Orígenes de la poesía castellana (1754) and Tomás Antonio Sánchez' Poesías anteriores al siglo XV (1779-1790). [13] Yet it is the Memorias which first speak to us of one of the oldest genres of Peninsular lyric poetry, the Galician cantigas de amigo, Sarmiento already stressing the inherently "lyric" nature of those former Celts now settled in northwestern Spain whose women, in direct contrast to the masculine-inspired verse of Castile and other regions, seem most responsible for the creation of these traditional love lyrics and their musical accompaniment. [14] Similarly, Sarmiento hypothesizes a Peninsular Arabic origin for most lyric verse in Spain and France (he did not need to know of the muwaššahas and jarchas to suggest that lyric poetry flourished in Spain three hundred years earlier than in France), assuming that the French availed temselves of the talents of Spanish poets who served as intermediaries, and, in a mental observation worthy of Américo Castro, defines just who these "Spanish poets" might be: "... no es del caso que los Españoles fuesen Mahometanos, Judíos, Apóstatas, malos, o buenos Christianos, como fuesen singulares en la Poesía rimada, en esta, u en otra lengua." [15]

Sarmiento's poetical aperçus are not confined to the purely lyrical zone. Alluding to the evolutionary character of the romances which have come down to us from the Siglo de Oro, and looking forward to the more specialized epic-ballad studies of Milá y Fontanals and Menéndez y Pelayo, he sees the lyrical romance as a derived form of the oral-anonymous epic tradition of the twelfth century that eventually "deteriorated" into the prose chronicle or libro de caballerías but which ultimately acquires its generic status from the poems of Homer himself. [16] This generic continuity between epic (or epic-ballad) and prose romance also marks his interest in other examples of chivalric fiction (we shall soon see it applied to the Amadís de Gaula), especially the Historia (not Poema) de Ruy Díaz de Vivar o del Cid Campeador, an extensive abstract of which he copies in 1750 (twenty-nine years

---

[13] For the Memorias, I have used the modern edition (Buenos Aires: Emecé, 1942).
[14] Ibid., p. 169.
[15] Ibid., p. 68.
[16] Ibid., pp. 169 and 172. Cf. too pp. 40 and 47.

before the publication of the poem by T. A. Sánchez!) and comments upon, together with abstracts of Berceo's poems (he had devoted a whole section of his *Memorias* to "El Poeta Castellano D. Gonzalo de Berceo, Benedictino," judging him to be the most archaic stylist in the Castilian language long before the Spanish Romantics discovered the primitive charm of their earliest-known poet) and a Castilian *Libro del Tesoro* of Brunetto Latini, whose thirteenth century lexicon had begun to fascinate him. It was during this period (1745-1750) that Sarmiento's interest in medieval language and literature was probably at its peak, [17] and his continued use of the word *historia* (several contemporary critics had applied it similarly), rather than *poema,* to describe the Poem of the Cid, doubtlessly bears out his own broad interpretation of epic *(épica),* chronicle *("chronica")* and chivalric romance *(libro de caballerías)* as belonging to the same literary species (i. e., the *historia*) which assumed different guises throughout the Middle Ages.

This panoramic view of the entire corpus of chivalric literature, both epic verse and prose romance, characterizes Sarmiento's unpublished essay on the *Amadís* entitled *Disertación sobre el Amadís de Gaula,* which I "discovered" at the Boston Public Library. Actually, according to a note sent by Pascual de Gayangos to George Ticknor and printed in the *Catalogue of the Spanish Library and of the Portuguese Books Bequeathed by George Ticknor to the Boston Public Library* (Boston, Printed by Order of the Trustees, 1879, p. 473), the *Disertación,* MS no. D. 6, forty-eight pages long, originally formed part of a more extensive unpublished essay entitled *La vida y escritos de Miguel de Cervantes Saavedra.* As a matter of interest, I found another note signed by "P. de G." inserted in the MS; it reads: "Esta disertación sobre el *Amadís de Gaula* compuesta por el famoso Padre Sarmiento existe original en la Biblioteca del Marqués de Villafranca entre otras obras suyas que todas hacen 22 tomos en folio." In other words, our MS is probably only a copy of the original still preserved in Spain.

---

[17] Cf. Chacón y Calvo, *op. cit.,* p. 149.

Except for the brief mention of the *Amadís* by the Portuguese Diogo Barbosa Machado and the Spanish Nicolás Antonio and Juan Antonio Pellicer, Sarmiento's essay (written after 1759, a date appearing on page 19 of the text) is the only extensive work of the eighteenth century dealing with Montalvo's book; indeed, it was probably the only such work written before Gayangos' "Discurso preliminar" to the *Amadís* appeared in 1857.[18] Like Gayangos, Sarmiento attempts to place the *Amadís* within the broad scope of Spanish chivalric literature which he separates into four stages or epochs. The first of these is characterized by the presence and influence of the *Historia Karoli et Rotholandi*, better known as the *Pseudo-Turpin*, throughout the eleventh and twelfth centuries; the second is the cycle of Crusades romances most typified in Spain by the thirteenth century prose tale, *La gran conquista de Ultramar;* the third encompasses the totally fanciful tales of the fourteenth and fifteenth centuries centering about "Héroes fingidos" or "Caballeros andantes" of which Amadís is the prime example; finally, we have the most lofty but genuinely human chivalric tale which ironically breaks with the past tradition of "pure" epic-romance and creates the new realistic mode, *Don Quijote de la Mancha.*

Interestingly enough, Sarmiento's use of the "epic mode" to define the ultimate source of all prose romance and, more specifically, Cervantes' novel, antedates Vicente de los Ríos' similar interpretation of the *Quijote's* "true" literary origins.[19] For Sar-

---

[18] Barbosa Machado mentions Vasco de Lobeira as the probable creator of the *Amadís* in his *Bibliotheca lusitana historica, critica, e cronologica* (Lisboa: I. Rodrigues, 1752), III, 775-776; Nicolás Antonio mentions both Vasco de Lobeira and Montalvo in his *Bibliotheca Hispana Nova* (Madrid: J. Ibarra, 1783), I, 515, II, 322 and *Bibliotheca Hispana Vetus* (Madrid: J. Ibarra, 1788), II, 105: Pellicer, under the heading "Del libro de Amadís de Gaula," discusses some basic points regarding the *Amadís'* origin in the introduction to his edition of: *El ingenioso hidalgo Don Quixote de la Mancha* (Madrid: Gabriel de Sancho, 197), I, XXXIX-LI. Gayangos' "Discurso preliminar" is really the introduction to his editions of the *Amadís* and *Esplandián* in *Libros de caballerías* (Madrid: Biblioteca de Autores Españoles, 1857), vol. XL, pp. III-LXII.

[19] For De los Ríos' interpretation of the *Quijote* as an epic, see his "Vida de Cervantes Saavedra y análisis del Quixote" in vol. I of *El ingenioso hidalgo don Quixote de la Mancha*, ...Nueva ed. Corr. por la Real academia española (Madrid: J. Ibarra, 1780), 4 vols.

miento the epic, be it verse or prose, lies at the center of man's being — it appeals to Youth's yearning for ideals and acts of heroism embodied in men with whom it can identify. Such, says he, was the cause of the tremendous wave of Carolingian epic that took hold of France, Spain and Italy in the eleventh and twelfth centuries. Such, too, was the origin of the romances surrounding Godefroid de Bouillon and the other heroes of the French campaigns in Palestine. But when false "literary" crusades were forcibly substituted for the historical Crusades, since Youth's thirst for these heroic tales is naturally unquenchable, the moral value of these tales began to be seriously undermined, and hence commenced the proliferation of a base literary form, "para que más se radicase en la juventud el error, la ociosidad e ignorancia y aun el vicio" (pages 14-15). In his *Memorias* (page 170), too, Sarmiento had viewed the *libro de caballerías* as a corruptive force in Spanish morality and, indeed, contributory to a false Spanish historical perspective: "Todos los referidos Poemas, aunque han dado algún ayre de valor a nuestra Poesía, han hecho mucho daño a nuestra Historia. ... los incautos creyeron ser historia lo que era fábula; y al contrario, ... han ocasionado que algunos discretos creyesen ser fábula lo que ha sido historia." In this area, Sarmiento is unlike those future Romantics who were to renovate the medieval chivalric tale and calls to mind the similar "rational" invectives against the genre by the sixteenth century Spanish moralists.

Sarmiento focuses attention on the *Pseudo-Turpin* as the real forerunner of the *Amadís* and all prose chivalric romance, thus anticipating Menéndez y Pelayo's more critical opinion of the next century. [20] We might remember here that Sarmiento had once been abbot of the monastery at Ripoll, that an intensely strong Carolingian oral and written tradition had attached itself to this abbey where a series of eleventh and twelfth century chronicles known as the *Rivipullenses* sought to connect Charlemagne with

---

[20] In his *Orígenes de la novela*, Menéndez y Pelayo writes: "...la *Crónica de Turpín*, que es uno de los libros apócrifos más famosos del mundo, y sin género de duda el primer libro de caballerías en prosa, aunque no vulgar, sino latina y de clerecía" (Madrid: Espasa-Calpe, 1946), vol. I, p. 210.

the founding of Ripoll. So, too, the latter houses one of the only two specimens preserved of the entire *Codex Calixtinus*, of which the *Pseudo-Turpin* forms the fourth book. By far the largest portion of this Latin chronicle consists of legends based on vernacular epics now lost but which obviously circulated in written as well as oral form in the last part of the eleventh century and first part of the twelfth.[21] Sarmiento correctly interprets the *Pseudo-Turpin* as literary propaganda contrived by some Frenchman of ca. 1090 to foment his country's political and military activities in the Peninsula. While he could not then know that the chronicle had been revised by Aimeri Picaud (ca. 1145) to blend with the rest of the *Codex* and hence present a falsely historical picture of Charlemagne's dual role in Spain as crusader and pilgrim to Santiago de Compostela, he was vehement against the French and Spanish for believing that Archbishop Turpin, dead hundreds of years before "his" work was supposedly written, could have composed such obvious falsehoods. For him there is no doubt that the "Turpin" to whom the work is fraudulently ascribed is actually Tilpin, for whom Charlemagne obtained the pallium from Pope Hadrian in 774, and "el cual ni fue Secretario ni compañero de Carlos Magno, ha sido docto y venerable." Hence Sarmiento is one of the earliest critics to equate Turpin with the historical Archbishop "Tilpinus" of Reims, so described by Flodoard in his *Historia Remensis Ecclesiae* some time before 948 [22]

Recognizing that the *Pseudo-Turpin* had always been circulating in variant MSS, he incorrectly assumes that medieval authors, like those Renaissance Spanish dramatists and poets who frequently based their themes on matter preserved in the *crónicas generales*, similarly exploited this chronicle for their epics and prose romances. While it is true that Nicolás de Piamonte's prose *Hystoria del emperador Carlomagno y de los doze pares de Francia* (1525) does indeed reproduce large portions of the *Pseudo-Turpin*, the latter, in Latin, had actually prosified verse epics originally dependent on an oral tradition, a process not dissimilar to that imposed on early medieval Latin literature by the equally

---

[21] See B. Sholod, *Charlemagne in Spain: The Cultural Legacy of Roncesvalles* (Geneva: Droz, 1966), pp. 111, 117, and 199.

[22] *Ibid.*, p. 28.

"authoritative" accounts of the Trojan War by Dictys of Crete and Dares the Phrygian, and possibly influential in creating such similar Latinized accounts of the French wars in Spain as a *Pseudo-Alcuin* or a *Pseudo-Gilles*, both contemporaneous with the *Pseudo-Turpin*.[23] Sarmiento is quick to point out that this prose chronicle, like the eleventh and twelfth century epics, is a pseudo-historical elaboration of Charlemagne's activity in Spain three hundred years before, and hence initiates that mixture of truth and fiction that denotes the "epic" quality of much chivalric romance and epitomizes the generic character of *Don Quijote*.

For Sarmiento the Carolingian epic, so "naturalized" in Spain by the twelfth century, was a device employed by the French to support their territorial claims in the Peninsula; this is essentially the same thesis he propounds regarding the origins of the *Pseudo-Turpin* (cf. above). Hence all the "conquests" attributed here and in the epics to Charles are actually those made by the Christian armies in Spain towards the end of the eleventh century and the Christian Emperor's dual concern for the "liberation" of Spain from Arab rule and the protection of Saint James' tomb is all too consistent with the policies of Alfonso VI of Castile and Alfonso I of Aragon to be a matter of coincidence. If anything, the French were clearly vying with the Spaniards for domination of the Peninsula. So effective had their propaganda in this direction become, that the Spaniards gradually rallied around their own epic tradition and created two "Anti-Rolands," Rodrigo de Vivar and Bernardo del Carpio, the latter serving as the basis for a whole new branch of Carolingian lore in Spain. Sarmiento had pointed these factors out in the *Memorias* too (pages 169-170), but it is here that he draws considerable attention to the oral Carolingian tradition still very much alive in his own day. He recalls hearing ballads of Roland, Oliver, and Bernardo sung by "mujeres y niños," "mozas de cántaro," and "mozos de mula," and mentions the influence exerted by the *Pseudo-Turpin* over the folk mentality of the populace (this was particularly true of Galicia, owing to the cult of Santiago), eager to hear "esta solemne patraña..., como historia verdadera y escrita con mitra y báculo por un Arzobispo, compañero de Carlo Magno y testigo de vista."

---

[23] *Ibid.*, pp. 21-22 and 115-116.

Just as the *Pseudo-Turpin* returns to centuries past for the bulk of its legendary material, so too *La gran conquista de Ultramar* reflects several periods of "crusades," including the actual Crusades of the twelfth and thirteenth centuries. Sarmiento, not yet aware of those "discoveries" in the epic to be made in the following century, once more fails to realize that much of the work consists of prosifications of epics, some of which probably circulated in oral form long before they were written down — hence the apparent "falsification" of the past by some unknown hand. Delighted with the thirteenth century Castilian of the manuscript at his disposal, as well as the actual manuscript itself, he points out that *La gran conquista* was one of several important prose works translated from the French during and immediately after the reign of Alfonso X. What Spanish poets had previously done with the French verse epics, Peninsular authors, still anonymous, were now doing with the prose tales. Yet Sarmiento, like so many critics after him, refuses to believe that the translation of *La gran conquista* was actually accomplished during the lifetime of the Rey Sabio (died 1284), but that it had merely been initiated by the latter and completed when so much other chivalric romance, such as the prose *Alexandre* and the *Historia troyana*, were already in full blossom.

Interesting is Sarmiento's discovery, antedating that of the nineteenth century critics, that the "frame" of *La gran conquista* is composed of a translation of William of Tyre's Latin account of the Crusades: "Comencé á leer... y á pocos capítulos que leí... noté que ya había leido aquel contesto en otra parte. Tardé poco en conocer que lo había leido en Willelmo o Guillermo Tirio; así saqué en limpio que la Conquista de Ultramar era traducción de la Guerra sagrada de Guillel-[sic] Tirio." Sarmiento stresses the anonymous and cumulative quality (a projection of his own "literary" inclinations?) of both the French and Spanish versions of the work, observing that this was to become characteristic of all fourteenth century chivalric prose, adding that such an interpolated tale as that of the *Caballero del Cisne* was at least as "chivalric" in context as was the soon-to-be conceived *Amadís de Gaula* or the much imitated "chivalric" chapters (based, as we now know, on former epics) of the older *Pseudo-Turpin*. So he writes: "Así jamás asentiré á que Amadís de Gaula y su libro haya sido el principio de los Libros de Caballerías."

The *Amadís* for Sarmiento is the best example of the combined spirit of epic and lyric poetry transmuted into the newly evolved prose of the fourteenth century that was gradually replacing the older "heroic" and "refined" genres among the new reading public. Even before declaring, "El Libro de Amadís es un Poema en prosa," he draws attention to the falsely-inspired crusading character of the work that doubtless sought to perpetuate the spirit of the more "genuine" Crusades romances, and to the fanciful geography so typical of the epic and sometimes apparently based on the Oriental onomastics made popular by the Crusades Cycle. Thus the very name "Amadís" would evoke the ancient Persian tribe of "Amadizes" mentioned by the Portuguese Pedro Texeyra in his *Relaciones* which describe the old Oriental kingdoms. Oddly enough, another primitive Persian tribe described here are the *Gaules* or *Gaulas*. Sarmiento therefore concludes: "El Autor del Amadís, o estuvo en la Persia, u leyó que hacia el seno Pérsico había pueblos Amadizes y Gaulas, y que eran muy valerosos y guerreros; así se valió de esos nombres para titular al héroe de su novela. Esto es Amadiz de Gaula, como que había nacido en los pueblos Amadizes y se había criado y vivido entre ellos y entre los Gaules para incorporar en ese fingido héroe el valor de los dos pueblos." He suggests, however, a possible confusion between the name of the Persian tribe and "Gallia" or France, since so much of the action in the *Amadís* takes place here, the latter hypothesis now being fairly well proved by Professor Place. [24] So, too, "Amadís" or "Amadiz" may depend on the Latin "amare," although the novel itself says that the hero was named for a saint and commentators have indicated both Saints Amandus and Amadeus as the saint in question. [25]

As for the name of the heroine, Oriana, Sarmiento proposes a Galician origin, for in the vicinity of Valdeorras the girls who traditionally searched for the gold granites alongside the riverbeds

---

[24] See Edwin B. Place, "Amadís of Gaul, Wales, or What," *Hispanic Review*, XXIII (1955), 99-107.

[25] Cf. G. S. Williams, "The Amadís Question," *Revue Hispanique*, XXI (1909), 50-51.

were wont to be called "orianas" or "ourianas" — and, indeed, it must be borne in mind that Oriana had "golden" hair. Throughout the seventeenth century the majority of Portuguese critics had attributed the *Amadís*' paternity to Vasco de Lobeira, who lived during the reign of "el Rei Dom Fernando" (1367-83) and was knighted by João I on the day of the famous battle of Aljubarrota (1385). No allusion to a Portuguese version of the *Amadís* exists prior to the fifteenth century, and while it is possible that such a version may actually have existed (Sarmiento feels that the Portuguese assertions rest solely on "su nacional pasión"), it does not necessarily follow that this version and that of Lobeira are one and the same. [26] Nor do we know the language in which Lobeira may have written his work. Was it Portuguese? Was it Galician? The *Pseudo-Turpin* and Arthurian prose romances were circulating in the latter language. Why could not some Peninsular imitator (Sarmiento, like most critics after him, discounts the possibility of a French origin for the *Amadís*) of the new chivalric mode have chosen to compose his own work in his native language? Our critic looks to his native Galicia, which preferred to ally itself with the Portuguese Ferdinand when Enrique II of Castile came to the throne, for the birthplace of Amadís. At that time thousands of Galician knights, including a number of Lobeiras, passed over into Portugal to pay hommage to Ferdinand. Many chose to stay there indefinitely. Sarmiento suspects that Vasco may have been among them. In any case, the surname "Lobeira," as used in both Galicia and Castile, would seem to have its source in the Castle or Tower of Lobeira, not far from the towns of So-Lobeira and Villagarcía on the Galician "ría" of Padrón. It is interesting that neither the *Noviliario* of the Conde D. Pedro nor the *Linhagens* of Antonio de Lima makes any mention of the name Lobeira, which is most irregular regarding a name supposedly "native" to Portugal. "El caso es que aunque el Amadís se haya fingido en Portugal, el autor no ha sido Portugués, sino un caballero Gallego, si el autor se llama Lobeira."

Sarmiento is right when he suggests it more likely that the Castilians would sooner have accepted a work composed in

---

[26] Cf. Place, *Amadís de Gaula*, vol. III, p. 925.

Galician or Galician-Castilian than one written in pure Portuguese, which they only looked upon as "un subdialecto champurrado de la lengua Gallega, dependiente sólo de la Latina." Not only had the Galicians become deeply attached to the Carolingian and Arthurian verse and prose romances, but they alone seem to have possessed the oldest tradition of lyrical poetry in the Peninsula, a fact already alluded to by Silius Italicus "en siglos más remotos," and evidently appreciated by Alfonso X in his choice of Galician as the language in which to express the florid sentiments of his *Cantigas de Santa María*. So imbedded in the soul of Galicia is the lyric strain that not only its men but also its rustic women, right down to the time of Sarmiento, could "instinctively" compose their own lyrics and music. Without going so far to demonstrate the lyrical capacities of the people who may have created Amadís, Menéndez y Pelayo likewise hints at a possible Portuguese or Galician origin for our tale, owing to this general region's close affinity with the Celtic nations, the "naturalization" of the French chivalric material here, and a comprehensible desire to make up for never having created a national epic of its own. [27] Angel Rosenblat, medievalist and author of the best modernized version of the *Amadís*, likewise suggests that its creator was "algún autor occidental, gallego o portugués— como prolongación de los poemas y novelas francesas del ciclo bretón." [28] Highly interesting was the "Galician" theory of García de la Riega who, on studying the onomastics alone of the *Amadís*, came to the conclusion that nearly all of the names of places and persons in the book are distinctly of Galician origin. [29] Most extraordinary along this line of thinking have been the recent findings of scholars who have studied the language of Rodríguez de Montalvo's "revised" Renaissance *Amadís* (after 1492, based on some precursor) as well as the fragments of an early fifteenth century manuscript which may or may not have been the same version upon which Montalvo relied for his own work. In either case, both Montalvo's

---

[27] See Menéndez y Pelayo, *op. cit.*, p. 276.
[28] See *Amadís de Gaula, novela de caballerías*, refundida y modernizada por Ángel Rosenblat (Buenos Aires: Losada, 1940), p. 9.
[29] See Celso García de la Riega, *Literatura galaica, el Amadís de Gaula* (Madrid: E. Arias, 1909), 194 pp.

text and the manuscript fragments reveal a preponderance of northwestern Peninsular lexical forms; neither version appears to revert to an original exclusively Portuguese or Castilian. Place writes: "Lo único que parece legítimo deducir es la intervención de alguna persona de larga residencia en la región fronteriza del extremo oriente de Galicia o del extremo occidente del territorio leonés-asturiano. Esta persona dejó en la obra bastantes huellas indicativas del habla de dicha región fronteriza; en efecto,... parece lícito conjeturar... que más bien que simple copista fuese el autor primitivo." [30] In other words, it is highly possible that the judgment of our intuitive eighteenth century scholar may indeed rest on certain insights rather than just another effort to prove the Galician origin of one more important Spanish literary genre.

With regard to the *Amadís*' literary classification or "genre," Sarmiento again indicates the general rise of prose in the fourteenth century, the latter period inviting the creation of two forms of non-poetical narrative— "chrónicas (historias) verdaderas y fingidas" and "novelas" or "apólogos y diálogos" (he never uses the word "cuento") of an amorous, political, moral, symbolic or alegorical nature. The popular animal tales, for example, would belong to the second category, the *libros de caballerías* to the first, although their "epic" character also stamps them as "poems in prose." Earlier, in his *Memorias*, when briefly alluding to the *Amadís*, Sarmiento had written: "Generalmente se coloca ácia la mitad de él [siglo 14]... la famosa Chrónica, ó Historia del Caballero Andante Amadís de Gaula, que ha sido el origen, y fuente de todos los demás Libros de Caballería, que después se escribieron en España, Francia, Italia, etc." (page 228). It is interesting to see the words "novela" and "apólogo" applied to non-historical and non-"epic" prose fiction, whereas those works which imply some historical or semi-historical foundation or "epic" character are invariably designated as "chrónicas" or "historias." The latter are the works which led to the creation of Cervantes' novel and the new "historical" or "epic" mode in modern letters.

---

[30] Place, *Amadís de Gaula*, vol. II, p. 597. Cf. too A. Rodríguez-Moñino et al., "El primer manuscrito del *Amadís de Gaula*," *Boletín de la Real Academia Española*, XXVI (1956), 199-225.

On a very subjective level, Sarmiento much prefers the "*chrónicas* generales" and moral and historical works of such authors as Pero López de Ayala and Alonso de Cartagena to the chivalric novels of the fourteenth and fifteenth centuries. For him, the sole value in wading through the "quiméricas composiciones" of this long period is the systematic study of their language, based, of course, on their chronological order, to determine the evolution of "las voces, y de las frases Españolas." Yet unlike those sixteenth century moralists who preached against the genre (see above), Sarmiento is not unaware of its charms. He realized that this chivalric fad, in which the forces of evil constantly yielded to those of virtue and righteousness, not only exalted the basic political and religious principles for which the Reyes Católicos had captured Granada, but also coincided with the marvelous New World discoveries and explorations made in the name of Spain by her *conquistadores*. Certain human qualities of the *Amadís*, stressing lofty ideals of love and loyalty, the latter dispelling the feudal concepts sustained by the Breton and Carolingian cycles, make of the work a veritable manual or "guide" for chivalric practices and ideas on kinship, sacrifice, faith, etc. And so, with such materials as these, "pudo el autor del Amadís de Gaula atraer los idiotas á su lectura, y de ese libro, como de un caballo Troyano, salió toda la canalla de la descendencia de Amadís de Gaula, y si Dios y Cervantes no hubiesen atajado ese chorrillo, aun hoy se multiplicarían esos ineptos y perniciosos libros." Sarmiento has spoken.

DRAMATIC TEXTS AND *ARS DICTAMINIS* IN MEDIEVAL ITALY

By Sandro Sticca
State University of New York

Historical and literary research on the relations and influences of one work of art upon another usually tends to be an excursus into daring and abstract generalizations whenever the investigation is not sustained by a critical and objective method that relates all comparative analyses to a cultural and thematic unity existing between the works under consideration. The existence in every epoch of a common cultural denominator would obviously facilitate the undertaking of such a research.

The purpose of this paper is to show the intimate connection existing between the twelfth-century Montecassino Latin Passion and the *Officium Quarti Militis*, a Passion fragment of the fourteenth century preserved in Sulmona, Italy, by giving emphasis to textual affinities, monastic ties, and their reliance on the poetical and rhetorical rules in vigor during the twelfth century.

The present investigation into dramatic influences is justifiable by a cultural and thematic unity between the two plays, a unity that we would call Catholic, and by the fact that these two productions share a technical-philological medium: the Latin language.

The Montecassino text is not complete: it records the events of the Passion from Judas' bargain to the Crucifixion and the

Planctus of the Virgin Mary.[1] The primary importance of the text is that it is a century older than any other Western Passion play yet known; paleographical evidence places it, in fact, in the twelfth century. The fourteenth-century Passion fragment known as the *Officium Quarti Militis*[2] was so named because it provides only the role of a subordinate character, the 'fourth soldier,' together with certain cues. The *Officium Quarti Militis*' distinctive position in the genesis and development of the medieval drama derives from the fact that, contrary to traditional and authoritative medieval scholarship,[3] it is not an isolated dramatic text but an integral part of the extensive twelfth-century Latin Passion play of Montecassino.

A comparison of the Montecassino Passion with the Sulmona fragment reveals indeed a close kinship. The Montecassino text not only supplies a number of missing scenes — Judas' bargain with Caiaphas, a few episodes in the betrayal scene, Peter's denial, the repentance of Judas, and that of the maid of the wife of Pilate — but it provides in addition the full text for passages alluded to in the fragment merely by incipits. By combining the two texts we get an extensive play of 543 lines, 317 coming from the earlier play, 226 from the fragment, with some 60 lines common to both; so that the earlier Passion from Montecassino offers us 257 new verses.

I have had occasion elsewhere to comment on the textual similarities between the two plays;[4] of greater importance, however, is a consideration of the monastic ties between the two communities for they are the principal agent in providing a logical and plausible reason for those similarities.

---

[1] Sandro Sticca, "The Priority of the Montecassino Passion Play," in *Latomus*, XX (1961), 381-391, 568-574, 827-839; also D. M. Inguanez, "Un Dramma della Passione del Secolo XII" in *Miscellanea Cassinese*, XII (1936), 7-38; reprinted, with the addition of the Sulmona fragment in *Miscellanea Cassinese*, XVII (1939), 7-50. Paolo Toschi, *Le Origini del teatro italiano* (Torino, 1955), 667-670.

[2] For text see Karl Young, *The Drama of the Medieval Church*, 2 vols. (Oxford, 1933), I, 701-8; or Inguanez, *Miscellanea Cassinese* (1939).

[3] Young, *op. cit.*, I, 537; Hardin Craig, *English Religious Drama* (Oxford, 1955), p. 46.

[4] Sandro Sticca, *The Latin Passion Play: Its Origins and Development* (Albany, 1970), pp. 84-88.

Any scholar of the Middle Ages is aware of the conscious transmission and utilization of ancient and contemporary literature from one monastic house to another and of the fact that this dissemination took place throughout Western Europe.[5] Students of the history of the religious drama have already remarked on its international character and on the fact it developed more or less contemporaneously in the various nations of the Catholic Western world. But if their studies have provided comprehensive and competent analyses of the dramatic development of singular countries, they have nevertheless failed to throw light on the influence of one country upon the other. In the study of medieval dramaturgy fruitful results are still to be achieved by investigating the means of communication among the various monastic houses, which were normally the places where the religious dramas were composed and copied and by determining the extent of the dissemination of the plays among the various countries. This methodology has immediate validity when applied to explain the textual similarities between the Montecassino Latin Passion and the Sulmona passion fragment from Abruzzi.

The abbey of Montecassino had kept for centuries close ties with Abruzzi through its dependent monastic houses;[6] one of the most famous beacons of Benedictine monachism in Abruzzi was the Abbazia of S. Clemente da Casauria. Founded in 822 by the Emperor Ludovico II, located near the historical Tocco da Casauria at a distance of a few miles from Sulmona, the abbey became a most important intellectual and religious center, particularly in the twelfth century, when, under the able hands of abbot Leonate, and his successor Gioele, it was completely reconstructed.[7] The *Chronicon Casauriense* written at the monastery, by Frate Giovanni di Berardo and decorated by Maestro Rustico at the instance of abbot Leonate, remains one of the

---

[5] Paul Lehman, "The Benedictine Order and the Transmission of the Literature of Ancient Rome in the Middle Ages," in *Erforschung des Mittelalters*, 3 (1960), 173-83.

[6] Inguanez, *op. cit.*, p. 17; Enrico Carusi, "Il '*Memoratorium*' dell'abate Bertario sui possessi Cassinesi nell'Abruzzo teatino, e uno sconosciuto vescovo di Chieti del 930," in *Casinensia* I (Monsecassino, 1929), 97-9.

[7] Benedetto Ventura, *San Clemente a Casauria* (Pescara, 1967), pp. 12-23.

richest mines of information on Benedictine monachism. Special relations were entertained between St. Peter Celestine — the founder, near Sulmona, in 1285, of the Badia of S. Spirito del Morrone — and Montecassino. [8] In addition, we know that the Celestines were followers of the rule of St. Benedict. [9] Dom Tommaso Leccisotti, archivista of Montecassino's monastic library, has recently indicated the importance for the study of the history of Montecassino of the monastic documents belonging to the Badia of S. Spirito del Morrone. [10] Given the relatively geographic vicinity of the Montecassino and Sulmona monastic houses, and the dissemination of Benedictinism in Abruzzi, it is not too difficult to imagine the exchange between them of ancient, biblical, patristic, and dramatic texts.

Even more striking in the relationship between the two plays is their preoccupation, for different reasons, with twelfth-century poetical and rhetorical modes. The Passion of Montecassino is in fact written in the type of Latin Sequence verse called *versus tripartitus caudatus*, the invention of which is attributed to Adam of Saint Victor (1110-1192).

Although Sequences were notably employed to celebrate canonical seasons, it is particularly in the twelfth century that one observes a growing relationship between Latin hymnody and the arts, the more obvious being the one between the sequence and the liturgical drama. Now the most popular and typical of the rhythmic and rhymed sequences of the twelfth century is precisely the trochaic stanza of two eight syllables couplets, with a third trochaic line of seven syllables as employed by the Montecassino author.

As Sequences were becoming quite prominent in liturgical dramatic representations, it is not surprising that our unknown dramatist should have chosen for the redaction of his drama the most widely used sequence form of his time, particularly since the monks of Montecassino distinguished themselves in the *artes*

---

[8] Inguanez, p. 17.

[9] Ignazio Baldelli, "La lauda e i disciplinati," *Rassegna della Letteratura Italiana*, 64 (1960), p. 401; Arsenio Frugoni, *Celestiniana* (Roma, 1954), p. 129.

[10] Tommaso Leccisotti, ed. *Abbazia di Montecassino. I Regesti dell'Archivio*, IV vols. (Roma, 1966), II, p. xlvi; III, pp. xii-xvii.

dictaminis and *cursus rhythmorum* which dominate the rhetoric of the twelfth century.

The invention of the Sequence is usually associated with Notker Balbulus (ca. 840-912), a monk of St. Gall, [11] although some question it. [12] After a transitional stage during the eleventh century, in which accentual meter, assonance and rudimentary rhyme were replaced by regular accentual meter, the Sequence reached the highest perfection with Adam and his school in the twelfth century, [13] and his type of Sequence, in particular, "became a prime favourite with other Sequence-writers, and remained so as long as Sequences continued to be written." [14]

This favorite strophe of Adam of St. Victor is the six-line stanza of accentual trochaic dimeters, of which lines 3 and 6 are catalectic in stanzas 1,2,3,4,9,10, acatalectic in 5,6,7,8. The rhyme, too, is usually: aabccd. L'Abbé E. Misset in *Les Proses d'Adam de Saint-Victor*, after having stated that Adam's verse rests on the triple basis of accent, syllabism, and rhyme, writes that

> les mots ne doivent y être considérés que comme une suite de syllabes accentuées et de syllabes non accentuées. S'ils sons monosyllabiques, ils prennent ou ne prennent pas l'accent *ad libitum*. S'ils ont deux syllabes, ils sont toujours accentués sur la pénultième. S'ils comptent plus de deux syllabes, ils reçoivent l'accent sur la pénultième, quand elle est longue, et sur l'antépénultième, quand la pénultième est brève. Dans ce cas, de deux syllabes, avant et après l'accent principal, ces mots reçoivent en autre un accent secondaire. [15]

---

[11] Heinrich Husmann, "Die St. Galler Sequenztradition bei Notker und Ekkehard" *Acta Musicologica*, XXVI-XXIX (1954-57), 6-18; J. F. Raby, *Christian Latin Poetry* (Oxford, 1927), p. 211; W. von den Steinen, "Die Angänge der Sequenze-dichtung" *Zeitschrift für schwizeren Kirchengeschichte*, XL (1946), 190-212, 241-268; XLI (1947) 19-48, 122-162.

[12] Egon Wellesz, "The Origin of Sequences and Tropes" in his *Eastern Elements in Western Chant* (Oxford, 1947), 153-74, pp. 158-9.

[13] Paul Zumthor, *Histoire littéraire de la France médiévale. VIe-XIVe siècles* (Paris, 1954), p. 139.

[14] F. Brittain, *The Medieval Latin and Romance Lyric to A. D. 1300* (Cambridge, 1951), p. 15.

[15] E. Misset, *Les proses d'Adam de Saint-Victor* (Paris, 1900), p. 29.

These are Adam's simple metrical rules. Now if we take for comparison one strophe from one of Adam's of S. Victor's hymns and one from the Montecassino Passion, we shall see how well the above rules apply. Before proceeding into the comparison it seems opportune to observe, however, that the Montecassino dramatist appears to have chosen Adams favorite Sequence-type with the intent of emulating by means of the dramatic form that exposition of the Scriptural truth so eminently practiced by Adam in his sequences. Ironically, our dramatist uses Adam's favorite Sequential form to dramatize the Passion of Christ, the one central Christian truth which Adam failed to treat in his sequences.

To provide a striking parallel in the comparison, we shall take the last stanza of Adam's hymn *De Trinitate* and one from the Passion of Montecassino.

Adam's *De Trinitate*	Montecassino Passion
Nós ĭn fĭdĕ glórĭĕmŭr	[I]ésŭs dólĭ sémĭnátŏr
Nós ĭn únă módŭlémŭr	Nóstrĕ géntĭs súpplăntátŏr
Fĭdĕĭ cŏnstántĭá:	tétrŏ fráudĭs nómĭné.
Trĭnăe sít laŭs Únĭtátĭ	Múltŏs nóstrŭm íam sĕdúxĭt
Sít ĕt símplăe trinitati	Ín ĕrrórĕm quós pĕrdúxĭt
cóaĕtérnă glóriá. [16]	fráudŭléntŏ nómĭné. [17]

It is obvious from the above that these two stanzas are metrically identical, both in meter and accent. Both are made up of verses which expand into a six-line stanza by doubling the first stave in a riming couplet twice and using the second stave between the two couplets and the riming end. Such is also the scheme of the Montecassino Passion, in general. The redaction of this Passion in the Victorine poetical sequence allows us to observe that although "sequences, such as those by Adam of St. Victor, did not find their way into the drama," [18] nevertheless the Victorine sequence was used for dramatic purposes and to

---

[16] Digby S. Wrangham, *The Liturgical Poetry of Adam of St. Victor*, 3 vols (London, 1881), I, 134.

[17] Inguanez, p. 21.

[18] Rembert Weakland, "The Rhythmic Modes and Medieval Latin Drama", *Journal of the American Musicological Society*, XIV (1961), p. 136.

invalidate the theory that the earliest Passion plays were written in Latin prose.[19]

It is not too surprising that the metrical Sequential type created by Adam in the twelfth century should have been available to the Montecassino author since the monks of that monastery distinguished themselves during the eleventh century in the composition of hymns (abbot Guaiferus, Peter Damian, Alphanus, Alberic of Montecassino being the most prominent)[20] and of the *artes dictaminis* (prose and verse) and *cursus rhythmorum*[21] which dominate the rhetoric of the twelfth century.

The poetic production of the twelfth century appears to have given preeminence particularly to three genres: the hymns, the tropes and the sequences,[22] and the evidence offered by the medieval Latin drama indicates that of these three poetic forms, especially in the twelfth century, it is the sequence which assumes an extraordinary popularity and wider diffusion.

An examination of the medieval drama seems to indicate that it evolved poetically and musically from rudimentary towards more complex rhythmic forms, particularly through the constant utilization of the hymnodic sequential technique.[23] Sequences such as *Victimae paschali laudes*, *Fideles animae*, *Planctus ante nescia*, appear in Latin dramas which exhibit a certain degree of dramatic sophistication both in themselves and through the presence of these lyrical additions.

A much more important reason for the use of the sequence form in the Montecassino Passion can be found in the fact that

---

[19] Eduard Hartl, "Das Drama des Mittelalters" in Wolfgang Stammler's, *Deutsche Philologie im Aufriss*, II (Berlin, 1954), p. 910; Marius Sepet, *Origines catholiques du théâtre moderne* (Paris, 1901), p. 59.

[20] Joseph Szovérffy, "L'hymnologie médiévale: recherches et méthodes" *Cahiers de Civilisation Médiévale*, IVe Année n. 4 (Octobre-Décembre, 1961), pp. 400-1.

[21] D. M. Inguanez and M. H. Willard, *Alberici Casinensis Flores Rhetorici* in *Miscellanea Cassinese*, XIV (1938), 9-59; Charles H. Haskins, "Albericus Casinensis" in *Casinensia*, I (Montecassino, 1929), p. 118; Owen J. Blum, "Alberic of Monte Cassino and the Hymns and Rhythms attributed to Saint Peter Damian", *Traditio*, XII (1956), *passim*, also pp. 124-7.

[22] J. De Ghellinck, *L'Essor de la littérature latine au XIIe siècle*, 2 vols. (Paris, 1946), II, 287.

[23] Giuseppe Vecchi, "Innodia e dramma sacro", *Studi Mediolatini e Volgari*, I-II (1953), 225-237, p. 237.

whereas the Latin hymn was traditionally tied in with daily secular worship and later with canonical monastic hours, the sequence was associated with the celebration of the divine sacrifice, [24] which is also the main theme of the Montecassino Latin Passion play.

Although the Sequence verse form had been traditionally associated with liturgical worship, the anonymous redactor of the Montecassino play seems to have employed the sequential *versus tripartitus caudatus* both because it was the most widely used sequence-form of his time and more particularly because in its rhythmic elegance and metrical precision well resumed the most prominent features of twelfth-century poetical tenets. Edgar de Bruyne has indicated that "l'idéal des poètes du XIIe siècle c'est l'élégance, la grâce, la vénusté fleurie." [25] Matthew of Vendôme, for instance, in his *Ars Versificatoria* states that "non enim aggregatio dictionum, dinumeratio pedum, cognitio temporum facit versum, sed elegans junctura dictionum, expressio proprietarum et observatum uniuscuijusque rei epithetum." [26] Geoffroi of Vinsauf echoes the same sentiments in his *Poetria Nova:*

> Semita versiculi... non vult tam grossa sed ipsas
> voces in forma gracili, ne corpus agreste
> verbi mole sua perturbet et inquinet illum
> vultque venire metrum tamquam domicellula, compto
> crine, nitente gena, subtili corpore, forma
> egregia. Seriem tantae dulcedinis auri
> nescit habere parem jocunda decentia metri. [27]

Matthew of Vendôme, in particular, points out that in a good poem the beauty of thought is sustained by that of the words and by the felicity of expression and that each complements the other for "in metro venustas interioris sententiae et superficialis verborum ornatus et qualitas discendi sese invicem hospitaliter recipiunt." [28]

---

[24] Ruth Ellis Messenger, *The Medieval Latin Hymns* (Washington, 1953), p. 45.

[25] Edgar de Bruyne, *Etudes d'Esthétique Médiévale*, 3 vols. (Brugge, 1946), II, 25.

[26] Edmond Faral, *Les Arts Poétiques du XIIe et du XIIIe siècle* (Paris, 1958), pp. 110-111.

[27] *Ibid.*, p. 254.

[28] *Ibid.*, p. 179.

The verse form chosen by the Montecassino dramatist demands of the poet a rigorous training in rhetoric and a systematic knowledge of all kinds of verbal figures and the ability to use varied patterns of both phrase and sound. The reoccurring rhyme within each stanza requires of the artist a supreme sensitivity to feeling and thought on the one hand, and word and rhyme on the other. The entire development is one of ordered exposition and progressive argumentation. Geoffroi of Vinsauf in his *Documentum de Modo et Arte Dictandi et Versificandi* cogently expresses the architectural and structural desiderata of any work of art: "Tria sunt circa quae cujuslibet operis versatur artificium: principium, progressus, consummatio." [29] He goes on then to indicate the difference, in such a work of art, between "artificial" and "natural" beginning, and states that "principium naturale est quando sermo inde incipit unde res geri incipit." [30]

The Montecassino Latin Passion play in its highly wrought stanzaic form and in its chronological representation of events clearly adheres to the concepts of *principium, progressus* and *consummatio*. The narrative too has a *principium naturale* since the play begins with Judas' betrayal and continues through a natural, progressive and chronological succession of events up to Christ's Crucifixion and Death on the Cross.

Although the Montecassino Passion dramatist's choice of the sequential form was dictated primarily by liturgical and dramatic considerations, there is no doubt that as a poet he adopted the *versus tripartitus caudatus* for it allowed him to combine the beauty of the matter (Christ's Passion) with the rhythmic elegance of the meter and the felicity and freshness of expression which where demanded by twelfth-century Poetics and which such meter best typified.

As a poet he is also one of the best representatives of that sequential liturgical tradition which beginning in the eleventh century with the *Victimae paschali laudes* reached its greatest florescence in the twelfth century where it came to be characterized by rhymed and rhythmic sequences based on regularity of rhythm,

---

[29] *Ibid.*, p. 265.
[30] *Ibid.*

constancy of rhyme in its bisyllabic composition and regularity of caesura at the end.

The sequential versification numbered a kaleidoscopic variety of rimed and rhythmic models such as the *leonini, caudati, claudicantes, alternati, conjugati, reciproci, concatenati*. Its most widely used form, however, particularly in the twelfth century, remained the trochaic stanza of two eight syllables couplets, with a third trochaic line of seven syllables as employed by the Montecassino dramatist.

Whereas the Montecassino text has made use exclusively of the Victorine measure, *versus tripartitus caudatus*, the Sulmona is polymetric. It contains predominantly the above verse form, and it has eight stanzas in hendecasyllabic lines and four in various other meters. There are obvious reasons for this metrical variety. The Sulmona fragment is truly sophisticated and of large proportions, encompassing a dramatization of the Passion and of the Resurrection; proof of this is the provision made for a separate and extensive text for a minor personnage. The fragment, moreover, shows a highly polished and refined technique and the general presentation of the various episodes and certain dramatic and literary allusions suggest that the compiler of the Sulmona passion possessed both a knowledge of the terminological resources of the religious drama and of literary traditions from which he drew at times in the redaction of the play. The writer combines rhetorical interests and literary reminiscences in one instances to vivify the dramatic action. He is indeed elaborating upon the Biblical account when he names one of the soldiers destined to guard Jesus' sepulchre Tristaynus.

The Montecassino dramatist's metrical choice was dictated, as we have seen, by liturgical and Christological considerations, whereas the Sulmona fragment redactor appears to have relied on a multiplicity of metrical schemes in order to provide poetical forms suited to convey the different moods of a passion which extended in many directions and whose amplitude one fully realizes from the number of characters involved in the fragment alone. Changing times and a different audience allowed the redactor to exercise a free hand in non-Biblical passages and to utilize his powers of inventiveness to achieve an edifying as well as an aesthetic experience. The fact remains that he saw fit to utilize predominantly the popular twelfth-century Victorine measure which, by its mere presence in a fourteenth-century text, bears witness to the dissemination and perpetuity of traditional liturgical and poetical modes.

The literary ties between the Montecassino and Sulmona plays provide a singular illustration of the widespread phenomenon of liturgical, literary, and poetical influences.

Modern essays on the history of the medieval drama have given prominence only to the timeless themes and literary dimension of that drama; its history will not be complete, however, until full investigation is undertaken of the poetical and rhetorical modes within which that drama was expressed.

BIBLIOGRAPHY OF MARIO A. PEI

A list of Mario Pei's writings, reflecting his vast range of interests that go well beyond the framework of philology, linguistics, and language in general, would fill many pages. Limitations of space have compelled the editors to exclude the folloving items from his rich production:

(a) Articles and reviews of a more popular nature, such as those in *The New York Times Magazine* and *Book Review, Saturday Evening Post, Holiday, Saturday Review of Literature, Reader's Digest, Chicago Tribune, Science Digest, Lingue del Mondo* (Florence), *Quinto Lingo, UNESCO Courier*, and many other newspapers, magazines, and periodicals both here and abroad. These run virtually into the hundreds;

(b) Articles on specific language topics in many encyclopedias, among them the *Americana, Collier's*, and *Funk and Wagnalls;*

(c) Articles in professional journals written on foreign-language teaching problems during World War II, cited in Paul Angiolillo's article;

(d) Reviews of textbooks in professional journals;

(e) Booklets and language guides intended primarily for the traveller, such as the well-known *Getting Along in* — (French, German, Italian, Portuguese, Russian, and Spanish) series, published both in hard-cover editions (Harper & Row, 1957-1958) and paperback (Bantam, 1959-1960), or *Talking Your Way Around the World* (Harper & Row, 1961, 1967, 1971).

(f) Papers, lectures, and communications delivered before professional societies, school and university audiences, and other groups, including radio and TV addresses, such as those prepared for the *Radio University of the Voice of America* in the early fifties.

The following list, then, arranged in chronological order (except for subsequent editions and translations of the same work), includes Professor Pei's books on language as well as his articles and reviews of deeper scholarship.

BOOKS

1. *The Language of the Eighth-Century Texts in Northern France.* New York: Carranza Press, 1932. (Doctoral Dissertation.)
2. *The Italian Language.* New York: Columbia University Press, 1941.
   Id. 2nd ed. New York: Vanni, 1954.
3. *Languages for War and Peace.* New York: Vanni, 1943.
   Id. 2nd. ed. rev. New York: Vanni, 1945.
4. *The World's Chief Languages.* (3rd. ed. rev. of *Languages for War and Peace.*) New York: Vanni, 1947.
   Id. British edition. London: Allen & Unwin, 1949.
   Id. 3rd. ed. New York: Vanni, 1960.
5. *French Precursors of the Chanson de Roland.* New York: Columbia U. Press, 1948.
   Id. Rept. from original edition by AMS Press, New York, 1967.
6. *A Comparative Grammar of French, Spanish, and Italian* by Oliver W. Heatwole. Ed. By Mario A. Pei. New York: Vanni, 1949.
7. *The Story of Language.* New York: Lippincott, 1949.
   Id. British edition. London: Allen & Unwin, 1952.
   — Italian translation, *La Meravigliosa Storia del Linguaggio.* Firenze: Sansoni, 1952.
   — French translation, *Histoire du langage.* Paris: Payot, 1954.
   — Spanish translation, *La Maravillosa Historia del Lenguaje.* Madrid: Espasa-Calpe, 1955.
   Id. Paperback edition. New York: The American Library, 1960.
   Id. New rev. ed. New York: Lippincott, 1965.
   Id. Rev. British edition. London: Allen & Unwin, 1966.
   Id. Rev. paperback edition. New York: Mentor (New American Library), 1966.
   — Hungarian translation, *Szabálytalan nyelvtörténet.* Budapest: Gondolat, 1966.
   Id. Japanese reduction, ed. with notes by Iwahito Higashitani. Tokyo: Nan'un Do, 1970.
8. *First Year French* (with Edmond A. Méras). New York: Dryden, 1950.
   Id. 2nd ed. rev. New York: Dryden, 1957.
9. *The Story of English.* New York: Lippincott, 1952.
   Id. British edition. London: Allen & Unwin, 1953 .
   Id. Paperback edition. New York: Premier-Fawcett, 1962.
10. *Liberal Arts Dictionary,* edited with Frank Gaynor. New York: Philosophical Library, 1952.

11. *Dictionary of Linguistics* (with Frank Gaynor). New York: Philosophical Library, 1954.
    Id. Paperback edition. New York: Wisdom Library, 1960.
12. *All About Language.* New York: Lippincott, 1954.
    Id. British edition. London: Bodley Head, 1956.
13. *Language For Everybody.* New York: Devin-Adair, 1956.
    Id. Pocket Book paperback ed. New York: Cardinal Giant, 1958.
    Id. New Paperback ed. New York: Devin-Adair, 1964.
    — Japanese reduction under the title of *Language in Human Society*, ed. and annotated by Tsuyoshi Amemiya and Hiroshi Saito. Tokyo: Kinseido, 1970,
14. *One Language for the World.* New York: Devin-Adair, 1958.
    — Condensed Icelandic translation, *Eitt Tungumál fyrir allan hoiminn*, serialized in *Lesbók Morgunsbladsins*, Reykjavik, December 1966-June 1967.
    — Icelandic translation issued in booklet form by Sérprentun úr Lesbók Morgunsbladsins, Reykjavik, 1968.
    Id. Rept. of original ed. by Biblo and Tannen, New York, 1968.
    Id. Abridged paperback ed. New York: Parents' Magazine Press, 1969.
15. *The Book of Place Names* (with E. Lambert). New York: Lothrop, Lee & Shepard, 1959.
16. *Our Names: Where They Came From and What They Mean* (with E. Lambert). New York: Lothrop. Lee & Shepard, 1960.
17. *The Families of Words.* New York: Harper & Row, 1962.
18. *Voices of Man.* New York: Harper & Row, 1962.
19. *Studies in Romance Philology and Literature.* (Studies in Romance Languages and Literatures, No. 44) Chapel Hill: University of North Carolina Press, 1963.
20. *Invitation to Linguistics.* New York: Doubleday, 1965.
    Id. British edition. London: Allen & Unwin, 1966.
    Id. Japanese reduction, ed. and anotated by Akisawa Kitayama. Tokyo: Aoyama, 1970.
21. *How To Learn Languages and What Languages To Learn.* New York: Harper & Row, 1966.
22. *Glossary of Linguistic Terminology.* New York: Doubleday-Anchor, 1966.
    Id. Hard-cover edition. New York: Columbia University Press, 1966.
23. *Language of the Specialists*, ed. with introduction by Mario A. Pei. New York; Funk & Wagnalls, 1966.
24. *The Adventure of Language* by Michael Girsdansky, rev. and ed. by Mario A. Pei. New York: Fawcett-Premier, 1967.
25. *The Story of the English Language* (rev. ed. of *The Story of English*). New York: Lippincott, 1967.
    Id. Paperback ed. New York: Simon & Schuster, 1968.
    Id. British edition. London: Allen & Unwin, 1968.
26. *The Many Hues of English.* New York: Knopf, 1967.
27. *Language Today* (with W. M. Marquardt, K. LeMée, D. L. Nilsen). New York: Funk & Wagnalls, 1967.
28. *What's In A Word?* New York: Hawthorn, 1968.
    Id. Paperback ed. New York: Universal, 1971.
29. *Words In Sheep's Clothing.* New York: Hawthorn, 1969.

— Japanese translation of six chapters with notes, serialized in *The Study of English*. Tokyo: Kenkyusha, 1970.

In addition to these books on language, the following works on socio-political topics should be mentioned:

1. *The American Road to Peace: A Constitution for the World*. New York: Vanni, 1945.
2. *The Consumer's Manifesto*. New York: Crown Publishers, 1960.
   — Japanese translation. Tokyo: National Diet Library, 1964.
3. *Our National Heritage*. Boston: Houghton Mifflin, 1965.
4. *The America We Lost*. Cleveland: World Publishing, 1968.
   Id. Paperback ed. with an introduction by William F. Buckley, Jr. New York: New American Library (signet), 1969.

Mario Pei also wrote three successful works of fiction:

1. *Swords of Anjou*. New York: John Day, 1953.
   Id. Paperback edition under the title of *Swords for Charlemagne*. New York: Graphic Publishing, 1955.
2. *The Sparrows of Paris*. New York: Philosophical Library, 1958.
3. *Tales of the Natural and Supernatural*. New York: Devin-Adair, 1971.

ARTICLES

1. "Old French Demonstratives," *Language*, 12 (1936), 47-51.
2. "Languages at the Crossroad," *French Review*, 9 (1936), 376-383.
3. "Accusative or Oblique," *Romanic Review*, 28 (1937), 241-267.
4. "French *icil*," *Modern Language Review*, 33 (1938), 260-261.
5. "Accusative versus Oblique in Portuguese," *Romanic Review*, 30 (1939), 189-191.
6. "Sull'uso della lettera *y* nell'anglo-sassone," *Lingua Nostra*, 1 (1939), 95-96.
7. "La Costruzione *In casa i Frescobaldi*," *Lingua Nostra*, 1 (1939), 101-103.
8. "La lingua italiana nell'inglese (pittura, scultura, architettura)," *Dante*, 1, No. 3 (1940), 18-20.
9. "La lingua italiana nell'inglese (teatro e musica)," *Dante*, 1, No. 4 (1940), 16-19.
10. "La lingua italiana nell'inglese (letteratura)," *Dante*, 1, No. 5 (1940), 16-17.
11. "French *-ier* from Latin *-ariu*," *Romanic Review*, 31 (1940), 380-395.
12. "Di un doppio esito fonetico italiano," *Lingua Nostra*, 3 (1941), 8-9.
13. "Latin and Rumanian," *Nunc et Tunc*, 8, No. 2 (1942), 15-16.
14. "Latin and Italian Front Vowels," *Modern Language Notes*, 58 (1943), 116-120.
15. "Intervocalic Occlusives in 'East' and 'West' Romance," *Romanic Review*, 34 (1943), 235-247.
16. "Languages in the World of Tomorrow," *Bulletin of the Linguistic Circle of New York*, 1, No. 2 (1943-1944), 15-16.
17. "The Problem of International Communication in a Global World," *American Esperantist*, 59, Nos. 5-6 (1944), 27-28.

18. "'The Loom of Language' and the Slav Tongues," *Slavonic Monthly*, September 1944, 5-6, p. 9.
19. "Suggestions for the Practical Teaching of the Sounds of Many Languages," *Modern Language Journal*, 19 (1945), 210-214.
20. "An Immortal Character in French Literature," *French Review*, 18 (1945), 189-195.
21. "Etruscan and Indo-European Case-Endings," *Italica*, 22 (1945), 73-77.
22. "Reflections on the Origin of the Romance Languages," *Romanic Review*, 34 (1945), 235-239.
23. "The Future of French Language Studies in the United States," *Tous Ensemble*, 1, No. 1 (1946), 5-7. Rept. in *French Review*, 19 (1946), 413-415.
24. "Languages for Post-War Trade," *Hispania*, 29 (1946), 258-261.
25. "Some Comments on Spelling Reform," *American Speech*, 31 (1946), 129-131.
26. "The State of Linguistics: Reply to a Mechanist," *Italica*, 23 (1946), 237-240.
27. "It Comes to Languages — But Is It Science?" *Modern Language Journal*, 30 (1946), 421-428.
28. "...Or Does It?" *Symposium*, 1 (1946), 51-59.
29. "One World? One Language," *Modern Language Journal*, 31 (1947), 11-14.
30. "The American Dialects," *Lingue Estere*, 12, No. 6 (1947), 132-133.
31. "An International Language for Science," *American Esperantist*, 62, Nos. 5-8 (1947), 37-39.
32. "Languages for the Very Young," *Modern Language Journal*, 32 (1948), 333-336.
33. "*Ab* and the Survival of the Latin Genitive in Old Italian," *Italica*, 25 (1948), 104-106.
34. "Some Notes on American Slang," *Lingue Estere*, 13, Nos. 8-9 (1948), p. 207.
35. "A New Methodology for Romance Classification," *Word*, 5 (1949), 135-146.
36. "Pidgin English Around the World," *Tomorrow*, 9 No. 5 (1950), 34-49
37. "Pacific Pidgins," *Lingue Estere*, 15, No. 8 (1950), p. 199.
38. "Fashions in Language," *German Quarterly*, 24 (1951), 239-249.
39. "The Practical Value of Knowing Foreign Languages," *French Review*, 26 (1953), 355-359.
40. "The International Prestige of French," *French Review*, 30 (1956), 62-63.
41. "Relativism in Linguistics," in *Relativism and the Study of Man*. New York: Van Nostrand, 1961, 216-235.
42. "The Dictionary as a Battlefront," *Saturday Review*, July 21, 1962, 44-46, p. 55.
43. "Reading in Different Languages," *Proceedings of the 19th Annual Reading Institute*, Temple University, 1962, 78-87.
44. "A Standard for English," *International Language Review*, 10, 31 (1963), 84-86.
45. "Remarks on the Esperanto Symposium," *International Language Review*, 10, 32 (1963). Rept. in *Universal Esperanto Documentation Center*, Rotterdam (1964), A/IV/4-6.

46. "Foreign Words and Phrases," in *The Complete Reference Handbook*. New York: Stravon Press, 1964, 261-286.

REVIEWS

Since the majority appear in *French Review, Modern language Journal, Romantic Review*, these journals will be coded as FR, MLJ, and RR, respectively.

1. "Chrestomathy of Vulgar Latin," by H. F. Muller and P. Taylor, *Medium Aevum*, 2 (1933), 231-237.
2. "La langue française," by Drapeau, FR, 7 (1934), 231-232.
3. "The Elucidation: A Prologue to the *Conte del Graal*," by Wilden Thomson, FR, 7 (1934), 232-234.
4. "Life of St. Alexis," by Dedeck-Héry, FR, 7 (1934), 413-415.
5. "Evolution et structure de la langue française," by W. von Wartburg, RR, 25 (1934), 409-413.
6. "Syntaxe du français Moderne," by Le Bidois, FR, 10 (1937), 409-412.
7. "Census of French and Provençal Dialect Dictionaries in American Libraries," by Adams and Woodard, RR, 29 (1937), p. 385.
8. "Geschichte der mittelfranzösischen Literatur II," by G. Gröber, RR, 29 (1938), 79-83.
9. "The Three Estates in Medieval and Renaissance Literature," by Mohl, FR, 11 (1938), 326-327.
10. "Répertoire des lexiques du vieux français," by R. Lévy, RR, 29 (1939), 194-195.
11. "Mélanges de linguistique et de philologie offerts à Jacques van Ginneken," RR, 29 (1938), 195-196.
12. "The Noun Declension System in Merovingian Latin," by F. Sas, *Medium Aevum*, 7 (1938), 153-159.
13. "The Medieval French *Roman d'Alexandre*," by Armstrong and Associates, RR, 29 (1938), 278-279.
14. "The French Language," by A. Ewert, FR, 12 (1938), 148-151.
15. "La Grammatica degli Italiani," by Trabalza and Allodoli, RR, 30 (1939), 315-321.
16. "History of the French language," by U. T. Holmes and Schutz, FR, 13 (1939), 147-149.
17. "Lingua contemporanea," by B. Migliorini, RR, 31 (1940), 92-95.
18. "Foundations of Language," by L. Gray, RR, 31 (1940), 194-198.
19. "La Canzone d'Orlando," by Rossi; "Roland-Orlando et l'épopée française et italienne," by Voigt; "Le Origini delle canzoni di gesta," by Siciliano, RR, 31 (1940), 285-292.
20. "The Spanish Language," by W. J. Entwistle, RR, 31 (1940), 304-309.
21. "La posizione della lingua italiana," by W. von Wartburg, RR, 32 (1941), 109-114.
22. "Bibliography of Italian Linguistics," by R. Hall, Jr., RR, 32 (1941), 442-445.
23. "The Latinity of Dated Documents in Portuguese Territory," by N. Sacks, RR, 33 (1942), 400-402.
24. "Storia della lingua di Roma," by G. Devoto, RR, 34 (1943), 116-120.
25. "Sulla lirica romanza delle origini," by Errante, FR, 17 (1944), 292-295.

26. "The Loom of Language," by F. Bodmer; "Interglossa," by L. Hogben, MLJ, 28 (1944), 633-639.
27. "Miscellania Fabra: Recull de traballs de linguistica catalana i romanica," RR, 34 (1945), 250-254.
28. "A Short Italian Dictionary," by A. A. Hoare, RR, 34 (1945), 337-339.
29. "Faire faire quelque chose à quelqu'un: recherche sur l'origine de la construction romane," by Dag Norberg, Word, 2 (1946), 90-92.
30. "Syntaktische Forschungen," by Dag Norberg, RR, 38 (1947), 87-91.
31. "Los elementos populares en la lengua de Horacio," by G. Bonfante, RR, 38 (1947).
32. "Perfiles de lingüistas: contribución a la historia de la lingüística comparada," by B. Terracini, RR, 38 (1947), 280-282.
33. "Linguistica," by B. Migliorini, RR, 38 (1947), 371-374.
34. "An Introduction to Linguistic Science," by E. H. Sturtevant, Symposium, 1 (1947), 114-118.
35. "Storia della lingua italiana," by B. Migliorini, RR, 39 (1948), 335-339.
36. "La Chanson de Roland e i Normanni," by Li Gotti, RR, 41 (1950), 129-130.
37. "Early Italian Texts," by C. Dionisotti and C. Grayson, eds., Speculum, 25 (1950), 395-397.
38. "Leave your Language Alone," by R. Hall, Jr., Symposium, 4 (1950), 291-295.
39. "Prontuario etimologico della lingua italiana," by B. Migliorini and A. Duro; "Dizionario Moderno," by A. Panzini, RR, 42 (1951), 71-73.
40. "Alcuin, Friend of Charlemagne," by E. Shipley Duckett, RR, 43 (1952), 54-56.
41. "Interlingua -English Dictionary": "Interlingua," MLJ, 36 (1952), 104-105.
42. "Die romanischen Sprachen," by A. Kuhn, Symposium, 6 (1952), 229-231.
43. "La Dialectologie," by S. Pop, RR, 45 (1954), 73-74.
44. "The Study of Language," by J. B. Carroll, MLJ, 38 (1954), 55-56.
45. "The Miracle of Language," by C. Laird, MLJ, 38 (1954), 156-157.
46. "Romance Trends in 7th and 8th Century Latin Documents," by R. Politzer and F. Politzer, RR, 45 (1954), 289-292.
47. "Profilo di storia linguistica italiana," by G. Devoto, Italica, 31 (1954), 249-251.
48. "Elementi di storia della lingua italiana," by A. Schiaffini, Symposium, 8 (1954), 365-367.
49. "The Spider King," by L. Schoonover; "Charlemagne," by H. Lamb, FR, 28 (1955), 272-274.
50. "Turoldo, La Canzone di Rolando," by S. Pellegrini, Symposium, 9 (1955), 168-170.
51. "Introduction to Descriptive Linguistics"; "Workbook in Descriptive Linguistics," by H. A. Gleason, MLJ, 39 (1955), 429-430.
52. "Aspects of Language," by W. J. Entwistle, MLJ, 39 (1955), 431-432.
53. "The Concise Usage and Abusage," by E. Partridge, American Speech, 30 (1955), 195-196.
54. "The Song of Roland," by C. Scott-Moncrieff, FR, 29 (1956), p. 366.
55. "Language: a Modern Synthesis," by J. Whatmough, MLJ, 40 (1956), 372-374.

56. "Modern Linguistics and the Teaching of English," by H. L. Smith, Jr., MLJ, 40 (1956), p. 374.
57. "Language, Thought, and Reality: Selected Writings of Benjamin Lee Whorf," by J. B. Carroll, ed., MLJ, 41 (1957), 106-108.
58. "Historische Grammatik der italienischen Sprache und ihrer Mundarten III (Syntax und Wortbildung)," by G. Rohlfs, *Erasmus*, 9 Nos. 17-18 (1956), 535-538.
59. "Language: An Inquiry Into Its Meaning and Function," by R. N. Anshem et al., MLJ, 42 (1958), 159-160.
60. "Esperanto and Interlingua Compared," by I. Reed, MLJ, 42 (1958), p. 210.
61. "Saggi Linguistici," by B. Migliorini, *Italica*, 35 (1958), 133-134.
62. "Readings in Applied English Linguistics," by W. B. Allen, ed., MLJ, 43 (1959), 55-56.
63. "Voci Romanesche," by P. Belloni and H. Nilsson-Ehle, *Modern Language Quarterly*, 20 (1959), 106-107.
64. "Short Etymological Dictionary of Modern English Origins," by E. Partridge, MLJ, 43 (1959), 302-303.
65. "Testi volgari abruzzesi del Duecento," by F. Ugolini, RR, 50 (1959), 202-203.
66. "Problemi di grammatica italiana," by E. Peruzzi, MLJ, 43 (1959), 355-356.
67. "Language Change and Linguistic Reconstruction," by H. M. Hoenigswald, MLJ, 44 (1960), 335-336.
68. "English-Italian, Italian-English Technical Dictionary," by C. Morelli, MLJ, 45 (1961), p. 332.
69. "Storia della lingua italiana," by B. Migliorini, RR, 52 (1961), 290-292.
70. "The Romance Languages," by W. D. Elcock, MLJ, 45 (1961), 375-376.
71. "A Linguagem dos foros de Castelo Rodrigo," by L. L. Cintra, RR, 53 (1962), 58-59.
72. "Language and Language Learning," by N. Brooks, MLJ, 46 (1962), 283-284.
73. "The Science of Language," by J. P. Hughes, MLJ, 46 (1962), 331-332.
74. "Teaching Foreign Languages in the Modern World," by T. Fotitch, ed., MLJ, (1962), 332-333.
75. "Historical Linguistics," by W. P. Lehmann, MLJ, 47 (1963), 137-38.
76. "What's What: A List of Useful Terms," by Donald D. Walsh, MLJ, 47 (1963), p. 340.
77. "The Adventure of Language," by M. Girsdansky, *Modern Language Review*, 47 (1963), 392-393.
78. "Garzanti Comprehensive Italian-English and English-Italian Dictionary," by M. Hazon, ed., MLJ, 48 (1964), 53-54.
79. "Perspectives in Linguistics," by J. T. Waterman, MLJ, 48 (1964), 111-112.
80. "The World's Living Languages," by S. Muller, MLJ, 48 (1964), 325-326.
81. "Idealism in Romance Linguistics," by R. Hall, Jr., RR, 56 (1965), 50-52.
82. "Langue et technique poétique à l'époque romane," by P. Zumthor, RR, 56 (1965), 56-57.
83. "Language and Style," by S. Ullmann, MLJ, 49 (1965), 196-197.

84. (Review article) "Some Current Trends in Linguistic Works" ("Structural Linguistics," by A. Shapiro et al.; "English as a Second Language," by M. Finocchiaro; "The ABC's of Language and Linguistics," by J. Ornstein and W. Gage; "The Study of Language," by C. Fries; "Elements of General Linguistics," by A. Martinet; "Introductory Linguistics," by R. Hall, Jr.), MLJ, 49, 375-383.
85. "Mélanges de linguistique et de philologie médiévale offerts à Maurice Delbouille" (J. Renson, ed.), *Modern Philology*, 58 (1966), 380-381.
86. "New Ways to Learn a Foreign Language, by R. Hall, Jr., MLJ, 50 (1966), 433-434.
87. "A Glimpse Into the Chinese Language: Peking's Language Reforms and the Teaching of Chinese in the U. S., by F. Shieh, MLJ, 50 (1966), p. 517.
88. "Linguistics, Language and Religion," by D. Crystal, MLJ (1967), 56-57.
89. "Canti e proverbi maieratesi," by J. V. Greco; "Italian Idioms with Proverbs," by V. Luciani; "A Dictionary of Colorful Italian Idioms," by Carla Pekelis, MLJ, 51 (1967), 62-63.
90. "Readings in Linguistics I, 4th ed." (M. Joos, ed.); "Readings in Linguistics II" (E. Hamp et al., eds), MLJ, 51 (1967), 312-314.
91. "The Italian Language," by B. Migliorini (tr. T. G. Griffith), *Italica*, 44 (1967), 244-247.
92. "The Romance Languages," by R. Posner, MLJ, 51 (1967), 424-426.
93. "Glossario degli antichi portolani italiani," by H. and R. Kahane, *Italica* 46 (1970), 437-439.

TABULA GRATULATORIA

E. Robert Adam
Paul F. Angiolillo
Robert Austerlitz
Menahem Banitt
E. B. Barnes
Jean-Albert Bédé
Sr. Virginia Belleggia, M. P. F.
Henry V. Besso
Dorothy R. Brodin
Jaroslav V. Broz
Victor Buescu
Arthur L. Campa
Adrienne Gokhalé Cannon
Fr. Luke M. Ciampi, O. F. M.
J. L. Collins, Jr.
Raymond J. Cormier
Joseph B. Costanzo
Sister Jane de Chantal
Ralph Paul de Gorog
Anita-Louise De La Garza
Giulio de Petra
Joseph F. De Simone
Arnold A. Del Greco
Robert T. Denommé
Henri Diament
Sylvia Klion Disenhof
Eugene Dorfman
Nathan Edelman
Sister Eloise Thérèse
Thaddeus Ferguson
Lena M. Ferrari
John Fisher
Joseph G. Fucilla
Paul A. Gaeng
Marinus C. Galanti
Devin A. Garrity
Frank M. Gatto
Michael Gertner
John L. Grigsby

Roger L. Hadlich
Joseph Graham Harrison
David Heft
Erik Hoder
Theodore Huebener
Willard S. Irle
Hisao Ishizuka
Istituto Italiano di Cultura
Mathilda Knecht
Milan S. LaDu
Pao-Ch'en Lee
Katharine LeMée
Jesse Levitt
Leonard Lieberman
Rosemary Lucente
Claude Lampkin
William A. Lydgate
Giuseppe Mammarella
Joan McConnell-Mammarella
J. P. McEvoy
Dorothy M. McGhee
José Martel
Nella K. Meyer
Bruno Migliorini
Nicholas J. Milella
René Muller
Dora A. Newson
Louis A. Pagnucco
Manuel de Paiva Boléo
Lawton P. G. Peckham
Alice Pianfetti
Frieda N. Politzer
Robert L. Politzer
John B. Post
Olga Ragusa
Salvatore Ramondino
Olga Razzari
Allen Walker Read
Louise Barbara Richardson

Kenneth H. Rogers
Gerhardt Rohlfs
David Romey
Paul Rosenzweig
S. Eugene Scalia
Ralph W. Scott
Barton Sholod
James P. Soffietti
Albert Z. Soletsky
Ernest V. Speranza
Mark Starr
Ted Stewart
Sandro Sticca
Benjamin Suhl
Abraham Tauber
Vito G. Toglia
Laura Torbet
Josephine Vallerie

Unicio J. Violi
Dorothy C. Walensky
Yvonne R. Weber
William C. Woolfson

COLLEGES AND UNIVERSITIES

Bryn Mawr College
Harvard University
Johns Hopkins University
Montclair State College
Princeton University
Stanford University
Stanford University, Florence, Italy
University of Notre Dame
University of Oregon
University of Virginia

The Department of Romance Studies Digital Arts and Collaboration Lab at the University of North Carolina at Chapel Hill is proud to support the digitization of the North Carolina Studies in the Romance Languages and Literatures series.

www.ingramcontent.com/pod-product-compliance
Lightning Source LLC
Chambersburg PA
CBHW022018220426
43663CB00007B/1123